"I like your Christ, I do not like your Christians. Your Christians are so unlike your Christ."
—Attr. Mahatma Gandhi

"The best evidence of Christianity is a Christ-like life, and the best evidence of the inspiration of the Word of God is found in the Word itself: when studied, loved, obeyed, and trusted, it never disappoints, never misleads, never fails."

—James Hudson Taylor

Copyright

The right of Duncan Matheson to be identified as the author of this work has been asserted to him under the Copyright and Design Patents Act 1988.

ISBN: 978-1-9164405-1-7 (paperback version).

ISBN: 978-1-9164405-4-8 (eBook version).

First published April 2019.

All rights reserved. Without limiting the rights under the copyright reserved above, no part of this publication may be reproduced, stored in or introduced into a retrieval system, or transmitted in any form or by any means (electronic, mechanical, photocopying, recording, or otherwise) without prior written permission.

For permission requests, please contact:

teachthemtoobey@gmail.com

Published by TTTO Ltd, Surrey, UK.

Scripture References

Unless otherwise noted, all Scripture quotations are taken from the HCSB®, Copyright © 1999, 2000, 2002, 2003, 2009 by Holman Bible Publishers. Used by permission. HCSB® is a federally registered trademark of Holman Bible Publishers[1].

Scripture quotations marked (NIV) are taken from the Holy Bible, New International Version®, NIV®. Copyright © 1973, 1978, 1984, 2011 by Biblica, Inc.™ Used by permission of Zondervan. All rights reserved worldwide. www.zondervan.com The "NIV" and "New International Version" are trademarks registered in the United States Patent and Trademark Office by Biblica, Inc.™

Definitions

Unless otherwise stated, all selected definitions used are taken from the online Merriam Webster dictionary at http://www.merriam-webster.com.

Annotations and Footnotes

Any square brackets contained within Scripture references are those of the author to provide clarification or amplification where considered necessary.

Footnotes cited in this material do not imply any endorsement or approval of any website or other external materials by the author. The veracity of the articles has not been determined and they are presented "as is" at the time of preparing this document. There is no guarantee that these links will continue to be valid.

Cover Design and Other images

All images are sourced from Pixabay.com and edited by the author.

Editorial Development

The *Christian Writer's Manual of Style* by Robert Hudson has been used in the editorial development of this book.

---

[1] Please note that the HCSB uses capitalised pronouns for references to God, Jesus and the Holy Spirit (e.g., Him, His and He etc.) unlike most other Bible versions.

Reader Interactions

You can interact with Duncan Matheson at the following links:

Twitter: @teachthemtoobey

Facebook: https://www.facebook.com/teachthemtoobey.uk/

Website: www.teachthemtoobey.co.uk and www.teachthemtoobey.uk

Reviewer Comments

"The last verses of Matthew's Gospel have been called the Great Commission. Many have emphasised the challenge to 'go' even though it is not actually a command in the text. Some have rightly seen the call to make disciples as the principal command but have not gone on to discuss the method set out for that discipleship making – teaching people to obey the commands of Jesus and incorporating them into a new community through baptism. Duncan's book goes some way to filling that gap.

Duncan has applied his professional expertise to look systematically at the commands of Jesus as recorded in the Gospels. He classifies them as three expanding categories of Kingdom Fundamentals, Kingdom Practices, and Kingdom Behaviours.

For a serious follower of Jesus, these books could prove a very useful guide for a pattern of self-examination. Church groups would benefit from studying the books together and helping one another in the path of discipleship. It would be great if as a result of Duncan's books many more Christians exhibited the reality of Christlike living so that others might be drawn to become Jesus's disciples."

— Ray Porter – Chair of Global Connections and OMF International (UK).

As a minister and a missionary, I have studied the Great Commission in Matthew 28 dozens of times, and I have desired to align my life with Jesus's last command. Not long ago, the significance of his words, *"teach them to obey everything I have commanded you"*, pierced my heart. For years, I glossed over the word *obey*, perhaps because I preferred to think of the task as merely listing the commands of Christ. Teaching to obey is another thing entirely. It requires my own obedience as I make disciples. Duncan Matheson's work in this book is vital for any Christian. He categorizes more than eighty of Jesus's commands into three Kingdom Fundamentals and nine Kingdom Practices. This isn't a watering down of the Scriptures; it is a simplification for the purpose of practical obedience. The fourteen study sessions in the accompanying Studies for Disciples book allow us to follow Christ more closely by helping us understand the commands and work obedience into our lives. Highly recommended.

—Rev. Craig McClurg – Youth with A Mission (YWAM), USA.

"I think this is an eminently worthwhile project, and you have done an amazing job in bringing this material together in a way that would benefit any congregation. There is always a need for different kinds of good studies everywhere, especially those like yours that take a slightly different approach."

—Dr. David Harley – Former General Director of OMF International and former Principal at All Nations Christian College, England.

"Seeing more than eighty commands of Jesus all presented in such an approachable and structured way has gripped us right from the first chapter. As we turned the pages, we felt a combination of awed fascination alongside a deep challenge to our spirits as we were lovingly confronted with all the ways our Saviour has commanded us to live and grow.

It is impossible to have all of these scriptures march across your heart and not be profoundly affected by them. It was not hard to imagine Jesus speaking them to us directly as he would have done with his disciples.

Duncan has laid a challenge squarely before us in producing this work. Are we willing to obey what Jesus has commanded with no ifs and no buts?

We are already considering how we might share this experience with others as we come to grips with what Duncan has so clearly drawn together in his books. We commend them highly for all those who are serious about their walk of discipleship. To read them will leave you changed."

—Mark & Sue Vening – Trustees of YWAM Cymru/Wales.

"Duncan Matheson has strategically and accurately composed a wonderful resource for pastors, churches, and new believers that is bound to strengthen and encourage all in their journeys with Jesus. The use of charts and study questions draws the reader into a deeper contemplation of their role in radical obedience and practical ways to respond. Teach Them to Obey is truly a gift to Christians to help unlock a life of blessing and effectiveness as witnesses unto Christ."

—Ryan Peters – Director of Donor Management - Christ for All Nations - Canada.

"If Christians are serious about following the commands of Jesus in their own lives, this book offers a very helpful tool for personal discipleship and growth. It encourages readers to think about over eighty specific commands from Jesus in Scripture summarised into twelve themes. It also prompts readers to reflect on how they can practically work these out in their relationship with God, how they themselves can grow spiritually, and how they relate to others."

—Trevor Warner – Assistant Director for Mobilisation OMF UK.

"Jesus makes it clear that the wise person is the one who both hears his words and practices them. In this way our lives are built on a sure foundation. The Holy Spirit empowers us to follow Christ, but we also have a part to play in learning Jesus's commands as well as to obey them. Teach Them To Obey provides resources to do just that along with a systematic way in which the commands of Christ can be understood, remembered, and learned by practicing them together. I recommend this study to small groups who believe that Jesus truly has all authority and who desire to follow him and make disciples. As we connect Jesus's commands with the narrative of Scripture and the stories of our own lives, we can become attuned to cooperating with the Holy Spirit and bear much fruit to glorify our Father."

—John Peachey - YWAM missionary for thirty-five years, facilitator of the University of the Nations Masters in Christian Formation and Discipleship.

"John chapter 10 has been one of my favourite passages throughout my adult life. Jesus says that "the sheep recognise his voice and come to him." Duncan Matheson is undoubtedly one of his sheep, and *Teach Them to Obey* is the call to all Christians to lean into Jesus's commands, hear his voice afresh and come to him. As Jesus explains later in the passage, "I tell you the truth, I am the gate for the sheep . . . Those who come in through me will be saved. They will come and go freely and will find good pastures." If you are searching for a practical way to understand your role in finding good pastures, read these books."

—Mike Forsey, Assistant Executive Director, Salvation Army Community Services, Calgary, Alberta, Canada.

"I've now had a chance to review your books. You thoroughly challenged me as I did so, and I think that you've done an incredibly thorough job using Jesus's teaching to distil your hierarchy of behaviours, key attributes, and central idea."

—Murray Johnstone – Former Global Head of Succession and Development at PA Consulting Group, London.

"Your books are covering a topic that is very valuable in helping a Christian believer understand how Jesus taught his disciples by example and expected them to apply what they were being taught. I am supportive of the breakdown analysis, the actual spiritual content, and the overall focus of the books."

—Pastor Glyn Thomas – Frimley Baptist Church, Surrey, England.

"Most would agree that we have been commanded to make disciples, teaching them to obey the commands of Jesus (Matthew 28:19-20). Duncan has grouped these commands in a novel way to make them easier to remember and has developed a useful diagram to explain how they all fit together. He also suggests how we might put the commands into practice, helpfully relating his own experiences. This book will be of maximum benefit if used in a group study. I believe that all those who put this teaching into practice will find it transforms their lives for the better. It will also enable them to be a great help to others."

—Rev. Mike Johnson MA MMin – Retired Assemblies of God minister and Bible School tutor, England.

Teach Them to Obey is a rich menu that excites the palate. Jesus reveals the heart and mind of God the Father. Rigorous and thorough. A helpful structure of kingdom fundamentals, practices, and behaviours. Challenging!! Let us be salt and light in this world".

—David Leeper – Christian mentor and Founder of Let Hope Arise International, Africa.

Acknowledgements

I would like to thank the following friends and colleagues for their thoughts and contributions on different sections or drafts of these books: Trevor Warner, Mark Vening, Rev. Mike Johnson, Allen McClymont, Rev. Ray Porter, Rev. Glyn Thomas, Dr Peter Rowan, Andy Smith, Murray Johnstone, my son Stuart, and daughter in law Amy Matheson. Many thanks too to Michele Hackney for her editorial support during the early drafting of these materials and subsequent careful proofreading.

A special mention for my sister Maggie Matheson for bringing both her theological training and career experiences of helping some of the most disadvantaged in society to challenge my text in each of the studies. I trust that this has made the material more robust and inclusive.

In particular I'd like to express my heartfelt gratitude to Jeanette Windle[2] for her diligent copy editing of these materials, her independent perspectives, and her advice concerning the publication process.

---

[2] http://jeanettewindle.com/editing-services/

I would also like to thank the fellow followers of Jesus in my house group (Chris and Dawn, Mary, Kath, Sue, Andy, Frances, and Mary-Anne) for their perseverance and feedback as we worked through the *Studies for Disciples* materials and for their friendship in Christ over many years. I also wish to thank my wife Mary-Anne for her support during the development of these books and our many years together leading up to it.

Pulling this all together, I am reminded of two scriptures:

> As iron sharpens iron, so one person sharpens another. (Proverbs 27:17, NIV)

and

> Plans fail for lack of counsel, but with many advisers they succeed. (Proverbs 15:22, NIV)

I have certainly benefited from the feedback of others, both personally and in regard to the development of the text, as I have attempted to make this material robust, defendable, readable, and theologically sound.

I hope that you enjoy this material and that it will become a blessing to you in your ongoing discipleship.

Preface

One of Jesus's final instructions to his disciples was that they should "teach them [other disciples] to obey everything that I have commanded you" (Matthew 28:20). However, his commands are peppered throughout the first five books of the New Testament and the early part of Revelation, so it is not easy to draw out the key themes of his teaching without some detailed analysis.

These Bible study books are the result of a comprehensive consideration of Scripture to identify Jesus's specific commands[3]. The material has been organised into a structural outline that can be readily comprehended and committed to memory by today's believers. In excess of eighty of Jesus's commands can be identified in the New Testament, each of which is presented in Figure 19.

---

[3] It should be noted that where various Bible translations highlight Jesus's spoken words, they provide text that is an interpretation/approximation to what he said as he spoke in Aramaic, the New Testament was written in Greek, and it has been translated subsequently into English and other languages.

The result of this analysis has been to group all of the scriptures from Jesus's commands into three top-level Kingdom Fundamentals. These are in turn supported by nine summary Kingdom Practices and a broader set of lower-level Kingdom Behaviours (comprising either single or strongly related commands). All together, these encompass the two "greatest commandments" and the "Great Commission" (please see note on terminology below). The aim has been to describe these Kingdom Fundamentals and Kingdom Practices in an easily understood manner suitable for study by individuals, couples, or groups.

The analysis is supported throughout by comprehensive references to the words of Jesus directly from the New Testament. In many senses, the words of Jesus alone should be enough as the many available translations of Scripture (in English at least) make his instructions and commands quite clear.

Innumerable books have been written to help address the challenges of the Christian life. In this book, however, the objective has been to focus wholly on those things Jesus commanded his followers (i.e., Christians) to put into practice. Jesus's other teachings and wider instructions for godly living from the Old and New Testaments are not covered, although relevant references are provided where appropriate.

No claim is made here that those scriptures containing Jesus's commands are more important than any other scriptures within the Bible. The Christian life encompasses more than these. However, if we were to implement his commands alone, we could not go far wrong in our walk as his disciples.

As author of this analysis, I am keenly aware of my own deficiencies and failings in terms of the effective practice of all the things Jesus seeks from his disciples. We all have to rest in his marvellous grace, recognising that we are all "under construction", relying upon the Holy Spirit, Scripture, trusted fellow believers, and sound biblical teaching to help us move forward in our practical discipleship.

Intended Readership

This material is for anyone, whether they are new or established believers, who wants to understand what Jesus commanded his disciples to do and how to apply his teachings to their own lives. This distillation of Jesus's teaching may also have applications in an outreach or missions' context to help others begin to understand what being a follower of Jesus means.

It may be that in the course of working through these studies you are prompted to consider where you are in your walk of faith. Or perhaps you are a non-believer reading this material to gain some understanding of Jesus's teaching. If either of these situations apply to you as a reader, then I encourage you to turn to Study 6 (Submit To Jesus's Lordship) before engaging with the rest of this book. This study will help set the context for you in terms of what people typically do when they take active steps to become Jesus's disciples. You may then want to look at Study 5 (Follow Jesus), followed by Studies 7 (Pursue Holiness) and 8 (Live Out Kingdom Values), which focus on how each disciple ought to develop in their personal response to Jesus, before considering the other sessions.

Terminology and Outline Structure

Within this book, three terms have been adopted instead of using the words "Commandment" and "Discipline" in an effort to avoid reader confusion. Those words tend to have very specific or traditional meanings in Christian circles. The three terms used are:

> Kingdom Fundamentals—used to describe the three most important elements that summarise and develop the book's central theme, "Teach them to obey all that I have commanded you."
>
> Kingdom Practices—used to define the key summarising themes that correspond to each Kingdom Fundamental.
>
> Kingdom Behaviours—used to denote the various commands of Jesus that generally correspond to each Kingdom Practice and two of the Kingdom Fundamentals.

Figure 1 illustrates this pictorially in four levels, beginning with the theme of this book and moving through each fundamental and its supporting practices and behaviours.

In addition, when using the term "God", this book generally refers to the Trinity as a whole rather than God the Father. The Father, Son (Jesus), and Holy Spirit are separately identified where considered appropriate.

The Structure of This Book

This book builds upon material already presented in the *All That I Have Commanded You* book, organising it into fourteen distinct Studies for Disciples. The purpose of these studies is so that we as modern-day followers can explore how implementing Jesus's teachings will help us become more like him and provide the basis for us to teach others.

It is my hope and prayer that Christians will come together to study these teachings of Jesus, but also to discuss and debate what is being presented. Working and learning in community was an important facet of life in the early church and provides a model for us today as well, helping us to shape and develop each other as we seek to be transformed by Jesus and for Jesus.

Figure 1 - Terminology and Structure

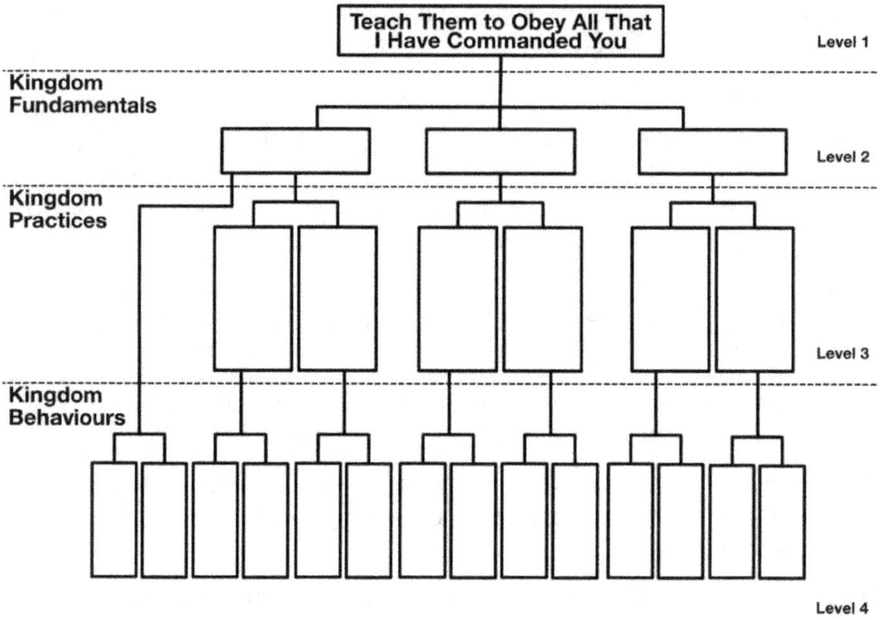

```
                    Teach Them to Obey All That
                        I Have Commanded You              Level 1
 ─────────────────────────────────────────────────────────────────
Kingdom
Fundamentals
                   ┌──────┐    ┌──────┐    ┌──────┐
                   └──────┘    └──────┘    └──────┘       Level 2
 ─────────────────────────────────────────────────────────────────
Kingdom
Practices
                                                          Level 3
 ─────────────────────────────────────────────────────────────────
Kingdom
Behaviours
                                                          Level 4
```

Following the introductory chapter, there are fourteen study sessions. These address the twelve themes derived from grouping, summarising, and structuring all of Jesus's commands. There are also two additional studies, the first and last. Study 1 focuses on every believer's essential need of the Holy Spirit in order to live a victorious life. Study 14 reviews the previous studies and draws out what others might see in us as we model Jesus better.

In preparing this material, I have analysed the scriptural content as presented in English-language translations. I am not a theologian. Neither am I a scholar of Greek or Hebrew. My main objective has been to develop these studies in a manner that is easy to understand, so that when readers have completed the material, they not only will have committed to memory the three Kingdom Fundamentals and nine Kingdom Practices but will be putting each of Jesus's commands into practice in their daily walk and witness as well as teaching them to others.

Some Notes on the Studies

Each study will present:

- An "Introduction" that reinforces where we are in the overall structure as presented in Figure 1 (and Figure 3), as well as study-specific diagrams.

- A "Biblical Support" section consisting of a subset of scriptures that underpin relevant elements of the Kingdom Fundamental or

Kingdom Practice principles and their supporting Kingdom Behaviours. This subset has been drawn from more comprehensive material presented in the *All That I Have Commanded You* book, Chapters 2 to 4.

- An "Our Context" section that provides perspectives on those scriptures so readers can better understand how they might apply to us today.

- A "Kingdom Fundamental/Kingdom Practice Application" section that includes thoughts on Jesus as our example, outlining where scriptures reveal Jesus effectively practising the Kingdom Fundamental or Practice under discussion, as well personal reflections on the relevant Kingdom Fundamental, Practice, and Behaviours.

- A "Kingdom Fundamental/Kingdom Practice Health Check". This includes:

    - Questions and issues for study participants to consider, discuss, and reflect upon, together with ideas for moving forward in your personal walk of faith.

    - Blank pages for you to make notes and jot down ideas to use in discussions with others in a group, as well as to record any important suggestions and views from others that can give you opportunities for reflection. Alternatively, you could use a separate notebook or journal to record these things.

    - A "Possible Action" prompt–i.e., a place to record and date any specific things that God through the Holy Spirit might be saying to you and/or any decisions, plans, or objectives you need to make.

    - An opportunity to help you reinforce learning the structure of Kingdom Fundamentals and Kingdom Practices as an aid to living out the practising of Jesus's commands. Each study includes a figure with some blank boxes for you to fill in as you work through Studies 1 to 14.

Responding to the Possible Action prompts is, of course, not compulsory. However, the whole purpose of these materials is to help us understand the commands Jesus is challenging us to obey and perhaps to change the way we live as a result. Whether as part of a group or alone, it is good practice to record your thoughts and responses to the material, particularly the questions in Kingdom Fundamental/Kingdom Practice Health Check subsections. Thoughts on the latter would be useful for:

- Any discussions you might have.

- Personal reflection in the short term.

- Contemplating how you may have developed in your spiritual walk after a passage of time.

You may also find it useful to read each scripture aloud and reflect on its meaning. You may want to refer to the other referenced parallel scriptures and read these too. Consider using different versions of the Bible if these are available to you to see how these translations (or paraphrases) differ in emphasis and phrasing.

When considering these Kingdom Fundamentals and Kingdom Practices, there may be a tendency to think of them in a legalistic way. This is not the intention of this book, and you must rely upon the Holy Spirit to prompt and influence you not to become dogmatic or burdened to practise these in your own strength. Doing this will weigh you down unnecessarily. At the same time, you should not stifle the Holy Spirit (1 Thessalonians 5:19) by such things as ignoring or rejecting his prompting, continually and wilfully sinning, disobeying Scripture, personal pride, or not giving space and time for the Holy Spirit to work.

Above all, may I encourage you to look at the "big picture" in each study. Consider whether you understand, agree, or disagree with the Kingdom Fundamentals, Kingdom Practices, and Kingdom Behaviours being discussed. Think about what implications there may be for you personally as a result of working through the material. In certain cases, the scriptures listed may feel contentious to you (just as they were in Jesus time and since) and possibly contradictory when read out of context. In creating material for personal or group study, there has been no attempt to explain each Bible reference, as this would increase the volume of text considerably and I as author am not suitably qualified to do this.

If at the end of the process, you are able to remember and practise the structure of the three Kingdom Fundamentals and nine Kingdom Practices more consistently, then your love for God, your love for your neighbour, and your own spiritual wellbeing will increase and I as author will have achieved my objective.

Table of Contents

Reviewer Comments	v
Acknowledgements	ix
Preface	xi
Foreword	xix
Introduction to the Studies	1
Study 1 - The Essential Need for the Holy Spirit in Our Lives	13
Study 2 - Love God - (KF1)	27
Study 3 - Listen to (Obey) God - (KP1)	41
Study 4 - Talk (Pray in Faith) to God - (KP2)	55
Study 5 - Follow Jesus - (KF2)	73
Study 6 - Submit to Jesus's Lordship - (KP3)	89
Study 7 - Pursue Holiness (Integrity/Purity) - (KP4)	105
Study 8 - Live Out Kingdom Values - (KP5)	121
Study 9 - Exercise Discernment - (KP6)	141
Study 10 - Love Your Neighbour as Yourself - (KF3)	159
Study 11 - Make Disciples - (KP7)	177
Study 12 - Forgive (Don't Judge) Others - (KP8)	193
Study 13 - Undertake Acts of Service/Generosity - (KP9)	213
Study 14 - Outcomes from Putting Jesus's Commands into Practice	229
Appendix 1 - Further Reading on Discipleship	243
Appendix 2 - Summary of the Biblical Analysis	245
Appendix 3 - Leaders' Notes and Advice	257

Foreword

The Church. Next to Jesus himself, the Church is God's best idea for the good of this world. Communities of Christ-followers organising around Jesus's teaching for the purpose of experiencing, expressing, and extending God's love into this world.

The Church. Next to Satan himself, the Church is the worst influence that ever happened to this world. No institution has done more damage to people's understanding of the God who is love and his Kingdom of peace than the Church.

Both of these sentiments are true. The Church is either the best or worst thing for the advance of the Good News of Jesus in our world. There is little in between. What makes the difference? The centrality and supremacy of Jesus. History bears this out. When the Church loses its central theme of following Jesus, of learning, loving, and living out his teachings, and of making more disciples (students of the way of Jesus), the Church falls in love with the power of God minus the humble, other-centred love of God. Then what we call the "kingdom of God" becomes really just another kingdom of this world, now backed by misguided religious zeal in the name of Jesus.

Simply admonishing Christians to read their Bibles is not enough. Again, history shows us that more Bible reading without the way and words of Jesus at the centre does nothing to decrease violence, hypocrisy, and judgmentalism. In the sixteenth century when Protestants split with the

Catholic Church, their cry of "Sola Scriptura" offered the Church a renewed hope to get back on track. But in reading the Bible without Jesus at the centre, too many Protestants used the Bible to justify violence against Catholics, Anabaptists and other Protestant groups with differing doctrines, Jews, supposed witches, or anyone else they deemed heretical. Putting the Bible in the centre of our spiritual lives is one step shy of what Jesus calls us to do. Rather than hold centre place in our lives, the Bible should operate more like John the Baptist, pointing to Jesus and crying out, "Behold!"

What the Church needs in this and every generation is a commitment to the Word of God in print that centres on the Word of God in Person. Let's be clear! Healthy Christians don't follow the Bible. They read the Bible, study the Bible, and immerse themselves in the Bible—so they can follow Jesus. There is a difference. Mature Christians believe in the authoritative, inerrant, infallible Word of God, and his name is Jesus!

To religious leaders who read the Bible, studied the Bible, memorized the Bible, and followed the Bible, Jesus said:

> And the Father who sent me has himself testified concerning me. You have never heard his voice nor seen his form, **nor does his word dwell in you**, for you do not believe the one he sent. You study the Scriptures diligently because you think that in them you have eternal life. These are the very Scriptures that testify about me, yet you refuse to come to me to have life. (John 5:37-40, emphasis mine)

Jesus says it is possible to know the Bible and not know the Word of God. It is possible to hold Scripture dear to our hearts and not have God's Word dwelling in us. Every Christian should sit up and take notice. We've got work to do.

This is why I am so excited about any book that helps realign the Christian church with Christ. So much is at stake! That is why I am grateful to Duncan Matheson for the work he has invested in this project, and I'm grateful to you, the reader, for the time and energy I trust you are about to invest. Nothing could be more important. I really believe that.

To be clear, a study of the four Gospels does not mean we are abandoning the rest of the Bible for the words in red. But it does mean that we are aware that really learning and living the words of Jesus will put the rest of the Bible in its proper context. Learn the teachings of Jesus, meditate on them, discuss them, apply them, and then go into the rest of Scripture with renewed vision and purpose. See how the Old Testament prepares the way for Jesus and how the rest of the New Testament reflects back on and discusses the application of the teachings of Jesus. In this way, the Bible will no longer be a painting we mount on the wall to look at, but a window we install in a wall to look through until we see the face of Jesus.

Something that Christians and non-Christians, believers, atheists, and everybody in between can all agree on is that this world would be a better place if Christians learned to be more Christ-like. Imagine a future where communities of Jesus-followers around the world are living simply, loving boldly, and are spreading the Good News of Jesus with inclusion, compassion, and gentleness. I want to be a part of that movement. I want to lean into that future. I hope you do too.

Peace.

Bruxy Cavey. Teaching Pastor, The Meeting House, Ontario, Canada.

Introduction

Introduction to the Studies

This book is designed primarily for groups of Christ-followers to work through in order to understand what Jesus has commanded them to do and to put those commands into practice under the guidance of the Holy Spirit. The commands are presented in an easy-to-remember structure of Kingdom Fundamentals and Kingdom Practices. Readers can study individually but would not have the advantage of discussing the questions and issues or listening to the views of others in each session. The material draws upon the broader New Testament analysis of Jesus's commands presented in the *All That I Have Commanded You* book, which is designed as a reference source for pastors and teachers (i.e., it is not essential for anyone to have read this to undertake these studies). This book is organised into this introduction and fourteen studies.

Situation

In the final verses of his Gospel, Matthew records what Jesus said to his disciples at the end of Jesus's ministry on earth:

> Then Jesus came to them and said, "All authority in heaven and on earth has been given to me. Therefore, go and make disciples of all nations, baptising them in the name of the Father and of the Son and of the Holy Spirit, and teaching them to obey everything I have commanded you. And surely I am with you always, to the very end of the age." (Matthew 28:18-20, NIV)

This text is known within Christianity as the Great Commission. James Hudson Taylor, founder of the China Inland Mission, is quoted as saying the following about it:

> The Great Commission is not an option to be considered; it is a command to be obeyed.

All who are Jesus's followers, in whatever context God has placed them, need to consider this as part of their life of witness.

This book contains a complete analysis of all Jesus's commands. But understanding exactly what Jesus commanded his disciples to do in such a way that can be readily remembered is not easy since Jesus gave his disciples in excess of eighty of them. One way to help us memorise his teaching is to summarise these commands into a smaller set of "themes".

Throughout this book, these themes are referred to as Kingdom Fundamentals and Kingdom Practices. They fall into two basic categories: specific commands from Jesus during his earthly ministry and teachings we can glean from what Jesus himself practised while on earth as well as his specific promises concerning the Holy Spirit.

As we study Jesus's commands, however, we must keep in mind that our salvation in Jesus is not based upon anything we do, either before or after we become his disciples. Our justification is by grace through faith in him alone. This is why the gospel is itself "Good News".

The price for our sins is paid by Jesus's sacrifice on the cross, his death, and subsequent resurrection by God the Father. If we repent of our sins and take him as our Saviour and Lord, we are given the assurance of everlasting life now. As a result, we should be motivated to undertake acts of service for him. However, our promise of eternal life is not conditional on how we "perform", as we read in Romans 8:1-2:

> Therefore, there is now no condemnation for those who are in Christ Jesus, because through Christ Jesus the law of the Spirit who gives life has set you free from the law of sin and death. (NIV)

On Judgement Day we will be rewarded on the basis of our actions as Jesus's disciples, whereas non-believers (those who have not accepted his free offer of salvation) will face judgement as God, who is sovereign, determines.

Complications

People may label themselves as Christian without a true understanding of what commands a genuine disciple of Jesus should be actively living out. Being a follower of Jesus is not only about trying to put these teachings into practice, but also about having a Christ-like heart and attitude. Wanting to implement Jesus's commands in our lives should be a response that flows naturally from our salvation. Likewise, striving for consistency between our inner perspectives and our outward actions, i.e., being authentic in terms of what we say and do.

To illustrate, there is a marked difference between the UK's 2011 census, in which 59.5% of the population (37.5 million) identified itself as Christian,[4] and actual church membership within the UK, which in 2010 stood at only 11.2% of the population (5.5 million).[5] Similarly, 2014 data from the Pew Research Centre indicates that in the United States 70.6% of the population identified themselves as Christian,[6] while only 39% or fewer actually attended church on a weekly basis.[7,8] From this it is clear that many who identify themselves as Christian are only nominally so.[9]

The global church has not done the best job in discharging Jesus's "Great Commission" (Matthew 28:18-20):

- Yes, we have gone.
- Yes, we have made converts/Christians, and many have become Jesus's disciples.
- Yes, we have also baptised a huge number of them.
- But no, we have definitely not systematically taught them to obey all that Jesus commanded.

In fact, the inconsistency of Christians in fulfilling what Jesus wants in terms of our actions, behaviours, and attitudes is one barrier to non-believers

---

[4] https://www.ons.gov.uk/peoplepopulationandcommunity/culturalidentity/religion/articles/fullstorywhatdoesthecensustellusaboutreligionin2011/2013-05-16
[5] Church Statistics - https://faithsurvey.co.uk/download/csintro.pdf - page 2
[6] http://www.pewforum.org/2015/05/12/americas-changing-religious-landscape/
[7] http://www.gallup.com/poll/166613/four-report-attending-church-last-week.aspx
[8] http://www.churchleaders.com/pastors/pastor-articles/139575-7-startling-facts-an-up-close-look-at-church-attendance-in-america.html
[9] The Lausanne Committee for World Evangelization (LCWE) defines a nominal Christian as "a person who has not responded in repentance and faith to Jesus Christ as his personal Saviour and Lord." The LCWE notes that such a one "may be a practising or non-practising church member. He may give intellectual assent to basic Christian doctrines and claim to be a Christian. He may be faithful in attending liturgical rites and worship services, and be an active member involved in church affairs."

coming to know Jesus. If we were more Christ-like, more people might come into God's kingdom through accepting Jesus as their personal Saviour.

That said, it is important to recognise that there are other reasons why people don't accept Jesus:

- Human beings are sinful and will resist the truth in Jesus because they don't want to face up to this.
- There is a spiritual battle going on, whether we realise this or not.

Muslim perceptions of Christians, for instance, are often confused by their classification of Western society[10] in general as being "Christian". The reality is, of course, far from this as secularism and atheism continue to increase in Western nations, while societal behaviours follow general cultural norms rather than any outworking of Christianity. To Muslim observers, Western practices such as poor moral standards, the eating of pork, and consumption of alcohol are in conflict with teachings in the Qur'an as well as the Old Testament. So, to them, Christianity is also seen to be in conflict since they interpret that behaviour as "Christian". It should be noted here that the Muslim religion is highly rules-based whereas the Christian life is one of a developing relationship with a God who transforms the believer.

Many other faiths, people groups (i.e., people with common language and customs that may cross what are today's national boundaries), cultures, and nation states also view Christianity negatively.[11] Some reasons for this are because they do not understand:

- The nature of salvation in Jesus.
- What the Christian life should encompass.
- What the Christian life means for the individual believer.
- How Jesus's disciples should live their lives in their community, whether at home or abroad.

That many Christians do not follow the teachings of Jesus as much as they should is where our collective witness falls down. In consequence, the term Christian has become devalued at the very least. Such poor witness by some

---

[10] For example, the European Economic Area, USA and Canada, Australia and New Zealand.
[11] http://www.opendoorsuk.org/persecution/country_profiles.php

believers may be one reason why Mahatma Gandhi is reported to have said, "I like your Christ, but I do not like your Christians. Your Christians are so unlike your Christ." Whether it was in truth Gandhi who said this or someone else is secondary. It is the relevance of the words themselves we need to consider.

Even if we are poor witnesses, it is important to understand that this does not affect our salvation in Jesus as we are saved through faith and not works:

> For it is by grace you have been saved, through faith –and this is not from yourselves, it is the gift of God –not by works, so that no one can boast. For we are God's handiwork, created in Christ Jesus to do good works, which God prepared in advance for us to do. (Ephesians 2:8-9, NIV)

Jesus tells us in Luke 6:41-42:

> Why do you look at the speck that is in your brother's eye, but do not notice the log that is in your own eye? Or how can you say to your brother, "Brother, let me take out the speck that is in your eye," when you yourself do not see the log that is in your own eye? You hypocrite, first take the log out of your own eye, and then you will see clearly to take out the speck that is in your brother's eye.

What Jesus is teaching here is that as followers of Jesus we need to put our own lives in some sort of order before looking at the lives of others. Of course we must also recognise we can never be perfect in this life. This is precisely why we need to understand what Jesus is teaching so we can apply it to our own lives. Only then can we begin to help other believers become better disciples too.

So how can we do this? By applying the original command we've been discussing: "Teach them to obey all that I [Jesus] have commanded you."

This call to action implies the question: what exactly did Jesus command us so that we can subsequently do as he directs and teach others to obey those commands? To imitate Jesus better, we have to first understand what he commanded. This in turn entails seeking out within Jesus's teachings what those commands are and putting them into practice. Once we have done this, we will see that the commands Jesus gives us in Scripture can be summarised in terms of three Kingdom Fundamentals.

The first Kingdom Fundamental is one of the two "greatest commandments" cited by Jesus in Mark 12:30: to love God [the Trinity - God the Father, God the Son (Jesus), and God the Holy Spirit] with all our hearts and souls and minds and strength.

The second Kingdom Fundamental is Jesus's call to "follow me" (Matthew 4:19). In other words, we are to emulate Jesus, assisted by the Holy Spirit. Indeed, it is in recognition of this that we call ourselves followers of Jesus. Obeying this command is necessary before we can begin to implement the

Great Commission as described in Matthew 28:18-20. In particular, we must become more like Jesus so that we can teach others to become more like him too. We will use the term Follow Jesus rather than "follow me" for this Kingdom Fundamental throughout the rest of this book.

The third Kingdom Fundamental is the second of the two commandments Jesus identifies as "greatest", which is to love your neighbour as yourself (Mark12:31). In other words, do to others as you would have them do to you (Luke 6:31).

We need to clarify that Jesus's command to love your neighbour as yourself is not a command to love yourself. On the contrary, the grammatical assumption in the text is that we already love ourselves, i.e., we put our own needs and wants naturally above those of others. This doesn't mean we shouldn't be comfortable with who we are. But Jesus's words here are much more about the need to live righteously, as we will discuss later.

If we look carefully, we can see that the two "greatest commandments", to love God and to love our neighbour, are both outward-focused, from us towards God and towards others. In contrast, the second Kingdom Fundamental, which is for us to follow Jesus, focuses upon us as individuals. Following Jesus is the most important thing we can do if we are to allow him to rule and reign within us.

God through the Holy Spirit wants to develop and mould us into the people he created us to be. We need to be informed by Jesus's teaching and allow it to alter our internal attitudes and motivations, then our external actions, i.e., putting it into practice. If our lives reflect all Jesus commanded, our impact on a wider society will be more marked, drawing others to him as we demonstrate how loving God and God loving us can transform our lives and those with whom we come into contact.

That said, we must also recognise the warning Jesus gives in Mark 13:13:

> Everyone will hate you because of me, but the one who stands firm to the end will be saved. (NIV)

The observation attributed to Mahatma Gandhi accurately highlights the difference between the character of Jesus as recorded in the New Testament and the witness of too many who identify themselves as being his disciples. It does not take too much searching on social media or on the internet to see how even Christian-themed accounts and websites can present a less than wholesome view of Christianity, certainly one that Jesus would not recognise.

As followers of Jesus, we are called to be salt and light in the world, and within the confines of freedom of speech provisions, we should be prepared to express our views on matters of the day. However, these should be presented in a constructive, non-judgemental manner. We are not responsible for others' reactions to these views, whether defamatory, blasphemous, or otherwise. But we are responsible for how we subsequently interact, if at all. This is not saying that there is only one Christian viewpoint. Clearly, there are many varying perspectives on secular and faith matters. However, we should seek to be Christ-like in our dealings with others, not through ridicule or intolerance of others' views.

If we are to live as Jesus commands, then it follows that we need to understand what he requires of us. James Hudson Taylor, founder of the China Inland Mission, wrote:

> The best evidence of Christianity is a Christ-like life, and the best evidence of the inspiration of the Word of God is found in the Word itself. When studied, loved, obeyed, and trusted, it never disappoints, never misleads, never fails.[12]

Kingdom Fundamentals and Practices Jesus Requires Us to Practise and Teach Others

Jesus's commands and teachings are recorded in the form of personal words he spoke throughout the four Gospels, the early part of the Acts of the Apostles, and in parts of the book of Revelation. If we are to be disciples who live and teach others authentically, we must seek to know, understand, and try to practise these commands in our lives. In particular, Jesus's commands, if obeyed, should help us model his example day by day as we:

- Deepen our relationship with God as our heavenly Father.
- Develop our own personality and character as we are led by the Holy Spirit to reflect Jesus more through our attitudes, behaviour, and actions.
- Try to be effective witnesses to others through our service to them, including teaching and discipling other believers.

At a simple level, this should look something like Figure 2. The prime focus is not on what we do or how we do it, but on the outcome of what we do as described in Matthew 5:16:

> In the same way, let your light shine before men, so that they may see your good works and give glory to your Father in heaven.

As followers of Jesus, everything we are about should bring glory to God. In particular, we are not seeking to do good works for their own sake (that

---

[12] https://archive.org/stream/HudsonTaylorsChoiceSayings-BroughtByPeter-johnParisis/HudsonTaylorsChoiceSayings-NotCopyrighted_djvu.txt

is legalism) or so that others will applaud us, but rather so that God alone gets the glory.

Figure 2 - Followers Should Seek to Become More like Jesus as They Also Deepen Their Relationship with God and Others

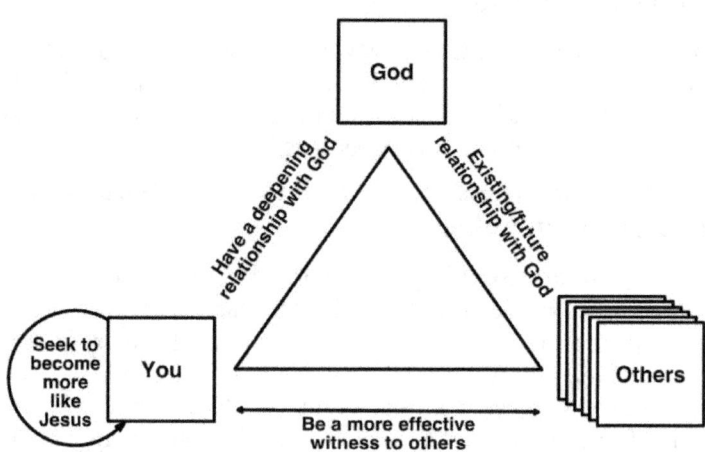

Figure 3 Builds upon Figure 2 and demonstrates that we have:

- A two-way relationship with God.
- A responsibility to let the Holy Spirit and the Bible help us become more like the people Jesus wants us to be.
- A requirement to live and work in community with others, who are our potential harvest field for God.

It also demonstrates:

- The Trinitarian nature of God: Father, Son, and Holy Spirit.
- That individuals can be characterised as comprising of body, mind, and soul/spirit.

Figure 3 - The Kingdom Fundamentals and Kingdom Practices Jesus Wants Us to Practise and Teach to Other Followers

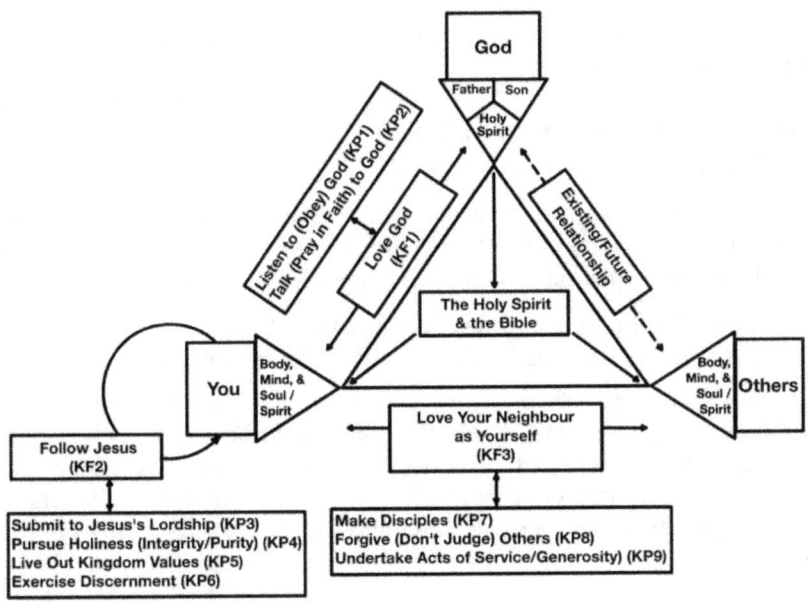

Figure 3 also highlights:

- Our need to love God (relate to God) with two linked Kingdom Practices under this.
- Our need to follow Jesus (live righteously) with four supporting Kingdom Practices under this.
- Our need to love our neighbour as ourselves (relate to others) with three related Kingdom Practices.
- That the Bible and the Holy Spirit are central to helping us and others grow in our knowledge of God and what he wants from us in Jesus.
- That some of those with whom we come into contact will already have an ongoing relationship with God as their heavenly Father. Others may come into a relationship in the fullness of time through accepting Jesus as their personal Saviour and Lord. This may be a result of our witness to them or through other believers, but most of all through the influence of the Holy Spirit.

Figure 3 summarises the essence of what we will be looking at as we work through Studies 1 to 13. Each study will focus on a specific theme from this figure, slowly building up the structure as we move forward to the next one.

In each study there will also be some images included to illustrate the Kingdom Fundamental or Kingdom Practice being discussed to help commit these points to memory.

Following this introduction chapter, there are fourteen studies that cover the set of twelve Kingdom Fundamentals and Kingdom Practices that were covered and discussed in the *All That I Have Commanded You* book plus two additional studies (1 and 14). You will find a list of these studies in the Table of Contents.

When trying to put Jesus's commands into practice, we need to recognise that we do not all have skills and gifting in equal measure, both in terms of practical gifts and spiritual gifts as Scripture makes clear:

> All these are the work of one and the same Spirit, and he distributes them to each one, just as he determines. (1 Corinthians 12:11, NIV)

This means that some tasks we undertake are likely to be better suited to our capabilities than others. However, we should not allow any self-perception of limited gifting or lack of skills to become an excuse for ignoring any urgent or important matters that might confront us, since all believers have the Holy Spirit as their helper, as the apostle Paul wrote to the church in Corinth:

> But he said to me, "My grace is sufficient for you, for my power is made perfect in weakness." Therefore I will boast all the more gladly about my weaknesses, so that Christ's power may rest on me. That is why, for Christ's sake, I delight in weaknesses, in insults, in hardships, in persecutions, in difficulties. For when I am weak, then I am strong. (2 Corinthians 12:9-10, NIV)

Part of our task as disciples is to become more like Jesus, no matter how long it takes. But if and when we fail, we are not condemned. That said, on Judgement Day God the Father will reward his followers according to what we have done for him in Jesus's name. This reward is beyond the gifts of salvation and eternal life we already received as followers of Jesus when we accepted Jesus as our Saviour and Lord, as denoted in Revelation 22:12-13:

> Look, I am coming soon! My reward is with me, and I will give to each person according to what they have done. I am the Alpha and the Omega, the First and the Last, the Beginning and the End. (NIV)

Christians themselves are not subject to judgement because Jesus has paid the price on the cross for us, as he makes clear in John 6:39-40:

> And this is the will of him who sent me, that I shall lose none of all those he has given me, but raise them up at the last day. For my Father's will is that everyone who looks to the Son and believes in him shall have eternal life, and I will raise them up at the last day. (NIV)

However, Jesus adds the following in John 12:47-49 about those who have not accepted Jesus:

> If anyone hears my words but does not keep them, I do not judge that person. For I did not come to judge the world, but to save the world. There is a judge for the one who rejects me and does not accept my words; the very words I have spoken will condemn them at the last day. For I did not speak on my own, but the Father who sent me commanded me to say all that I have spoken. (NIV)

And in Revelation 20:12-15, the apostle John describes:

> And I saw the dead, great and small, standing before the throne, and books were opened. Another book was opened, which is the book of life. The dead were judged according to what they had done as recorded in the books. The sea gave up the dead that were in it, and death and Hades gave up the dead that were in them, and each person was judged according to what they had done. Then death and Hades were thrown into the lake of fire. The lake of fire is the second death. Anyone whose name was not found written in the book of life was thrown into the lake of fire. (NIV)

Part of the inspiration for writing these studies was a recognition of truth in the observation commonly attributed to Mahatma Gandhi about how Jesus's disciples are frequently not like him. Only by understanding and responding to Jesus can we really fulfil the potential for which he created us.

The life of a follower of Jesus should be one in which we respond to God out of love, not out of duty nor out of personal pressure, whether from ourselves or from others. This is why the critical influence of the Holy Spirit is presented as part of the first study as he is key to living life as God intended for us. Trying to implement the Kingdom Practices without the Holy Spirit would just result in stress, guilt, and a sense of failure. Accepting Jesus frees us from this burden and, to the extent that we allow him, helps us live under the Holy Spirit's guidance day by day.

As the body of Christ, the church in its global sense, we are part of a mystery. We are broken and whole at the same time, called to serve each other, to help restore our brothers and sisters, and to have the grace to accept the help of others in times of need. The body of Christ should ideally be a place of friendship, love, and a commitment to the good of all. We all have skills and talents to contribute to the extension of God's kingdom on earth in keeping with his sovereign plan, whether through simple quiet service in our own community or pioneering activity on some foreign field.

Questions

> - Given the material presented in Figures 2 and 3 and the Kingdom Fundamentals and Kingdom Practices that have

been identified (corresponding to the topics in studies 2 to 13), what is your initial reaction to what has been outlined?

- Does it surprise you? If so, in what way?
- Is there anything missing in these figures you might have expected to see at this point? If so, it should appear as you work through each of the individual studies.
- Conversely, is there something in Figure 3 that you might not have considered before?
- With an emphasis on putting Jesus's commands into practice, how do you think you'd score on your application of the Kingdom Fundamentals and Kingdom Practices presented? Where might you most need to grow? Are you struggling with any of these things as you currently understand them at this point in the book? This is just something to consider and reflect upon, not for self-criticism.

In the subsequent studies we will look at each of these Kingdom Fundamentals and Kingdom Practices in more detail, together with some of the relevant commands and quotations of Jesus from which these principles have been derived.

However, before we address the individual Kingdom Fundamentals and Kingdom Practices, we must first understand our essential need for the Holy Spirit within us to lead and guide our lives as believers.

Study 1 - The Essential Need for the Holy Spirit in Our Lives

Subtitle: The Precious Gift from God to Lead Us into All Truth and Help Us Become More like Jesus

Study 1 - Introduction

First of all, welcome to this set of studies about the commands of Jesus and how you may be able to put them into practice better through the power of the Holy Spirit. Before we focus on the commands and how they have been categorised into a set of Kingdom Fundamentals and Kingdom Practices, it is important to consider the role of the Holy Spirit in the life of all followers of Jesus. This is what our first study introduces.

Figure 4 visualises how the Holy Spirit is central to interacting with each of us. Firstly as we seek to undertake the three Kingdom Fundamentals to love God, follow Jesus, and love our neighbour as ourselves. Secondly as we seek to implement the Kingdom Practices that correspond to these fundamentals.

Subsequent studies will each include a different version of this diagram related to the Kingdom Fundamental or Kingdom Practice under discussion. This will build until the final version in Study 14, which will be identical to that shown in the Introduction to the Studies in Figure 3.

Figure 4 - The Essential Need for the Holy Spirit in Our Lives

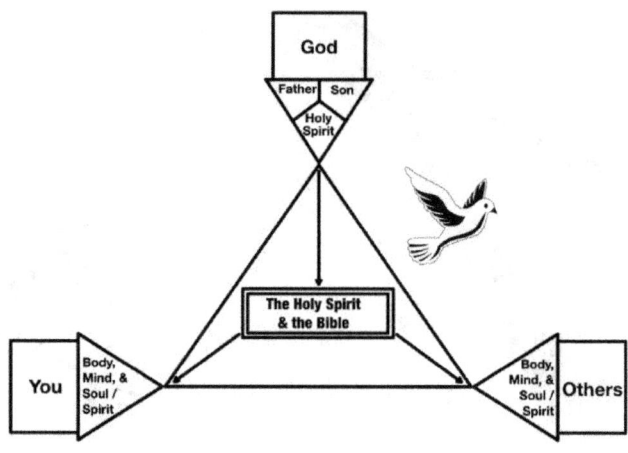

Study 1 - Biblical Support for the Importance of the Holy Spirit

The Holy Spirit is God's active force on earth, indwelling every believer. The Holy Spirit and the Bible represent two of the main spiritual influences for those actively seeking to live as followers of Jesus. The Bible itself is, of course, inspired by the Holy Spirit:

> All Scripture is God-breathed and is useful for teaching, rebuking, correcting and training in righteousness, so that the servant of God may be thoroughly equipped for every good work. (2 Timothy 3:16–17 NIV)

However, there are other influences impacting believers that we must consider. Some of these are positive, faith-reinforcing interactions such as prayer, corporate worship, biblically-based church teaching, fellowship with other believers, Christian books, and Christian media.

But there are negative influences as well. These include some aspects of secular media or even media claiming to be Christian that espouse false messages such as the prosperity gospel. Other negative input can include watching and/or reading inappropriate material or allowing ourselves to be in situations with others where our integrity may be compromised:

> Do not be misled: Bad company corrupts good character. (1 Corinthians 15:33, NIV)

That said, just plain "going it alone" as Christians isn't the answer as we are called to reach the lost. Not all Christians may be in a place where they feel fully confident in their faith. Even so, we still need to come alongside and befriend unbelievers so they can see Jesus in us and hopefully respond to what they see in a positive manner. Yes, we live in this world, but as Jesus's followers we are in fact citizens of the Kingdom of God, called to make disciples from the world. Jesus, after all, spent a huge amount of his time with the most marginalised of society. As God prompts us, we should be prepared to reach out to the lost and marginalised too.

During his earthly ministry, Jesus spoke of teachings he could not yet share fully because he had not yet submitted himself to his unjust death by crucifixion and subsequent resurrection by God (Acts 2:24, Acts 10:40). The most important of such teachings concerned the sending of the Holy Spirit as a promise to every believer, which could only be accomplished once Jesus had ascended into heaven.

After Jesus returned to heaven, we see the active influence of the Holy Spirit in the lives of the disciples and apostles, especially as detailed in the book of Acts. Through the direct inspiration of the Holy Spirit, the New Testament was written. The following scriptures are important truths for us as disciples to believe and understand that the Holy Spirit remains active in the lives of Christians today:

> Nevertheless, I am telling you the truth. It is for your benefit that I go away, because if I don't go away the Counsellor will not come to you. If I go, I will send Him to you. (John 16:7)

> "Repent," Peter said to them, "and be baptised, each of you, in the name of Jesus Christ for the forgiveness of your sins, and you will receive the gift of the Holy Spirit. For the promise is for you and for your children, and for all who are far off, as many as the Lord our God will call." (Acts 2:38-39)

> After they went down there, they prayed for them, so the Samaritans might receive the Holy Spirit. For He had not yet come down on any of them; they had only been baptised in the name of the Lord Jesus. Then Peter and John laid their hands on them, and they received the Holy Spirit. (Acts 8:15-17)

> The purpose was that the blessing of Abraham would come to the Gentiles by Christ Jesus, so that we could receive the promised Spirit through faith. (Galatians 3:14)

These references show specifically that Jesus had to leave the earth so that the Holy Spirit could come and live in us as believers. The Old Testament book of Joel foretells the time when God will pour out his Spirit on all flesh (Joel 2:28-32). The time period Joel referenced in this passage is that following the death, resurrection, and ascension of Jesus, as the apostle Peter himself affirmed in Acts 2:17-21.

Some Christian traditions teach that this outpouring of the Holy Spirit has already come and gone, whereas other Christian groups live in the reality that God's Spirit remains an active force in the lives of believers today—and even in the lives of unbelievers in terms of drawing them to faith in Jesus.

Study 1 - Our Context

So how does this teaching relate to us today? When compared to other religions, one key truth of Christianity is the wonderful reality that God promises to give part of himself, the Holy Spirit, to live within every believer. Additional differentiators from other religions include:

- God stepping down into his creation to experience life as a human (Jesus), yet living without sin and, in fact, paying the price for humanity's sins through his sacrifice on the cross.

- Salvation by grace alone (Ephesians 2:8-9) so that by accepting Jesus as Saviour and Lord we can know that our sins are forgiven once and for all and we can receive the gift of eternal life now and forever.

- That these other religions do not offer such assurance, but require the follower to obtain salvation (or an equivalent such as nirvana) by works, so that only upon death and/or their day of judgement will they find out if they have done "enough".

The Holy Spirit does not possess or control us in the sense we see described in Scripture of demon possession since God's way of being involved in our lives will never be forceful or against our will. But as we allow him, the Holy Spirit will prompt us and bring things into our consciousness. As we grow in our knowledge of Scripture and as our faith and obedience develop, we will be better able to recognise the Spirit's promptings in a range of situations. The Holy Spirit is given to help us overcome challenges and temptations we face in our fallen world. He is not a guarantee of "success" as the world or even the prosperity gospel defines it but is always available to help us in our daily struggles. Indeed, the Spirit can also restore, encourage, comfort, and bring healing and is at work in places and situations of which we are not even aware.

The Holy Spirit is a spiritual Being so is not generally felt in a physical sense, although believers may testify they can "feel" his presence from time to time. Sensing may be a more accurate description. Certainly, many believers have shed tears or felt other emotions when they experience their first or a subsequent filling of the Holy Spirit.

We are encouraged to keep on being filled with the Holy Spirit (Ephesians 5:18), principally because Christians still have a sinful nature and unconfessed sin tends to diminish the Spirit's influence within us. The image conveyed is that we are "leaky vessels" and that is why we need to be continually filled. Also, as we are God's children, he wants to be intimately involved in our lives.

More specifically the Holy Spirit will communicate with us in a variety of ways that are set out in Scripture, including:

- Dreams and visions (Acts 2:17, 2 Corinthians 12:1-2, Acts 9:10-12)
- Words of Scripture, i.e., a quickening by the Holy Spirit when reading the Bible (John 6:63, 2 Peter 1:19-21)
- Explicit revelation (Ephesians 3:1-6, 1 Corinthians 2:9-10)
- Prophecy via others (Acts 11:27-28, Acts 6:8-11, Acts 21:9-11)
- Specific directions (Acts 8:26-29, Acts 10:19-21)
- Direct leading (Galatians 5:16-18, Acts 16:6-7, Genesis 24:27, 1 Samuel 10:6)
- An inner witness (Romans 8:16, 1 John 5:6-8)

May I encourage you to look up the above biblical references so that you understand how the Holy Spirit works in each case. You can find a much more comprehensive description at the reference below[13].

While I don't wish to downplay the validity of any believer's personal experience, I do urge that we be careful not to rely on our "feelings" in seeking or responding to what we might perceive to be the Holy Spirit,[14] as the apostle Paul admonishes in Ephesians 5:15-21:

> Pay careful attention, then, to how you walk –not as unwise people but as wise –making the most of the time, because the days are evil. So don't be foolish, but understand what the Lord's will is. And don't get drunk with wine, which leads to reckless actions, but be filled by the Spirit: speaking to one another in psalms, hymns, and spiritual songs, singing and making music from your heart to the Lord, giving thanks always for everything to God the Father in the name of our Lord Jesus Christ, submitting to one another in the fear of Christ.

When the Holy Spirit communicates with us, it will never be in a way that contradicts Scripture. Any prompting, direction, or challenge from the Holy

---

[13] http://pneumareview.com/six-ways-the-holy-spirit-will-communicate-with-you-by-charles-carrin/
[14] For a deeper consideration of this, see Chapter VI - Counterfeits of the Divine in *War on the Saints* by Jesse Penn-Lewis and Evan Roberts.

Spirit will always be in accordance with God's Word. If you feel you are being led by the Holy Spirit in a particular direction, I would also encourage seeking the advice of other godly disciples, so that they too can consider the matter in prayer and by searching the Scriptures for confirmation.

We are in a constant battle between the physical world with its related attractions and our desire to please God in response to our salvation in Jesus. The Holy Spirit is our primary God-given resource to help us.

As we mature in our faith, our thinking should develop into a more Christ-like approach to the things we face. The external evidence that we are becoming more like Jesus will be demonstrated in the fruit of the Holy Spirit as outlined in Galatians 5:22-23:

> But the fruit of the Spirit is love, joy, peace, patience, kindness, goodness, faithfulness, gentleness, self-control. Against such things there is no law.

It is important to understand that the Holy Spirit within us is the critical piece of the puzzle that helps Christians overcome temptation to sin and live victorious lives that are pleasing to God. Just as it was impossible for the Jews to obey without fault the Ten Commandments and other religious laws given in the Old Testament, it is impossible for us to practise Kingdom Fundamentals and Kingdom Practices successfully in our own strength. In the Old Testament, the Holy Spirit was given to a very small number of people, mainly prophets such as Moses, Elijah, and Elisha, but also some of Israel's kings, such as Saul, David, and Solomon, as well as other important leaders like Samson and Gideon. In contrast, from Pentecost forward, the Holy Spirit is given to all who come to accept Jesus as their Saviour and Lord.

Study 1 - Application

In this next section, we are challenged to listen to the Holy Spirit as we apply what we have just studied. We will look at examples from the life and ministry of Jesus himself as well as some personal anecdotes of the Holy Spirit's working in the believer's life.

Jesus as Our Example

The Holy Spirit is seen from the outset of Jesus's ministry when Jesus requests that John the Baptist baptise him:

> Then John gave this testimony: "I saw the Spirit come down from heaven as a dove and remain on him. And I myself did not know him, but the one who sent me to baptise with water told me, "The man on whom you see the Spirit come down and remain is the one who will baptise with the Holy Spirit." I have seen and I testify that this is God's Chosen One." (John 1:32-34, NIV. See also Mark 1:10 and Luke 3:21-22)

This Scripture passage highlights that Jesus is the person through whom the Spirit will be given. In the Gospel of Luke, chapter three, we read further that directly after his baptism Jesus was full of the Holy Spirit and entered into the desert to fast, where he was subsequently tempted by the devil. Was Jesus better able to withstand the temptation because he was full of the Spirit, or could he have done so in any case because he was the incarnate Son of God? Or are both true? While the Scriptures do not specify here, we can see a distinct connection between being full of the Spirit and resisting Satan's temptations.

Jesus himself refers to the Holy Spirit on a number of occasions.

When Jesus was in Nazareth, he read a prophetic scripture from Isaiah 61:1-2 and confirmed that he himself was that scripture's fulfilment as set out in Luke 4:14-21:

> Jesus returned to Galilee in the power of the Spirit, and news about him spread through the whole countryside. He was teaching in their synagogues, and everyone praised him. He went to Nazareth, where he had been brought up, and on the Sabbath day he went into the synagogue, as was his custom. He stood up to read, and the scroll of the prophet Isaiah was handed to him. Unrolling it, he found the place where it is written: "The Spirit of the Lord is on me, because he has anointed me to proclaim good news to the poor. He has sent me to proclaim freedom for the prisoners and recovery of sight for the blind, to set the oppressed free, to proclaim the year of the Lord's favour." Then he rolled up the scroll, gave it back to the attendant and sat down. The eyes of everyone in the synagogue were fastened on him. He began by saying to them, "Today this scripture is fulfilled in your hearing." (NIV)

The apostle John also records in his Gospel that Jesus promises the Holy Spirit to help his followers:

> If you love me, keep my commands. And I will ask the Father, and he will give you another advocate to help you and be with you forever— the Spirit of truth. The world cannot accept him, because it neither sees him nor knows him. But you know him, for he lives with you and will be in you. (John 14:15-17, NIV)

In his teaching on prayer, which we will consider in more detail in Study 4, Jesus also indicates God's willingness to pour his Spirit on those who ask him:

> If you then, who are evil, know how to give good gifts to your children, how much more will the heavenly Father give the Holy Spirit to those who ask Him? (Luke 11:13)

As followers of Jesus, Romans 8:26 provides us additional reassurance:

> In the same way, the Spirit helps us in our weakness. We do not know what we ought to pray for, but the Spirit himself intercedes for us through wordless groans. (NIV)

In Ephesians 6:10-18, we are commanded to put on the full armour of God, which includes the sword of the Spirit:

> Take the helmet of salvation and the sword of the Spirit, which is the word of God. (v. 17, NIV)

And 1 Corinthians 10:13 assures us:

> No temptation has overtaken you except what is common to humanity. God is faithful, and He will not allow you to be tempted beyond what you are able, but with the temptation He will also provide a way of escape so that you are able to bear it.

The Holy Spirit is given to the believer to lead, teach, and guide. He is God within us, something unique to Christianity, as we discussed earlier. The indwelling Holy Spirit helps us live and work victoriously to the extent that we allow him to influence us. This is something not available to the non-believer.

Jesus had to suffer, die, and be raised to life, then return to his Father in heaven, so that God the Father could send the Holy Spirit. We see in the early part of Acts the effect this had on the community of believers who had seen Jesus after his resurrection. From hiding away for fear of the Jews, they were transformed by the Holy Spirit into a bold group who proclaimed the gospel with such power that a huge number of listeners also became believers within a short space of time (Acts 2:41). In particular, the gift of speaking in other languages enabled these early converts to testify of God's work to the many different people groups (i.e., nationalities) assembled in Jerusalem for the festival of Pentecost (Acts 2:5-12).

Some Brief Personal Reflections on the Holy Spirit

The indwelling of the Holy Spirit can be a cause of some concern for those coming to faith. When I accepted Christ, it was very much an act of faith that God would demonstrate his reality to me as I began and continued my walk with him. This he has done time and again over the years, particularly in terms of answered prayer, although explicit God-instances (what the world would refer to as coincidences) that reinforce faith have diminished a little as I have become surer of his presence and his promises in Scripture.

Recently some missionary friends recounted how they were seeking God as a couple for the next phase of their ministry. The wife does not usually remember dreams, but did so on this occasion and upon waking shared her dream with her husband. The Holy Spirit was clearly at work because her husband had experienced the exact same dream. The message each received was to wait for a guide for the next step of their journey.

Some believers may have a particular experience of the Holy Spirit in a meeting or group, possibly through the laying on of hands by a fellow believer. This was true in my own case when I went forward at a conference and subsequently welled up with many tears. But not every believer should expect to undergo the same experience, as God works differently in each of us. What is important is that we should put our trust in the Bible, particularly the New Testament references to the Holy Spirit, rather than go chasing after spiritual experiences at different meetings, conferences, and so on. God is working in us and through us by his Spirit as we allow him.

So in my walk of faith, I am aware of the Spirit's prompting, but not on a continual basis even though he is walking with me constantly. Maybe this is because I am not listening as well as I should or because I do not always attribute to the Spirit things that he is doing and bringing to my consciousness. Some examples when I know the Spirit is at work include hearing particular passages of music, especially certain hymns, that make emotion well up in me so that tears come to my eyes. Or a passage of Scripture I may have read many times before jumps out at me because of its relevance to my context at that time.

However, when I have urgently needed the Holy Spirit's input due to important issues or particular circumstances in my life, I have been very aware of ideas and thoughts coming into my mind that were definitely not my own but from the Holy Spirit. On one occasion I was speaking long-distance to a young Christian man who was going through a difficult time following the untimely death of his father. A believing family had befriended him in his loss, including one daughter to whom he had formed a strong attachment.

It seemed that the young man had been exaggerating his credentials and achievements to this young woman. This had reached a crisis point, and I had been asked to speak with him. As I prayed before the call, I received a distinct message from the Holy Spirit that I needed to advise the young man to be honest with the girl, the family, and himself. In retrospect, this may seem obvious advice, but at the time I needed clear guidance on what to say as counselling others on Christian life and behaviour was (and is) difficult for me.

More recently when I was seeking to develop the material for this book, the Holy Spirit spoke to me distinctly concerning how to illustrate the Kingdom Fundamentals and Kingdom Practices that have been presented. In the middle of the night, I awoke with a very clear sense that I should be considering Jesus as the ideal example of each Kingdom Fundamental and Kingdom Practice. Consequently, I sought out further scriptures concerning the narratives of Jesus in ministry and at other times. Some examples are straightforward parables. Some are references to Jesus's actions outside the ministry context. Others relate to his direct interactions with people to whom he ministered. For us as disciples, Jesus should be our only role model, and it seems entirely consistent that Jesus practised what he commands us to do.

I undertook a missions trip to South India in late 2017 to teach this material. In the course of praying for people during a number of sessions, I was very aware of the Holy Spirit being at work. I was praying for these people in English with someone translating their needs to me from their native Tamil, so they did not necessarily understand what I was praying for on their behalf. But on some occasions, I could actually sense God's power flowing from me to them. I didn't receive any immediate feedback or visible results on the outcome of these prayers, but I trust that God was answering them in his good time.

Study 1 - Health Check - Questions and Issues to Consider
Biblical Support Section
- In your cultural context, what awareness is there of the spirit world, and what effect does this have on the lives of those around you?

Our Context Section
- Is the reality of the Holy Spirit something you have experienced, whether on particular occasions or as a regular part of your daily walk?
- How does the Holy Spirit interact with you, or how do you interact with him?

Application Section
- Have you any experience of being tempted where you sensed the Holy Spirit prompting you to turn away or providing a way out?
- What happened, and how did you respond?

Study 1 - Possible Action
Consider whether the Holy Spirit is prompting you to take a further step concerning his involvement in your life. Why not write this down in the text box provided (or in your journal/notebook) in the form of a prayer, then record the date.

My Response/Prayer and Date

Space For You To Record Responses To Questions, Make Notes, Etc.

Study 1 - The Essential Need for the Holy Spirit in Our Lives

Study 1 - Memorising the Structure

Can you fill in the blank boxes without looking at the figure displayed at the beginning of this study?

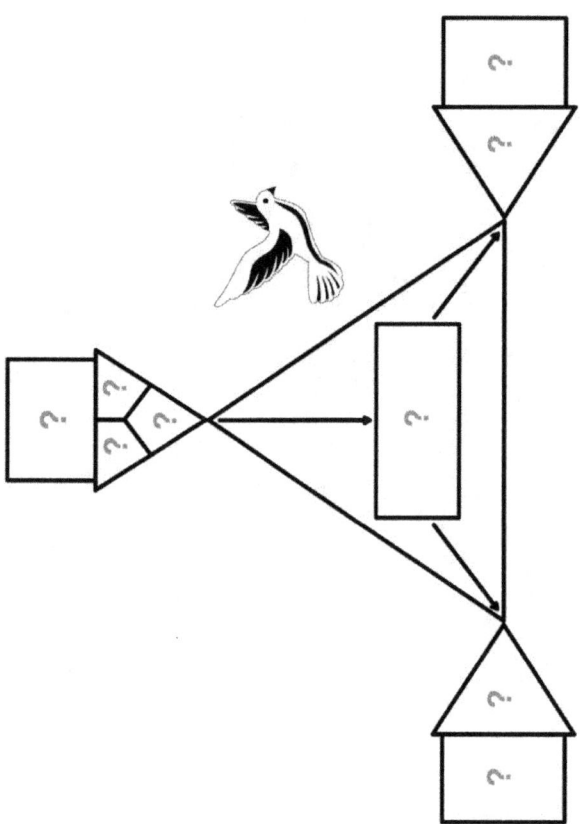

Study 2 - Love God (the Trinity) - (KF1)
Subtitle: What It Means to Make God the Most Important Thing in Our Lives as Jesus's Followers

Love:
> Love is patient, love is kind. It does not envy, it does not boast, it is not proud. It does not dishonour others, it is not self-seeking, it is not easily angered, it keeps no record of wrongs. Love does not delight in evil but rejoices with the truth. It always protects, always trusts, always hopes, always perseveres. (1 Corinthians 13:4-7, NIV)

God: The Being perfect in power, wisdom, and goodness who is worshipped as creator and ruler of the universe.

Study 2 - Introduction

This study focuses on the first "great commandment" to love God. This is for us as individuals and for those we are journeying with and/or teaching as followers of Jesus.

Figure 5 demonstrates that the commandment to love God is a two-way relationship between each of us and the Trinity. A strong influence from the Holy Spirit and the Bible is essential to helping us love God more effectively.

Figure 5 - Kingdom Fundamental 1 - to Love God

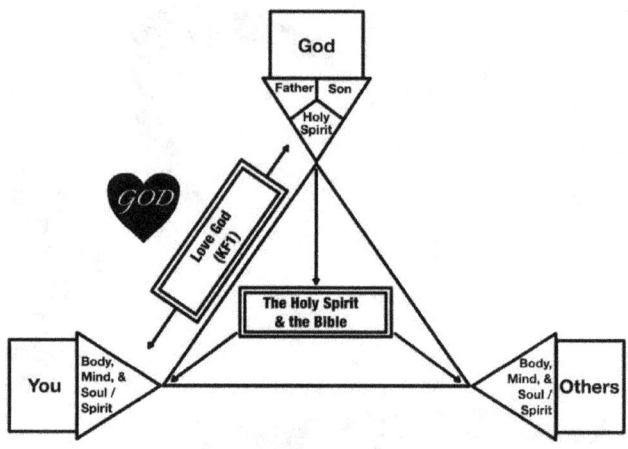

Study 2 - Biblical Support for This Kingdom Fundamental

First and foremost, as Jesus's disciples we need to love God/the Lord as set out in the first "great commandment":

> Love the Lord your God with all your heart, with all your soul, with all your mind, and with all your strength. (Mark 12:30. See also Matthew 22:37-38 and Deuteronomy 6:5)

Interestingly, Jesus does not quote the first of the Ten Commandments here as set out in Deuteronomy 5:7 and in particular Exodus 20:3:

> You shall have no other gods before me. (NIV)

The phrasing in Deuteronomy 6:5 seems to be a "better definition" as far as Jesus is concerned:

> Love the Lord your God with all your heart, with all your soul, and with all your strength.

All these texts would have been very familiar to Jesus's listeners.

It is also interesting that Jesus adds the term "all your mind" in his statement in Mark 12:30 when compared with Deuteronomy 6:5. As to why, we see in their discussion that both the teacher of the law and Jesus seem to agree that understanding God encompasses both soul and mind, leaving the heart perhaps as an emotional response and strength as our will or sheer determination. Verse 34 tells us that Jesus recognises that the man has answered wisely:

> "Well said, teacher," the man replied. "You are right in saying that God is one and there is no other but him. To love him with all your heart, with all your understanding and with all your strength, and to love your neighbour as yourself is more important than all burnt offerings and sacrifices." When Jesus saw that he had answered wisely, he said to him, "You are not far from the kingdom of God." And from then on no one dared ask him any more questions (Mark 12:32-35, NIV).

As disciples we try to understand that God is three indivisible persons as Father, Son, and Holy Spirit. That is, God is 100% Father, 100% Son, and 100% Holy Spirit. The Trinity works and operates together in seamless harmony, upholding the whole of creation and intervening in the lives of believers and unbelievers. In response, we should put God (the Trinity) first in our lives constantly and consistently while seeking God's will on a daily basis as we attempt to walk step by step with him. We all face the challenges this poses wherever we live. Such things as secularism, consumerism, and material comforts do their part to entice people away from putting God uppermost in everything.

Regardless of what upbringing we experienced, God as our heavenly Father loves each one of us unconditionally and equally, no matter who we are or what we've done. He made each one of us complete with our own particular skills, capabilities, and gifts. He longs for us to have a relationship with him, which is only possible through accepting Jesus as our Saviour and Lord. He wants us to interact with him through prayer, reading his Word, worship, or simply spending quiet time alone with him, whether outdoors in nature or some other place where we can be away from the distractions of life. As with any other relationship, building our love for God requires time, effort, and commitment. We should look forward to our time with him as we would with any person dear to us.

Jesus tells us in Matthew 16:24:

> Whoever wants to be my disciple must deny themselves and take up their cross and follow me. (NIV. Mark 8:34 and Luke 9:23)

This means that as his disciples we are to deny ourselves to fulfil what Jesus requires of us. There is a cost to being a disciple, just as there was a cost for Jesus to be our Saviour on the cross. Examples of this cost could include:

- Being unpopular because people do not like the message of Jesus and the cross.

- Denial of some worldly pleasures and benefits because we are led to follow a simpler lifestyle than those around us.[15]

- Prejudice in some form, whether racial, class, educational, cultural etc., because we are led to live, work, and/or serve in a different context than our own birth place.

- Death to pride as we rely upon God the Holy Spirit to work within us.[16]

Thankfully, we do not have to do this in isolation but as part of a community of believers who can walk with us and share our challenges as well as our joys. We will look at this in more detail in subsequent studies.

Taking up our cross and following Jesus does not mean that we will all become preachers or missionaries in a foreign land. Rather, it is an ongoing action to seek God's will for our lives on a daily basis by:

- Reading the Scriptures regularly.

- Being sensitive to the promptings of the Holy Spirit.

- Listening to others and testing their suggestions in the context of Scripture.

- Responding appropriately to events that affect our personal lives and the wider world.

- Seeking God's will and direction in prayer.

- Committing all we do, once we have some sense of what is being asked of us, to God for his glory.

An important part of living out our love for God is understanding that Jesus wants us to be in fellowship with him on a continual basis. This can be much harder than it may seem as it is easy to separate our daily living from our prayer and study times. Jesus reminds his disciples in John 15:7:

---

[15] Many people have left a potential life of comfort to go and minister as missionaries in remote rural or other contexts. John Wesley's annual expenditures remained the same in his published accounts despite raising huge sums for the work of the Kingdom.
https://www.christianitytoday.com/pastors/1987/winter/8711027.html
[16] Adapted from OMF International training material "The Way of the Cross".

> If you remain in Me and My words remain in you, ask whatever you want and it will be done for you.

In other words, we are to seek to be in constant contact[17] with God and Jesus through the power of the Holy Spirit. This is particularly important as we strive for Christ-like attitudes and thoughts and to carry out actions and responses that are consistent with these. Being authentic in what we say and do should be our main focus according to Jesus's own teaching and commands.

Just as human relationships only develop when we spend quality time with people, so our relationship with God in Jesus can only deepen as we read the Bible (listen to God) and pray (speak to him), sharing with him the joys, successes, challenges, and struggles of our lives. In other words, we need to treat our relationship with Jesus as if he were with us all the time, which he is through the power of the Holy Spirit.

The first "great commandment" could be considered an encapsulation of the first three of the Ten Commandments (see Exodus 20 and Deuteronomy 5):

- We must not have other gods before God.
- We must not make any graven image.
- We must not take God's name in vain.

In our love for God as his disciples, we should be striving to live out these commandments under the guidance of the Holy Spirit.

Study 2 - Our Context

While Jesus offers no specific parables related to his command to love God, he does provide two back-to-back analogies that show how important it is to accept his offer of salvation and to become a citizen of his heavenly kingdom. In effect, these analogies are illustrations of how important and superior a relationship with God in Jesus is when compared to worldly things:

> The kingdom of heaven is like treasure hidden in a field. When a man found it, he hid it again, and then in his joy went and sold all he had and bought that field. Again, the kingdom of heaven is like a

---

[17] What "continual" and "constant" mean above is open to personal interpretation. However, the point is that God want us to be in frequent contact with him, not just first thing in the morning or last thing at night or whenever we set aside time for our formal study/prayer time.

merchant looking for fine pearls. When he found one of great value, he went away and sold everything he had and bought it. (Matthew 13:44-45, NIV)

Our own specific context—home, employment, health, financial, family, religious, cultural—will present different things that attract and motivate us, some of which may be at odds with putting God first. By this world's standards, there are three principal drivers and motivators for living successfully: love (including sex), money (including greed for things and possessions), and power (control over others or prestige or status). While not necessarily universal, most people seek to pursue at least one of these to some degree. But pursuing these can prevent us from loving God as fully as we should. Among those things people strive for are:

- Being loved or loving someone (love).
- Owning their own home (money).
- Providing for a comfortable retirement through building up a good "pension pot" (money).
- Owning one or more vehicles, including possibly an expensive one (money/status).
- Wearing the latest fashion items and owning things from specific labels and brands (money/possessions).
- Seeking seniority and influence at work, i.e., achieving high professional status (power).

Also to a lesser extent:

- Idolising pop-stars, actors, actresses, and sports personalities (love).
- Living and staying connected on the internet (love/status).
- Pursuing hobbies and pastimes (love/money/power).

In some cultural contexts, what people strive for may also include:

- Being seen to be at work most of the hours available each week and even spending non-work time with colleagues, a business "norm" in places like Japan (sense of love and duty).
- Being in harmony with family, colleagues, and neighbours, a strong motivator in East Asia where needs of the group take precedence over individual priorities (love/harmony). This is not a bad thing!
- Putting the needs of the community ahead of personal desires and aspirations (love). Again, this is not necessarily negative if this is sacrificial giving in a Christian context where God is at the centre of motivation.

- Pursuing personal wealth, which seems to be almost a universal goal (money).

In many places, all people may be seeking is enough for self and family to survive from one day to the next, including access to clean water, food, shelter, and clothing. Education, healthcare, or provision for old age aren't even a consideration, while those unfortunate enough to live in conflict zones are focused on simply remaining alive and protecting those they love.

From a personal perspective, I am unqualified to comment on how difficult life is for countless millions who live with the daily reality of poverty, intimidation, violence, and persecution. The good news is that God in Jesus is not constrained by our circumstances and loves each of us equally since he is our Creator and heavenly Father. What he wants from us is to put him first, upon which his Word promises that he will then provide for our needs, if not necessarily all our wants, as we will examine further in Study 6.

In summary, making our relationship with God the highest priority in our life is not easy, especially when we are constantly bombarded with marketing messages about bigger, better, tastier, smarter, and faster.

Study 2 - Kingdom Fundamental Application

Jesus as Our Example

Our challenge now is to put loving God into daily practice. To accomplish this, we can look at the loving relationship between God the Father and Jesus as shown in Scripture:

> As soon as Jesus was baptised, he went up out of the water. At that moment heaven was opened, and he saw the Spirit of God descending like a dove and alighting on him. And a voice from heaven said, "This is my Son, whom I love; with him I am well pleased." (Matthew 3:16–17, NIV)
>
> Aware of this, Jesus withdrew from that place. A large crowd followed him, and he healed all who were ill. He warned them not to tell others about him. This was to fulfil what was spoken through the prophet Isaiah: "Here is my servant whom I have chosen, the one I love, in whom I delight; I will put my Spirit on him, and he will proclaim justice to the nations. He will not quarrel or cry out; no one will hear his voice in the streets. A bruised reed he will not break, and a smouldering wick he will not snuff out, till he has brought justice through to victory. In his name the nations will put their hope." (Matthew 12:15-21, NIV)
>
> While he was still speaking, a bright cloud covered them, and a voice from the cloud said, "This is my Son, whom I love; with him I am well pleased. Listen to him!" (Matthew 17:5, NIV)
>
> For the law was given through Moses; grace and truth came through Jesus Christ. No one has ever seen God, but the one and only Son,

> who is himself God and is in closest relationship with the Father, has made him known. (John 1:17-18, NIV)
>
> I and the Father are one. (John 10:30, NIV)

From the John 10 reference, we understand that Jesus and the Father were "as one". On at least two occasions, we also see God the Father stating clearly his love for Jesus. And Jesus in turn has already highlighted that to love God is the most important command of all. He practised this as he went about his ministry, supported by prayer and then obedience to the Father's will.

Some Brief Personal Reflections on Loving God

Loving God in a way that always puts him first is difficult for everyone, and I too continue to fail in doing this as fully as might be possible. As I prepare this material, I am only too conscious of my own weaknesses. Which is why I appreciate Jesus's analogies of the buried treasure and pearl as they convey the excitement of someone entering God's kingdom. The focus is upon allowing God to change us rather than us trying to change ourselves.

I try to be diligent in what I am doing as set out in Ephesians 6:7-8:

> Serve wholeheartedly, as if you were serving the Lord, not people, because you know that the Lord will reward each one for whatever good they do, whether they are slave or free. (NIV)

This is part of the answer. Whatever my task, whether at work, at leisure, with family, in church, or elsewhere, I seek to give my best as though serving God directly. Still, like you I am human, so my earthly nature is "at war" with my spiritual nature as the apostle Paul also discovered (Romans 7:14-25). I take comfort from recognising that if someone who wrote a major portion of the New Testament found these things a challenge, I should expect them to be a challenge for me too.

That said, I have the knowledge that God lives in me by his Holy Spirit, so he will be at work within me whether I am conscious of it or not. Ultimately God knows my motivations, how much I love him, and how I respond to his promptings.

In some senses, preparing this Bible study material has been an outworking of my love for and obedience to God. My career in consultancy and the nature of my training there was perhaps what prepared me to undertake an analysis like that presented in the *All That I Have Commanded You* book. I strongly sensed that God was asking me to create these materials as a means to explain Jesus's commands to others and to help us live them out in our daily lives, and I trust he will use this material for his glory.

Study 2 - Kingdom Fundamental Health Check
Biblical Support Section
- What does loving God mean in practice?

Our Context Section
- In your cultural context, what is the widespread view of the God of creation and the commandment to love him?
- Is knowing God in Jesus like the pearl of great price or the buried treasure in the field for you? Describe how you feel about your relationship with God.
- What do you currently put first in your life and why?

Kingdom Fundamental Application Section
- What does it mean for you to love God with all your heart, soul, mind, and strength?
- To what extent do you feel that this is a reality in your own life or in the lives of other disciples that you know?
- Is the love you have for God the same as the love you have for other people? If not, how is it different?
- Can we make ourselves love God or people, or is it an active choice?
- Is there anything that prevents you from experiencing God's love as demonstrated on the cross?
- Have you bought into your local culture's worldview (system of thinking) rather than that of God's Kingdom, or has addressing the cares of this world taken priority?
- What might you feel God needs to do for you to love him more? (He sent his Son Jesus to pay the price once and for all for our sins, past, present, and future and gave us eternal life; what else would you ask for?)
- What strategies might you use to help you overcome any difficulties and further develop your relationship of love with God? What positive behaviour change(s) might you make?

The Following Studies
As we look at Jesus's commands in detail, two Kingdom Practices stemming from Jesus's teachings fall under and correlate to the Kingdom Fundamental of Love God:

- Listen to (Obey) God.
- Talk (Pray in Faith) to God.

We will consider these in depth in the following two studies. However, it is immediately apparent that these topics are consistent with our normal lives in community with others. If we want to love someone deeply, we can only really do this by listening to and talking with them. As we begin to show our love for them by doing things that help to improve their well-being and they do things for us, our relationship with them will deepen. This applies to our relationship with God too.

Study 2 - Possible Action

Consider whether the Holy Spirit is prompting you to take any steps concerning how you could love God more. Why not write this down in the form of a prayer and then record the date in the outlined text box provided (or your notebook/journal).

Health Warning

Remember that you should not respond to this Kingdom Fundamental in a legalistic way. It is much more about serving God as an outpouring of our love for him because of our salvation in Jesus. We will become more like Jesus the more we allow the Holy Spirit to lead and guide us day by day. As we do so, God will get the glory.

My Response/Prayer and Date

Space For You To Record Responses To Questions, Make Notes, Etc.

Study 2 – Love God

Study 2 - Memorising the Structure

Can you fill in the blank boxes without looking at the figure displayed at the beginning of this study?

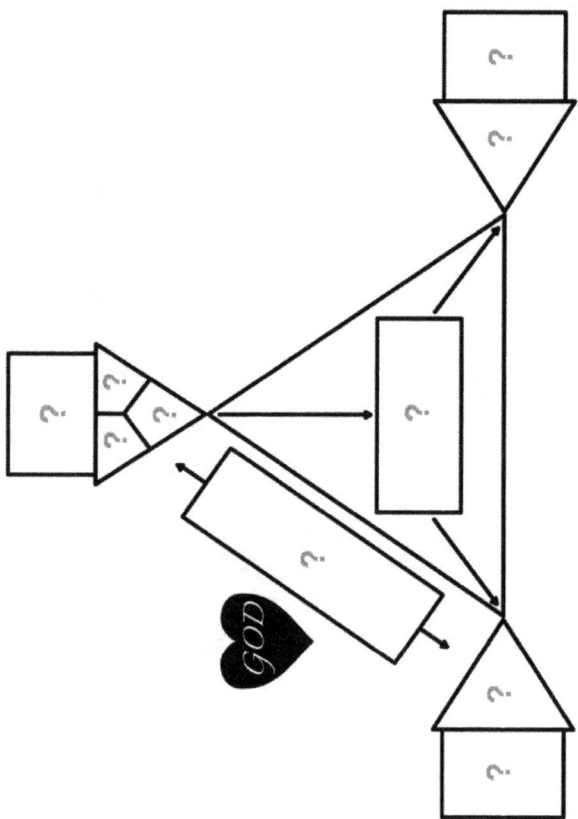

Study 3 - Listen to (Obey) God - (KP1)
Subtitle: How God Communicates What He Wants from Us and the Challenge to Obey

Listen: To hear what someone has said and understand that it is serious, important, or true. To pay attention to someone or something in order to hear what is being said, sung, played, etc[18].

Obey: To follow the commands or guidance of. To conform to or comply with.

Study 3 - Introduction

In this study we will be looking at the first Kingdom Practice that correlates to the Kingdom Fundamental to Love God. This is part of the process of transforming our lives and those of other disciples we may teach into the type of disciple that God in Jesus designed us to be.

---

[18] You might like to consider the following article:
http://www.northumbriacommunity.org/articles/listening-to-god/

The Kingdom Practice to Listen to (Obey) God is also a two-way process between us and the Trinity. There is again a strong influence from the Holy Spirit and the Bible as discussed under the Kingdom Fundamental to Love God. The "listening" part refers to being attentive to what God is saying to us through the Bible and the Holy Spirit. The "obeying" part is our response to his prompting. Figure 6 shows the interactions between the Kingdom Practice and the Kingdom Fundamental to which it corresponds.

Figure 6 - Kingdom Practice 1 - to Listen to (Obey) God

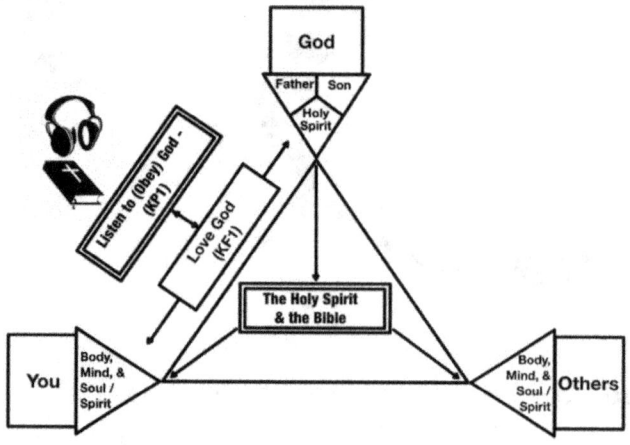

Study 3 - Biblical Support for This Kingdom Practice

This first Kingdom Practice is not so much about hearing an audible voice from God as about being open and receptive to undertaking one or more of the following activities:

- Read the Bible in a structured way so that we can learn and discern what God wants for us individually as the Holy Spirit leads.

- Use daily Bible reading notes or other aids such as concordances and commentaries to help us understand the Scriptures better and improve our ability to witness as disciples of Jesus.

- Reflect on the teaching we receive during worship services, conferences, etc. and whether it has implications for us moving forward spiritually and practically.

- Seek guidance and input from others whom we trust as a way to help clarify, confirm, or even contradict what we may think God is saying to us.
- Be conversant with world events and issues, seeking to understand what God may be saying to us through them.
- Listen to any prompting by the Holy Spirit.
- Be reflective, meditating on a portion of Scripture or an issue and seeking God's guidance and leading.

We can do any or all of these things on our own, but we can also do them as part of a community of believers who are collectively seeking God's will on matters of concern.

We will be looking at six aspects of Jesus's commands that have been drawn out from New Testament teachings of Jesus. These teachings are grouped primarily in terms of God communicating with us as God the Father, God the Son, and God the Holy Spirit. They have been characterised in terms of Kingdom Behaviours as follows:

- Listen to Jesus's voice.
- Be obedient.
- Fear God and not mankind.
- Receive God's power in the Holy Spirit.
- Allow the Holy Spirit to speak through us in time of testing.
- Be steadfast.

Taking each in turn, we will look below at examples and their underpinning Bible references that summarise Jesus's teachings on these topics (see Appendix 2 or the *All That I Have Commanded You* book, Chapter 2.1, for a complete set of scriptures).

3.1 - Listen to Jesus's Voice

On a number of occasions, Jesus states that people need to listen to what he is saying:

> Anyone who has ears should listen. (Matthew 11:15)

This is in response to recognising who Jesus is.

3.2 - Be Obedient

Jesus repeatedly states that we need to obey his teachings, which draw upon the following supporting Kingdom Behaviours:

Keep Jesus's Commands

The commands of Jesus are summarised throughout these studies and the *All That I Have Commanded You* book.

> If you love Me, you will keep My commands. (John 14:15)

Put Jesus's Words and God's Will into Practice

Our challenge as followers is to be not only hearers but doers too (James 1:22-25):

> Not everyone who says to Me, "Lord, Lord!" will enter the kingdom of heaven, but only the one who does the will of My Father in heaven. (Matthew 7:21)

Do Our Duty

Even when we have done what Jesus asks, we have only discharged our responsibilities to him:

> Which one of you having a slave tending sheep or ploughing will say to him when he comes in from the field, "Come at once and sit down to eat"? Instead, will he not tell him, "Prepare something for me to eat, get ready, and serve me while I eat and drink; later you can eat and drink"? Does he thank that slave because he did what was commanded? In the same way, when you have done all that you were commanded, you should say, "We are good-for-nothing slaves; we've only done our duty." (Luke 17:7-10)

Hold To and Obey Jesus's Teachings

By being obedient to Jesus, we will demonstrate our love for God and through the Holy Spirit will be liberated by the truth of God's Word:

> To the Jews who had believed him, Jesus said, "If you hold to my teaching, you are really my disciples. Then you will know the truth, and the truth will set you free." (John 8:31-32, NIV)

> Jesus replied, "Anyone who loves me will obey my teaching. My Father will love them, and we will come to them and make our home with them. Anyone who does not love me will not obey my teaching. These words you hear are not my own; they belong to the Father who sent me." (John 14:23-24, NIV)

Don't Fail to Keep Jesus's Words

We have to respond to Jesus's teachings. If we reject them, then they will be the evidence against us:

> If anyone hears my words but does not keep them, I do not judge that person. For I did not come to judge the world, but to save the world. There is a judge for the one who rejects me and does not accept my words; the very words I have spoken will condemn them at the last day. (John 12:47-48, NIV)

The sense here is that the text is directed at those who reject Jesus's message (non-Christians). However, it might also be considered as applying to those Christians who choose to ignore some of what Jesus is saying.

3.3 - Fear God Not Mankind

Jesus highlights that we need to fear God[19] and not people:

> Don't fear those who kill the body but are not able to kill the soul; rather, fear Him who is able to destroy both soul and body in hell. (Matthew 10:28)

3.4 - Receive God's Power in the Holy Spirit

Receive: To act as a receptacle or container for. To permit to enter.

Jesus promises that our lives as his followers will be empowered by the gift of the Holy Spirit:

> But you will receive power when the Holy Spirit has come on you, and you will be My witnesses in Jerusalem, in all Judea and Samaria, and to the ends of the earth. (Acts 1:8)

3.5 - Allow the Holy Spirit to Speak through Us in Time of Testing

When we face difficulties, Jesus reminds us that we should not worry about what we are to say as the Holy Spirit will speak on our behalf:

> Whenever they bring you before synagogues and rulers and authorities, don't worry about how you should defend yourselves or what you should say. For the Holy Spirit will teach you at that very hour what must be said. (Luke 12:11-12. Matthew 10:19-20 and Mark 13:11)

3.6 - Be Steadfast

Collectively, the following supporting Kingdom Behaviours can be summarised as the need to be steadfast:

Stand Firm to the End

We need to keep to Jesus's teachings in all circumstances:

> You will be hated by everyone because of me, but the one who stands firm to the end will be saved. When you are persecuted in

---

[19] The term "Fear God" is different from the concept of being terrified of something or someone. It is generally considered to include awe, adoration, respect for, and reverence towards God, although that is not immediately apparent in the quotations that are referenced.

one place, flee to another. Truly I tell you, you will not finish going through the towns of Israel before the Son of Man comes. (Matthew 10:22-23, NIV. Matthew 24:13 and Mark 13:13)

Do Not Be Ashamed of Jesus

Jesus requires us to be true to him, particularly among unbelievers:

> For whoever is ashamed of Me and of My words in this adulterous and sinful generation, the Son of Man will also be ashamed of him when He comes in the glory of His Father with the holy angels. (Mark 8:38. Luke 9:26 and Luke 12:8-9)

Be Victorious

Jesus makes a series of promises in Revelation for those who remain obedient to him. One example is given below:

> Anyone who has an ear should listen to what the Spirit says to the churches. I will give the victor the right to eat from the tree of life, which is in God's paradise. (Revelation 2:7)

Study 3 - Our Context

To understand how these principles and behaviours relate to us today and what Jesus wants us to do as individuals, it is vital that we read and study the Scriptures in depth. Jesus's own knowledge of Old Testament Scripture was extensive, and he quoted passages from the Old Testament many times in the Gospels, including to refute Satan when he was tempted in the wilderness. In his Gospel, the apostle John refers to Jesus as being the "Word", and as believers we recognise that the Bible as a whole is God's Word. It is important for disciples to understand that our witness to others will be influenced strongly by our understanding and practice of biblical teaching in the way we live our lives. We need to study both the Old and New Testaments if we are to be led into all truth by the Holy Spirit:

> All Scripture is inspired by God and is profitable for teaching, for rebuking, for correcting, for training in righteousness, so that the man of God may be complete, equipped for every good work. (2 Timothy 3:16-17)

In Matthew 21:28-32, Jesus told a parable that illustrates the issue of listening and then being obedient or disobedient:

> "What do you think? There was a man who had two sons. He went to the first and said, "Son, go and work today in the vineyard." "I will not," he answered, but later he changed his mind and went. Then the father went to the other son and said the same thing. He answered, "I will, sir," but he did not go. Which of the two did what his father wanted?". "The first," they answered. Jesus said to them, "Truly I tell you, the tax collectors and the prostitutes are entering the kingdom of God ahead of you. For John came to you to show you the way of righteousness, and you did not believe him, but the tax

collectors and the prostitutes did. And even after you saw this, you did not repent and believe him." (NIV)

Later in the same chapter, Jesus goes on to say:

> Therefore I tell you that the kingdom of God will be taken away from you and given to a people who will produce its fruit. (Matthew 21:43, NIV)

I wonder how many of us go about our lives believing that we are good followers doing the right things, but in reality not doing them at all or to a very limited degree. Are we in effect being blinded by our own righteousness and acting like the second brother even while we fool ourselves into believing we are the first brother?

Conversely, perhaps there are some aspects of Jesus's teaching that we think we cannot do, make a conscious decision not to do, or do not set out to do. And yet as we allow the Holy Spirit to have greater influence upon us and our behaviours, when the time comes we end up carrying them out after all. We initially downplay our abilities and don't want to get involved, but as we grow in our faith, the Holy Spirit gets to work on us, and we become like the first brother.

In subsections 3.1 to 3.6 above, we see that the Bible, and in particular the teachings and commands of Jesus, sets out what God the Father and Jesus want us to do as disciples. If we study the Bible and allow the Holy Spirit to speak to us, we should discern our role and task for that period or season. Our role and/or task will most likely change with time as we grow and as circumstances around us change. The challenge for us is which brother we intend to be like. In answering that challenge, we need to see it in the context of loving God with all our heart as discussed in Study 2.

Looking at the scriptures above, we can see that there is some important teaching here about our ongoing response in listening to and acting upon what God tells us as a demonstration of our love for him. We will consider some aspects of our personal discipleship and challenges for our own behaviours in terms of obedience in Study 8. Here the focus of Jesus's commands is on our intimate relationship with Father, Son, and Holy Spirit and our need to listen to each of them. We do this through studying the Bible more broadly, through Jesus's specific commands, and by being sensitive to the leading and prompting of the Holy Spirit in our daily lives.

Study 3 - Kingdom Practice Application
Jesus as Our Example

A variety of scriptures confirm that Jesus both listened to and obeyed God the Father during his earthly life. The following scriptures illustrate Jesus's listening and knowledge of Scripture:

> Do not think that I have come to abolish the Law or the Prophets; I have not come to abolish them but to fulfil them. For truly I tell you, until heaven and earth disappear, not the smallest letter, not the least stroke of a pen, will by any means disappear from the Law until everything is accomplished. (Matthew 5:17-18, NIV)

> He went to Nazareth, where he had been brought up, and on the Sabbath day he went into the synagogue, as was his custom. He stood up to read, and the scroll of the prophet Isaiah was handed to him. Unrolling it, he found the place where it is written: "The Spirit of the Lord is on me, because he has anointed me to proclaim good news to the poor. He has sent me to proclaim freedom for the prisoners and recovery of sight for the blind, to set the oppressed free, to proclaim the year of the Lord's favour." Then he rolled up the scroll, gave it back to the attendant and sat down. The eyes of everyone in the synagogue were fastened on him. He began by saying to them, "Today this scripture is fulfilled in your hearing." (Luke 4:16-21, NIV)

> He said to them, "How foolish you are, and how slow to believe all that the prophets have spoken! Did not the Messiah have to suffer these things and then enter his glory?" And beginning with Moses and all the Prophets, he explained to them what was said in all the Scriptures concerning himself. (Luke 24:25-27, NIV)

Jesus's obedience in complying with Scripture is also evident in the following verses:

> He went away a second time and prayed, "My Father, if it is not possible for this cup to be taken away unless I drink it, may your will be done." (Matthew 26:42, NIV)

> "Put your sword back in its place," Jesus said to him, "for all who draw the sword will die by the sword. Do you think I cannot call on my Father, and he will at once put at my disposal more than twelve legions of angels? But how then would the Scriptures be fulfilled that say it must happen in this way?" (Matthew 26:52-54, NIV)

We see in these references that Jesus listened to his Heavenly Father, knew his Father's will, and was obedient. He fulfilled the Old Testament laws and did what his Father wanted, even to the point of submitting to his death on a cross. In addition, an account from Jesus's early life reveals that he was obedient to his earthly parents as well, specifically when he stayed behind in Jerusalem and was subsequently found in the temple:

Then he went down to Nazareth with them and was obedient to them. But his mother treasured all these things in her heart. (Luke 2:51, NIV)

Some Brief Personal Reflections on Listening to God

I worship God in church on Sundays and set aside time to read the Bible daily. In the past I have at times focused on reading the Bible in its entirety by taking a chapter or more a day. These days I am finding it more helpful to read a smaller section of text each day and allow time to think about the passage and how to apply it. Before I read, I pray that the Holy Spirit will bring to my attention anything specific he wants me to know or understand. In other words, I invite the Holy Spirit to lead me forward. I don't receive any specific "message" every time I read, although sometimes reading will speak directly to me and my situation (see Study 1 - Our Context to review how the Holy Spirit speaks to us).

In addition, I read a daily biblical thought/message for the day that offers different perspectives on the Christian life and its challenges as well as strategies and biblical approaches to addressing these. This is a matter of intention and personal commitment. I undertook to do this daily some years back, not out of some feeling of duty but because I wanted to commit to my relationship with God. There are many online and print Christian resources that offer such a daily devotional focus to build us up in our faith. Sometimes circumstances, particularly where my routine is different (usually when I'm away from home), conspire to prevent me from having my normal quiet time.

I tend to be on the slow side in picking up on what God is saying to me. So if God wants to get something through to me, it may take the form of multiple communications, usually from different sources, before I begin to take notice or take action. However, once the message has finally got through to me and I have decided to respond appropriately, then I generally don't find myself prompted subsequently by the Holy Spirit on that subject.

Obedience can be more difficult than listening. There are many things Jesus commanded his followers to do that I have not done. For example, I have not undertaken the washing of people's feet (which is probably inappropriate in a Western context today but is still a common practice in some places, especially rural regions of Africa, Asia, and the Middle East). While we have invited people to our home whom we would not expect to repay us, I suspect there is always more we could do in terms of hospitality.

I do not share Jesus with all those with whom I come into contact either, as for me this is a process of building rapport and relationship before being invited or feeling welcome to share my faith. I do not consider myself to be an evangelist. Teaching seems to better fit my skill set. However, when acquaintances who may not be believers share health or other problems, I routinely ask if they would like me to put them and their concerns on my prayer list, and I will follow up with them on their situation. This demonstrates to them my faith in God, and hopefully as they see answers to prayer, they will also see that God has been at work.

Study 3 - Kingdom Practice Health Check

Biblical Support Section

➢ What does listening to God mean for you?

Our Context Section

➢ In your cultural context, what is the view of the wider community where you live or work to reading the Bible and the relevance of its truth to daily living?

➢ Which of the two brothers in the parable above do you believe yourself to be like?

➢ Is God speaking to you about something he wants you to do? If so, why are you putting this thing off?

Kingdom Practice Application Section

➢ How difficult do you find it to listen/obey?

➢ What things possibly undermine your attempts to listen/obey? Is there anything you could do about it?

➢ How do you approach your personal Bible study? Do you look at things randomly or study systematically?

➢ Do you set aside time, ideally daily, for Bible study? If not, how could you do this?

➢ Are there people you could study with if you don't already? Working together can help you to grow.

Why not take a little time to reflect on one of the scriptures in 3.1 to 3.6 above. Practise being in God's presence. Listen carefully in order to develop healthy and helpful skills. As you are able, consider using a well-respected study guide to help you. There are many Bible study resources for individuals or group study that typically focus on a particular book or theme.

Study 3 - Possible Action

Consider whether the Holy Spirit is prompting you to do something that would help you listen to (obey) God better. Why not write this down in the form of a prayer and then record the date in the outlined text box provided (or your notebook/journal).

Health Warning

Remember that you should not respond to this Kingdom Practice in a legalistic way. It is much more about serving God as part of our love for him because of our salvation in Jesus. We will become more like Jesus the more we allow the Holy Spirit to lead and guide us day by day, and God will get the glory.

My Response/Prayer and Date

Space For You To Record Responses To Questions, Make Notes, Etc.

Study 3 - Listen to (Obey) God

Study 3 - Memorising the Structure

Can you fill in the blank boxes without looking at the figure displayed at the beginning of this study?

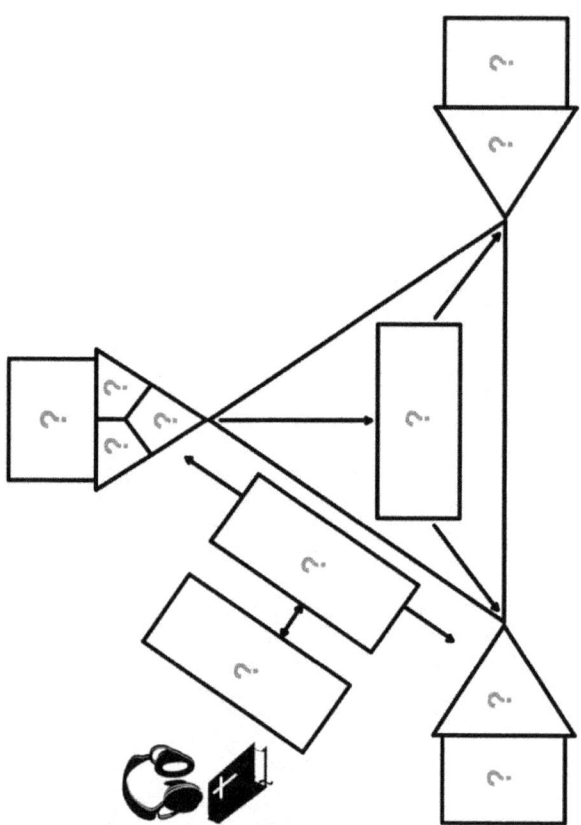

Study 4 - Talk (Pray in Faith) to God - (KP2)

Subtitle: Prioritise Prayer as the Main Means for Developing a Living Relationship with God and Jesus

Talk: To use (a language) for conversing or communicating. To deliver or express in speech.

Pray: To address God or a god with adoration, confession, supplication, or thanksgiving.

Faith:

> Now faith is confidence in what we hope for and assurance about what we do not see. (Hebrews 11:1, NIV)

Study 4 - Introduction

In this fourth study we are looking at the second Kingdom Practice that correlates to the Kingdom Fundamental to Love God, which is to Talk (Pray in Faith) to God.

How this Kingdom Practice sits relationally to its corresponding Kingdom Fundamental is illustrated in three distinct elements in Figure 7. We can be prompted and assisted by the Holy Spirit to pray. We can use the Bible as an aid to prayer, including the use of scriptures we understand to be relevant to our situation. Thirdly, we can respond through our prayers to God, both with our minds and through the help of the Holy Spirit.

Figure 7 - Kingdom Practice 2 - to Talk (Pray in Faith) to God

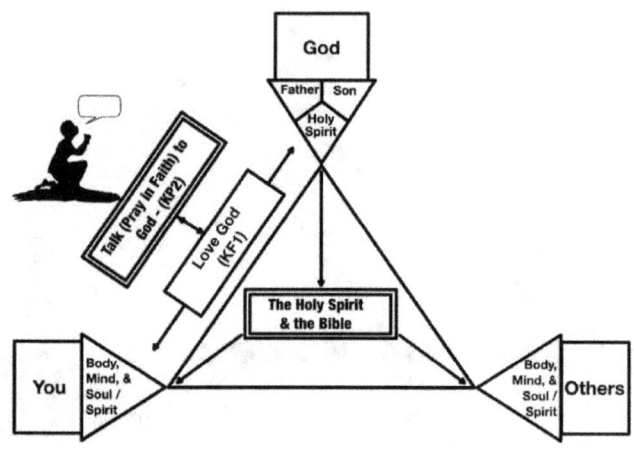

Study 4 - Biblical Support for This Kingdom Practice

Prayer is a challenge for most of us. We may think we are not good at it. Or maybe we have a negative and incorrect view that God won't listen to us, let alone respond. Too often, we don't make it a priority and hence don't set aside time for it. We can become distracted, particularly if we are not alone, and both noise and silence can lead our minds to wander.

We are encouraged to pray at all times in Ephesians 6:18:

> And pray in the Spirit on all occasions with all kinds of prayers and requests. With this in mind, be alert and always keep on praying for all the Lord's people. (NIV)

This means we need to develop an attitude of being ready to pray about anything as our day progresses. Our praying does not need to be audible or visible to others, but we can offer silent prayers as we go about our daily routine or find ourselves in various situations.

Prayer is the privilege we have of being able to share our inmost needs, concerns, and issues with the Creator of the universe. He wants to hear from us and is already at work when we pray. His answers may come quickly or may take years. Indeed, we may not see the answers in our lifetime. Regardless, we are encouraged to come before God enthusiastically, regularly, and expectantly in conversations that can have dramatic consequences for us and the world in which we live. If we persevere, prayer can become a real joy, something to anticipate. We share with our heavenly Father things that have gone well and the challenges we face as we would with a non-judgemental friend.

We can pray alone or with other disciples to discern God's will in a situation and to ask God to act. We should look forward to speaking with him in the same way as we do when we see someone we love, whether our spouse or a close friend.

The importance of prayer can be illustrated in the life of J. O. Fraser, who experienced many years of challenge and fruitlessness in taking the gospel to the Lisu people of China. After some of his immediate family and their friends committed to pray together, he wrote:

> You will see from what I am saying that I am not asking you just to give "help" in prayer as a sort of side-line, but I am trying to roll the main responsibility of this prayer warfare on you. I want you to take the burden of these people upon your shoulders. I want you to wrestle with God for them [20].

Subsequently within a four-month period, six hundred Lisu representing one hundred-twenty-nine families committed to follow Jesus Christ. The conversion of the Lisu is one of the great stories in missions history. Today there are an estimated three hundred thousand Lisu Christians in China, with more among the Lisu living in Myanmar and Thailand. In 1922, J. O. Fraser wrote the following to his prayer partners:

> I used to think that prayer should have the first place and teaching the second. I now feel that it would be truer to give prayer the first, second, and third place, and teaching the fourth [21].

Six aspects of Jesus's commands have been grouped under this heading, summarised in terms of the following actions (Kingdom Behaviours):

- Ask, seek, and knock.
- Ask in Jesus's name.

---

[20] https://omf.org/us/about/our-story/quotes/ (J O Fraser tab - Behind the Ranges: The Life-changing Story of J.O. Fraser. Geraldine Taylor. Singapore: OMF International (IHQ) Ltd., 1998, 269).

[21] https://omf.org/us/about/our-story/quotes/ (J O Fraser tab - Behind the Ranges: The Life-changing Story of J.O. Fraser. Geraldine Taylor. Singapore: OMF International (IHQ) Ltd., 1998, 269).

- Believe you have received.
- Pray for people to spread the gospel.
- Pray for those who persecute us.[22]
- Watch and pray so that we will not fall into temptation.
- Do not babble when you pray.

Let's consider each of these Kingdom Behaviours through reviewing relevant Bible references (see Appendix 2 or the *All That I Have Commanded You* book, Chapter 2.2, for a complete set of supporting scriptures).

4.1 - Ask, Seek, and Knock

Jesus tells us to keep asking in prayer for the things that concern us:

> So I say to you: Ask and it will be given to you; seek and you will find; knock and the door will be opened to you. (Luke 11:9, NIV. Matthew 7:7-8)

4.2 - Ask in Jesus's Name

When we pray, we are to ask in Jesus's name as we do not have any right to ask in our own name:

> I assure you: The one who believes in Me will also do the works that I do. And he will do even greater works than these, because I am going to the Father. Whatever you ask in My name, I will do it so that the Father may be glorified in the Son. If you ask Me anything in My name, I will do it. (John 14:12-14)

4.3 - Believe You Have Received

Jesus states that we will be rewarded if we believe that God will answer when we pray:

> Therefore I tell you, all the things you pray and ask for –believe that you have received them, and you will have them. (Mark 11:24. Matthew 21:22)

4.4 - Pray for People to Spread the Gospel

Jesus highlights that we need to pray for more people to spread the gospel:

---

[22] Open Doors "World Watch List" — http://www.opendoorsuk.org/persecution/

He told them: "The harvest is abundant, but the workers are few. Therefore, pray to the Lord of the harvest to send out workers into His harvest." (Luke 10:2. Matthew 9:37-38).

4.5 - Pray for Those Who Persecute Us

This is a particular challenge from Jesus to pray positively for those who mistreat us:

> But I tell you, love your enemies and pray for those who persecute you. (Matthew 5:44. Luke 6:27-28)

4.6 - Watch and Pray So We Will Not Fall into Temptation

Jesus commanded his disciples to be vigilant, especially in the face of worldly things around us:

> Stay awake and pray, so that you won't enter into temptation. The spirit is willing, but the flesh is weak. (Matthew 26:41)

4.7 - Do Not Babble When You Pray

Jesus tells us to be concise and to the point when we pray:

> And when you pray, do not keep on babbling like pagans, for they think they will be heard because of their many words. Do not be like them, for your Father knows what you need before you ask him. (Matthew 6:7-8, NIV)

Study 4 - Our Context

In understanding how these teachings apply to us today, Jesus again provides some illustrations or parables that set out the approach to prayer we should adopt, including a call to persistence and anticipation that God will act:

> He also said to them: "Suppose one of you has a friend and goes to him at midnight and says to him, "Friend, lend me three loaves of bread, because a friend of mine on a journey has come to me, and I don't have anything to offer him." Then he will answer from inside and say, "Don't bother me! The door is already locked, and my children and I have gone to bed. I can't get up to give you anything."
> I tell you, even though he won't get up and give him anything because he is his friend, yet because of his friend's persistence, he will get up and give him as much as he needs. So I say to you, keep asking, and it will be given to you. Keep searching, and you will find. Keep knocking, and the door will be opened to you. For everyone who asks receives, and the one who searches finds, and to the one who knocks, the door will be opened. What father among you, if his son asks for a fish, will give him a snake instead of a fish? Or if he asks for an egg, will give him a scorpion? If you then, who are evil, know how to give good gifts to your children, how much more will the heavenly Father give the Holy Spirit to those who ask Him?" (Luke 11:5-13)

In this passage, Jesus shows us that we need to persevere in prayer, come before God in boldness, and expect God to answer. Making prayer a priority can be a challenge for most of us, but it is as vital as the need to love God above all other things (Study 2) and listening to (obeying) God (Study 3).

Prayer is the primary means through which we communicate with God. But prayer is just another way of talking. Speaking to God, either audibly or silently, can be just as easy as chatting with our friends or family. There are many ways we can do this, but the Lord's Prayer provides a great model for us. While many treat the Lord's Prayer as a prayer in itself, we read that Jesus provided it as a model for prayer in response to a specific request:

> He was praying in a certain place, and when He finished, one of His disciples said to Him, "Lord, teach us to pray, just as John also taught his disciples." (Luke 11:1)

As a model for prayer, it can be broken down into the following six elements:

- **Praise** – "Our Father in heaven, your name be honoured as holy."

- **Promotion** – "Your kingdom come. Your will be done on earth as it is in heaven."

- **Provision** – "Give us today our daily bread."

- **Pardon** – "And forgive us our debts, as we also have forgiven our debtors."

- **Protection** – "And do not bring us into temptation, but deliver us from the evil one."

- **Praise** – "For yours is the kingdom, the power and the glory, for ever and ever. Amen."[23]

Each phrase can represent a springboard for us to petition God for specific requests relating to ourselves or family, friends, colleagues, governments, employers, etc. These requests may be in terms of loved ones coming into God's kingdom, for health, and/or many other needs. A number of books

---

[23] Note that the emboldened text in these bullets is slightly different from the approach set out in footnote 24.

have been written on the Lord's Prayer that can be real aids to improving our prayer lives.[24, 25]

I have recently become aware of the Temple/Tabernacle Prayer approach, which mirrors the Old Testament process of entering the tabernacle and/or Solomon's temple. The praying person "stops" for prayer at each area and feature that was present in those structures, finally proceeding to the Holy of Holies to make our requests to God. Examples for this prayer pattern can be found in footnotes. [26, 27, 28]

Some people adopt the simpler model of Thank You, Sorry, Please (TSP) or Adoration, Confession, Thanksgiving, Supplication (ACTS) for their prayer life as these headings are easy to remember.

Collectively, the scriptures above give some of Jesus's instructions on how to pray. In addition to the instructions in 4.1 to 4.6 above, we can also consider the following:

Remain (abide) in Jesus.

This includes maintaining an ongoing communication with the Lord and talking directly to him as we live our lives through prayer:

> Remain [Some versions say "abide"] in me, as I also remain in you. No branch can bear fruit by itself; it must remain in the vine. Neither can you bear fruit unless you remain in me. (John 15:4, NIV)

Pray in secret.

Private prayer should ideally be done in seclusion (see Matthew 6:6-8). Corporate prayer at a fellowship or other gathering of believers is something different where Jesus promises to be amongst us:

---

[24] One book on the Lord's Prayer that I have found very helpful is *Could you not tarry one hour?* by Larry Lea.
[25] http://emmausumc-nj.org/wp-content/uploads/2017/05/Lords-Prayer-Prayer-Pattern.pdf
[26] http://lovemyword.com/wp-content/uploads/2014/10/Tabernacle-Prayer-by-Pastor-Cho1.pdf
[27] http://www.bethelupc.org/bulletin/2010/Praying-Through-the-Tabernacle(screen).pdf
[28] http://www.vdrc.org/English/Tools/The%20Temple%20Approach%20to%20Prayer.pdf

> For where two or three gather in my name, there am I with them.
> (Matthew 18:20, NIV)

Our faith that God will answer our requests is almost a prerequisite before we can expect to see a reply, however long it takes and in whatever form.

One extreme example is George Müller,[29] who established orphanages and cared for ten thousand orphaned children in Bristol during the 19th century. Mueller never made appeals for money, trusting implicitly in God. In answer to prayer, he received in total in excess of £1,500,000, which in today's market would value well over £86,000,000.

Another example is James Hudson Taylor, who in 1865 felt that God was calling him to create what became the China Inland Mission to reach people groups in the heart of China. On the flyleaf of his Bible, he wrote, "Prayed for twenty-four willing, skilful labourers at Brighton, June 25, 1865." A bank account under the proposed name of China Inland Mission was opened with the small sum of ten pounds and, as Taylor phrased it, "all the promises of God." Less than a year after that Brighton beach decision, Hudson Taylor with his wife and four children and a party of sixteen other missionaries sailed for China. The call for twenty-four missionaries was being answered.[30]

We are not all asked to exercise our faith like Mueller and Taylor, but we can respond to things God has laid on our heart to pray for. As we see God answering our prayers and experience God bringing us through challenges and difficulties, our faith will grow so that we are able to trust him more.

Keep in mind that God's reply may also not be the outcome we were seeking.

The time of day we can set aside for prayer may vary with our weekly and daily schedules and how we organise our time. For some people early mornings are best, while others will find a different time slot more effective.

Faith is a spiritual gift from God that we can all develop. While some people may have a greater faith than others, we can all grow in our faith through such exercises as taking a small step of faith, seeing God work in response to that, then being prepared to take bigger steps for him. In the same way that an athlete develops his muscles through using them, we need to be people who strive to exercise the faith we have.

---

[29] https://www.mullers.org
[30] https://omf.org/us/about/our-story/james-hudson-taylor/

We must also recognise that at times God may respond to our requests with silence such as when Jesus requested his heavenly Father in the garden of Gethsemane to let the cup of suffering pass from him. This can be a potential cause of stress or frustration. We may have to live with unresolved issues and try to reconcile that with knowing that God loves us and wants the best for us. We may have to try and take some comfort from Romans 8:28:

> And we know that in all things God works for the good of those who love him, who have been called according to his purpose (NIV).

Sometimes the answer might be to wait. We may have a strong vision for something but have to hold onto that while God equips us with the skills and characteristics to be able to fulfil it. For example, you might have a calling to work in the medical profession, but no one would let you loose on real people unless you had received the relevant training and shown proficiency – a process that might take years. Similarly you might want to reach out to a particular people group as a missionary. But before you could be effective, you'd need to learn their heart language and cultural norms and behaviours – again a process that may take many years.

God is at work in his creation today, bringing about change in people and circumstances, but God is always looking at the bigger picture in which you are a part. The Holy Spirit is active in literally billions of situations. Some of our prayers may not have the outcome we hope for, maybe because he is simultaneously working to answer the prayers of others that are all part of his bigger plan:

> "For My thoughts are not your thoughts, and your ways are not My ways." This is the LORD's declaration. "For as heaven is higher than earth, so My ways are higher than your ways, and My thoughts than your thoughts." (Isaiah 55:8-9).

This is not because God can't answer our prayers but may be because granting our requests would create a different outcome than the ones he wants to achieve.

It may be difficult to reconcile scriptures that instruct us to believe we have received with results that don't appear to reflect that belief (see Mark 11:24). Ultimately, God is sovereign and is in control. When his answers are not what we want, this is not necessarily a reflection on our lack of faith, lack of perseverance, unrighteousness at that time, or wrong motives. We need to understand that God's ways and our ways are different.

One example is the story of King David when he fasted, slept on the ground, and dressed in sackcloth while praying for his new-born son, conceived in adultery with Bathsheba, to be restored to health. After his prayers were not answered and the child died, David washed, dressed, went to worship God, and then ate–all contrary to the expectations of his servants (2 Samuel 12:1-25). Why? David explained that he'd fasted and prayed in the hope that God would change his mind and heal his son, but once his son died, there was no longer any purpose in begging God to change his mind, so he returned to normal life.

Can we change God's mind through prayer? In certain circumstances, Scripture seems to indicate this may be possible. One such example was when the patriarch Abraham raised concerns that righteous people might be living in Sodom and Gomorrah after God had indicated he was going to destroy those cities (Genesis 18 and 19). Another is when God threatened to destroy the rebellious nation of Israel after they made and worshipped the golden calf. God relented or "changed his mind" after Moses reminded God of his promises to Israel. Moses expressed concerns that the enemies of Israel would be able to say that God had rescued the Israelites from Egypt only to kill them in the desert (Exodus 32:11-14). Still, even in such circumstances, we must keep in mind that God in his sovereignty already knew the full situation and what would be his final decision.

Study 4 - Kingdom Practice Application

Jesus as Our Example

Some scriptures we can apply to our own lives that show how Jesus prayed to the Father include:

> At that time Jesus, full of joy through the Holy Spirit, said, "I praise you, Father, Lord of heaven and earth, because you have hidden these things from the wise and learned, and revealed them to little children. Yes, Father, for this is what you were pleased to do. All things have been committed to me by my Father. No one knows who the Son is except the Father, and no one knows who the Father is except the Son and those to whom the Son chooses to reveal him." Then he turned to his disciples and said privately, "Blessed are the eyes that see what you see. For I tell you that many prophets and kings wanted to see what you see but did not see it, and to hear what you hear but did not hear it." (Luke 10:21-24, NIV)

> So they took away the stone. Then Jesus looked up and said, "Father, I thank you that you have heard me. I knew that you always hear me, but I said this for the benefit of the people standing here, that they may believe that you sent me." When he had said this, Jesus called in a loud voice, "Lazarus, come out!" The dead man came out, his hands and feet wrapped with strips of linen, and a cloth around his face. Jesus said to them, "Take off the grave clothes and let him go." (John 11:41-44, NIV)

> My prayer is not for them alone. I pray also for those who will believe in me through their message, that all of them may be one, Father, just as you are in me and I am in you. May they also be in us so that the world may believe that you have sent me. I have given them the glory that you gave me, that they may be one as we are one—I in them and you in me—so that they may be brought to complete

unity. Then the world will know that you sent me and have loved them even as you have loved me. (John 17:20-23, NIV)

We have already seen that Jesus and God the Father had great love for one another (Study 2). And we understand that while our entire universe was created through Jesus (John 1:1-3), during his ministry here on this earth Jesus had to rely on prayer for the power to heal and minister to others.

Some Brief Personal Reflections on Prayer

Over the years I found that getting up earlier than was necessary just to get ready for work was the most effective way for me to set aside time to pray. Others of my household were generally not about, and I could concentrate on reading Scripture, daily notes, and prayer. When I had a long commute to work, I read and prayed on the train as well. These days I still pray early in the morning before starting my activities but a little later than when I commuted to London.

More recently, I have created a prayer spreadsheet that provides:

- A four-week programme that addresses subjects of prayer for each day of the week along with those things I will pray for on specific days of each month.
- Short and long-term prayer requests from those in my weekly house group.
- A list of missionaries with whom I have connections.
- Specific countries for which I pray.
- A list of blessings for which I can be thankful, including spiritual and personal blessing as well as family, other people, or physical possessions.

This spreadsheet helps me be intentional about what and whom I pray for, covering daily, weekly, and monthly issues as well as people and organisations that are close to my heart. While I am committed to using this, I don't do it in a legalistic way and am flexible when my routine differs from its norm. I also work through a range of missionary prayer letters and monthly country/ministry prayer diaries during the course of each month.

Both my parents died of cancer. My father's cancer was a rare form associated with an industry with which he had never been involved. Having served in Christian ministry for over twenty-five years, he questioned why this had developed. Although we prayed for my father, his initial recovery from surgery did not last. However, God was still at work as he died on the day he was due to start morphine injections to help manage pain. We were thankful that his suffering was not prolonged.

In a different way, God was also gracious at the end of my mother's life. She was diagnosed with an aggressive brain cancer, and the treatment she received initially gave her a new lease of life. God also answered prayer for her to be looked after in a Christian hospice, enabling her to have a bed after we'd been told three days before that there were no places available. She was peaceful about the whole process, had enjoyed a happy life, and at eighty-nine was ready to go home to her heavenly Father.

In contrast, when someone close to us was expecting a baby, the first two scans highlighted an area of the baby's bowel that does not usually show. This may have been nothing but also may have indicated signs of an echogenic bowel or Hirschsprung's disease, which could mean the baby would need surgery soon after birth. Many prayed for this baby's health and safe delivery. After much prayer, the third scan showed no signs of the potential issue previously present, and a healthy baby was born with no surgery needed. We were naturally very thankful for this.

Collectively, the house-group I am part of has seen many wonderful answers to prayer, often as part of an even wider community of people praying. Specifically, a lady we know was diagnosed with cancer in a number of places in her body. In human terms, the outlook was bleak, but almost from the outset, the family felt that God was communicating with them that she would come through this. Over an extended period of time, many courses of chemotherapy, and the ongoing prayers of people around the globe, this lady came to the point where she had no active cancers in her body. At the time of completing this book, she underwent a further course of chemotherapy for a different type of cancer and has reached an outcome where again there is now no active cancer.

However, it is necessary to note other situations both I and others have prayed for where the result has either not yet been seen or turned out differently from what we'd hoped. For example, we have prayed for friends and family members to come to faith who have not yet done so. Others have had their health deteriorate to the point where they did not recover. As indicated previously, we are called to pray constantly, but that does not mean that everything we seek is in God's will. The way God works and his purposes often remain a mystery to us.

In practice, I find it difficult to think about praying while going about the course of my day. Some are able to manage this better. Personally, I've found there is a balance to be struck between stopping for prayer every time I face a situation and using my God-given skills and capabilities to just get on with what needs to be done. In summary, while I am getting better at it, I can admit honestly that I too still find it difficult to implement a life of constant prayer.

Study 4 - Kingdom Practice Health Check
Biblical Support Section
➢ What does talking (praying in faith) to God mean for you?

Our Context Section
➢ In your cultural context, how important is prayer? Is it different from the processes described in this session?

➢ How do the two points listed in the Our Context Section—Remain (Abide) in Jesus and Pray in Secret—affect the practice of prayer?

➢ Is there anything in our coverage of this topic you think might be missing? If so, what?

Kingdom Practice Application Section
➢ What answers to prayer have you seen that have encouraged you?

➢ Are there any things you've prayed about where the answer was different from what you hoped for/expected? How did you respond to that?

➢ Are you intentional about your prayer life?

➢ Is there something that might improve your prayer life moving forward?

While answers may not come in the form or timeframe we wish, nothing is too difficult for God, and he wants us to pray to him about all issues, great and small, that trouble us (as we saw in Ephesians 6:18 above).

Some believers keep a journal where they record prayer requests and any answers to those prayers. They might also write down particular scriptures to which God is drawing their attention. Listening to hymns, songs, or other music may also be helpful for opening up to God in prayer.

A prayer partner can also be a blessing. This entails meeting at regular intervals with a friend to share joys and challenges, then praying for one another and wider world concerns. In choosing a prayer partner, you will want to find someone you can trust to keep things confidential.

There are also many online Christian resources that can help you improve your prayer life. Consider choosing one or more such options to write down in the Possible Action point a couple of pages further on.

Study 4 - Possible Action
Is the Holy Spirit prompting you to do something that would help you improve your prayer life? Why not write this down in the form of a prayer

and then record the date in the outlined text box provided (or your notebook/journal).

Health Warning

Remember that you should not respond to this Kingdom Practice in a legalistic way. It is much more about serving God as part of our love for him because of our salvation in Jesus. We will become more like Jesus the more we allow the Holy Spirit to lead and guide us day by day, and God will get the glory.

My Response/Prayer and Date

Space For You To Record Responses To Questions, Make Notes, Etc.

Study 4 - Talk (Pray in Faith) to God

Study 4 - Memorising the Structure

Can you fill in the blank boxes without looking at the figure displayed at the beginning of this study?

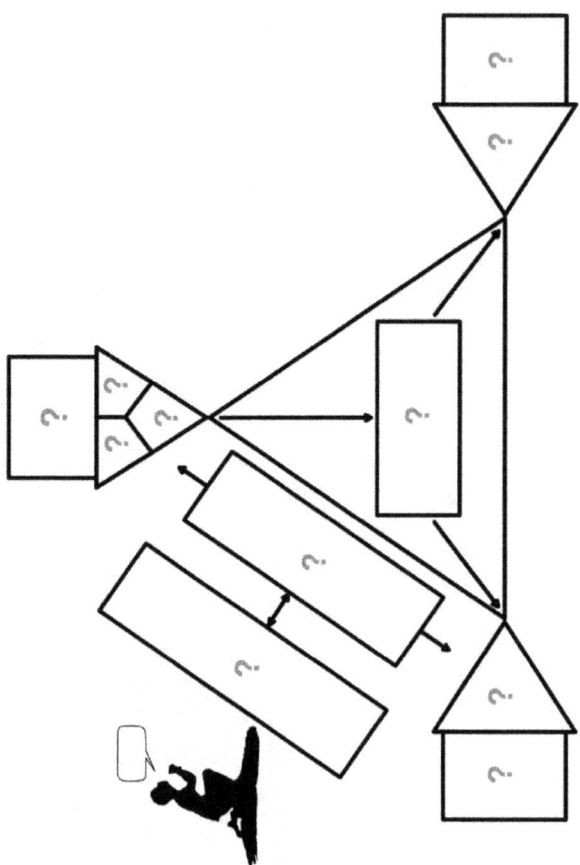

Study 5 - Follow Jesus - (KF2)
Subtitle: Consider the Call of Jesus So That You Can Grow and Become More like Him

Study 5 - Introduction

We have already considered the Kingdom Fundamental to Love God and two Kingdom Practices under this (Studies 2 to 4). In this study we will start to look at the second Kingdom Fundamental to Follow Jesus as we respond to the challenge to "teach them to obey all that I have commanded you."

Figure 8 demonstrates that the challenge to Follow Jesus is primarily a personal response in which we allow ourselves to be influenced by the Holy Spirit and our reading of the Scriptures.

Time and time again during his ministry, the call Jesus gave to all was to "follow me." Indeed as Christians we refer to ourselves as being followers, or disciples, of Jesus. Later after his resurrection, Jesus commanded his followers to Make Disciples (Matthew 28:19), a command we will look at in Study 11 as this is one aspect of loving others. We share our faith with others because we love them and want them to know salvation in Jesus.

Figure 8 - Kingdom Fundamental 2 - to Follow Jesus

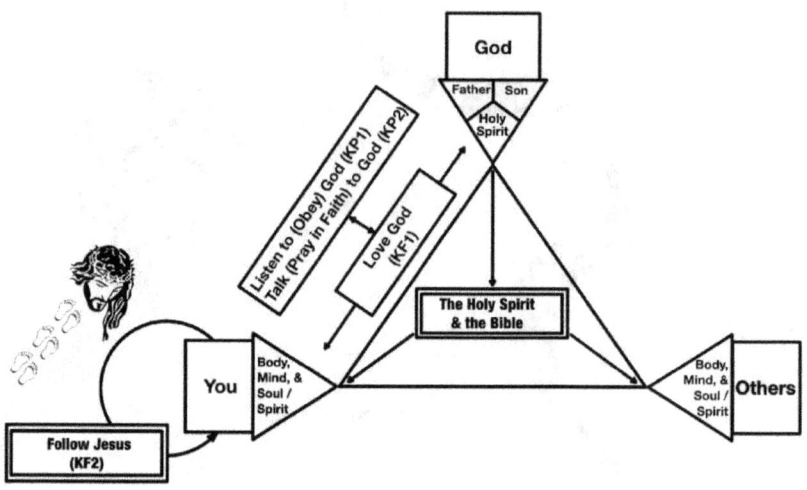

Study 5 - Biblical Support for This Kingdom Fundamental

Six Kingdom Behaviours have been grouped under the call to Follow Jesus:

- Respond to the call to follow.
- Don't make excuses.
- Know Jesus's voice.
- Follow and serve Jesus.
- Calculate the cost (deny yourself and take up your cross).
- Receive rest from Jesus.

We will consider each of these in slightly more detail below through reviewing some relevant Bible references (a complete set can be found in Appendix 2 or in the *All That I Have Commanded You* book, Chapter 3).

5.1 - Respond to the Call to Follow

Jesus called specific people to "follow me." He calls us to do the same, so we need to decide how we will respond:

> "Follow Me," He told them, "and I will make you fish for people!" (Matthew 4:19)

5.2 - Don't Make Excuses

If we are to respond to the call of Jesus, we must not delay in doing so:

> As they were travelling on the road someone said to Him, "I will follow You wherever You go!" Jesus told him, "Foxes have dens, and birds of the sky have nests, but the Son of Man has no place to lay His head." Then He said to another, "Follow Me." "Lord," he said, "first let me go bury my father." But He told him, "Let the dead bury their own dead, but you go and spread the news of the kingdom of God." Another also said, "I will follow You, Lord, but first let me go and say good-bye to those at my house." But Jesus said to him, "No one who puts his hand to the plough and looks back is fit for the kingdom of God." (Luke 9:57-62. Matthew 8:18-22)

5.3 - Know Jesus's Voice

As we grow in our knowledge of Jesus, we will become more familiar with his voice:

> My sheep hear My voice, I know them, and they follow Me. I give them eternal life, and they will never perish -ever! No one will snatch them out of My hand. My Father, who has given them to Me, is greater than all. No one is able to snatch them out of the Father's hand. (John 10:27-29)

5.4 - Follow and Serve Jesus

Just as Jesus came as a servant, we must adopt this role if we are to truly follow him:

> If anyone serves Me, he must follow Me. Where I am, there My servant also will be. If anyone serves Me, the Father will honour him. (John 12:26)

5.5 - Calculate the Cost (Deny Yourself and Take Up Your Cross)

We must consider the cost of being a disciple because Jesus does not promise that all our troubles will stop when we make a decision to follow him:

> Then Jesus said to His disciples, "If anyone wants to come with Me, he must deny himself, take up his cross, and follow Me. For whoever wants to save his life will lose it, but whoever loses his life because of Me will find it." (Matthew 16:24-25. Mark 8:34-35 and Luke 9:23-24)

> Now great crowds were travelling with Him. So He turned and said to them: "If anyone comes to Me and does not hate his own father and mother, wife and children, brothers and sisters -yes, and even his own life -he cannot be My disciple. Whoever does not bear his own cross and come after Me cannot be My disciple. For which of you, wanting to build a tower, doesn't first sit down and calculate the cost to see if he has enough to complete it? Otherwise, after he

has laid the foundation and cannot finish it, all the onlookers will begin to make fun of him, saying, "This man started to build and wasn't able to finish." Or what king, going to war against another king, will not first sit down and decide if he is able with 10,000 to oppose the one who comes against him with 20,000? If not, while the other is still far off, he sends a delegation and asks for terms of peace. In the same way, therefore, every one of you who does not say good-bye to all his possessions cannot be My disciple." (Luke 14:25-33)

5.6 - Receive Rest from Jesus

Jesus offers people with troubles and challenges a specific invitation to come to him and receive the rest only he can give:

> Come to Me, all of you who are weary and burdened, and I will give you rest. All of you, take up My yoke and learn from Me, because I am gentle and humble in heart, and you will find rest for yourselves. For My yoke is easy and My burden is light. (Matthew 11:28-30)

Study 5 - Our Context

That you have reached this far in working through this material implies you have already responded to the call to Follow Jesus. Or perhaps you are considering it seriously but are still working out for yourself what following Jesus means. Indeed, following Jesus means different things to different people. In its simplest form, it focuses on the need to listen to and apply what Jesus commands under the guidance of the Holy Spirit. The breadth and complexity of this teaching is what these studies seek to simplify, hopefully in a manner than can be understood and remembered.

Our purpose in following Jesus is to bring glory to God through what we do by seeking to reflect his example. This includes showing love, compassion, and forgiveness as well as being generous to others just as God has been to us in Christ (covered in Studies 10 to 13). This is made explicitly clear in Matthew 5:16:

> In the same way, let your light shine before men, so that they may see your good works and give glory to your Father in heaven.

Over time as we respond to Jesus's call, we learn more about what he wants from us through listening to him (Study 3), through prayer (Study 4), and through learning from other believers in worship and fellowship (Study 10).

Following Jesus is not something we should do in our own strength. It's not about having a big to-do list of how we are expected to behave and work and serve, but about responding to God's leading. Most importantly, we learn through the prompting of the Holy Spirit as Jesus states in John 16:13:

> When the Spirit of truth comes, He will guide you into all the truth. For He will not speak on His own, but He will speak whatever He hears. He will also declare to you what is to come.

Study 5 - Follow Jesus

We need to seek God's will on matters that confront us and be prepared to do things we might not feel comfortable doing, i.e., sharing our story with others. Following Jesus is also about being servant-like when we do even the little things that might go unnoticed by others but not by God:

> And whoever gives you a cup of water to drink because of My name, since you belong to the Messiah—I assure you: He will never lose his reward. (Mark 9:41. See also Matthew 10:42)

Ideally, we should not be drawing attention to what we do in any event (see Matthew 6:3-4). In John 15:15, Jesus says:

> I do not call you slaves anymore, because a slave doesn't know what his master is doing. I have called you friends, because I have made known to you everything I have heard from My Father.

This passage contains an important message that being a follower of Jesus is not a role of servitude but one where we can count ourselves friends of Jesus and of God the Father. Yes, we are to obey (Study 3), but not in a legalistic way. Jesus wants us to journey with him as companions, not as servants, as he leads us by means of the Holy Spirit.

We should recognise and consider the cost of being a disciple too, as Jesus warns that difficulties will come to those who accept the challenge to follow him. Just what difficulties will vary according to our particular context, where we live, and with whom we come into contact. In Study 4 we saw that we should pray for those who persecute us. Many people around the world are currently suffering for their faith in Jesus (see footnote 22) and even being martyred.[31]

But Jesus also appeals to those who are facing challenges in their own lives as we saw in the prior reference from Matthew 11:28-30. Maybe you are in a place where you are heavy laden and need to come to Jesus to find rest. Maybe you are a disciple of Jesus but are not happy with who you are. This may be because you have suffered or are suffering hurt, trauma, or abuse. Examples of such include:

- A difficult childhood or dysfunctional family life.
- The breakdown of an important relationship such as a divorce.
- The death of a close friend or relative.

---

[31] http://www.christianpost.com/news/90000-christians-killed-in-2016-1-every-6-minutes-study-172464/

- A chronic health condition or some form of disability.
- Bullying or other forms of abuse, including verbal, physical, racial, ageist, or sexual.
- Unrealistic demands people put on themselves such as poor body image in the young or not-so-young.
- A lack of education or career choices, leading to a sense of unfulfillment.
- Gender and gender orientation struggles.
- The aftermath of some criminal activity or event.
- Prior involvement with cults, other religions, or ongoing spiritual attacks or possession.
- Prejudice of some form (e.g., cultural differences).

This list is far from exhaustive, but the impact of any of these may result in low self-esteem, guilt, depression, self-harm, or even thoughts of suicide. Some people carry the consequences of their past as an ongoing physical or psychological condition. This may make them very emotional or conversely lacking in emotions, leading to ongoing relationship challenges. To compensate, people may seek to manage the hurt they have experienced in things like:

- Inflicting the same abuse they have suffered upon others.
- Over or under-eating (eating disorders).
- Substance abuse such as alcohol and drugs.
- Use of pornography[32] or using casual sex as a form of intimacy.

All these things have serious negative effects not only on the individual but also those close to them. They are not things that as disciples we should be practising. Thankfully, the good news is that we are not expected to change ourselves but to rely upon God through Christ and the Holy Spirit to transform us day by day into the new creation that Jesus has already made us spiritually when we accepted him as our Saviour:

---

[32] Consider reading this article about the impact of pornography: http://www.challies.com/articles/5-ways-porn-lies-to-you

> Therefore, if anyone is in Christ, the new creation has come: The old has gone, the new is here! (2 Corinthians 5:17, NIV)

Most of us are only too aware of our failings and limitations, both in human and in spiritual terms, because we know that we are far from perfect. In a later study we will discuss how Jesus commands us to be perfect (subsection 7.1) and what that means. But we need to recognise that when God looks at us he sees a deeply loved son or daughter. He has promised to forget our sins, which have been forgiven once and for all in Jesus. But he also recognises that we may still carry injuries and brokenness from past hurts.

From a practical perspective, we should be trying to move beyond our past. This may necessitate seeking healing as well as learning to forgive others or ourselves (Study 12). We cannot face our challenges or difficult situations in isolation but need to draw upon God's power. Much of Jesus's ministry was concerned with restoring the mental, spiritual, and physical health of those who came to him. He never refused to heal anyone, and he is still in that business today.

We also need to understand the power of fellowship with other believers as a healing community. We are called to bear one another's burdens, pray for each other, and even confess our sins to each other:

> Brothers and sisters, if someone is caught in a sin, you who live by the Spirit should restore that person gently. But watch yourselves, or you also may be tempted. Carry each other's burdens, and in this way you will fulfil the law of Christ. (Galatians 6:1-2, NIV)

> Therefore confess your sins to each other and pray for each other so that you may be healed. The prayer of a righteous person is powerful and effective. (James 5:16, NIV)

Sharing with trusted brothers and sisters in Christ can be a powerful step towards healing and freedom. Satan likes to tell Christians that they are the only ones struggling with a particular sin, but this is a lie. We may not realise how many others around us are dealing with the same issues because we keep them to ourselves.

If any of the above has brought issues to the surface in your own life, then consider what practical steps you might take to allow God to restore you. One first step is prayer. A second step is to seek out other Christians who will share your burden, commit to pray with you, and from whom you can receive friendship, love, and support. Seeking Christian counselling may be another step that can help you work through unresolved issues so that they do not hold you back from following Jesus.

It is immensely difficult for us to disclose our addictions, whether we are Christian or not. As an alternative to the above, you could consider searching for relevant help via websites or through anonymous helplines. Remember that you are still God's beloved son or daughter regardless of your past or present circumstances. This can be very hard to accept when addiction creates so much damage for us and for others.

Study 5 - Kingdom Fundamental Application

Jesus as Our Example

From the start of his ministry, Jesus reached out to all spheres of society, teaching, healing, challenging people, and announcing the kingdom of God. He began his work by calling specific people to leave their careers and families and follow him. Many passages in the Gospels highlight the huge crowds that gathered to listen to Jesus teach and experience his healing touch, including:

- Feeding five thousand men plus women and children (Matthew 14:13-21, Mark 6:33-44, Luke 9:12-17, John 6:1-14).
- Feeding four thousand men plus women and children (Matthew 15:32-38, Mark 8:1-9).
- Large crowds that gathered for the Sermon on the Mount and other times Jesus preached (Matthew 4:25, Matthew 5:1, Matthew 7:28-8:1, Matthew 9:36, Matthew 19:2, Matthew 23:1, Mark 10:1, Luke 5:15, Luke 11:29).

Jesus's aim was to point people towards God and to show that God's true nature was different from their understanding of him. Jesus knew the Scriptures (Study 3) and was in constant contact with God (Study 4), so he knew what to do in the situations that faced him. Jesus also understood the Old Testament prophesies concerning the Messiah. While he could not actively make them all come to pass, he allowed God to bring them to completion. In his final journey to Jerusalem and particularly in the garden of Gethsemane, Jesus recognised that fulfilling God's purposes would mean giving his life as a sacrifice on behalf of the sins of all mankind.

In fact, Jesus recognised that his death and resurrection would itself be a means through which people could come to the point of making a decision to follow him:

> "Now My soul is troubled. What should I say—Father, save Me from this hour? But that is why I came to this hour. Father, glorify Your name!" Then a voice came from heaven: "I have glorified it, and I will glorify it again!" The crowd standing there heard it and said it was thunder. Others said that an angel had spoken to Him. Jesus responded, "This voice came, not for Me, but for you. Now is the judgement of this world. Now the ruler of this world will be cast out. As for Me, if I am lifted up from the earth I will draw all people to Myself." He said this to signify what kind of death He was about to die. (John 12:27-33)

It is worth highlighting that there is at least one biblical reference to Jesus refusing to let someone follow him. In Mark 5:18-20, Jesus refuses to let the demon-possessed man he has just healed travel back across the Sea of Galilee with him. Instead, he commands the man to return to his own community to be a witness to God and Jesus there. Jesus was not refusing to let the man be his follower, but was sending him to be a witness in the context of where he could be most effective.

Some Brief Personal Reflections on Following Jesus

In trying to follow Jesus, perhaps my own greatest challenge has been allowing my mind to be renewed by the Holy Spirit so that I am thinking and acting more and more as Jesus would. This is a lofty goal and so an ongoing challenge for me. As I allow the Holy Spirit to influence me day by day, the attitude of my heart should reflect Jesus more. Others should see this though my love for them, through mercy, forgiveness, compassion, service, and generosity.

Someone once remarked to a well-known Christian, "How is your walk with God?" Somewhat perplexed, the well-known Christian was not really able to answer. When the Christian later met the same person, he was asked the same question. He was still at a loss how to respond when the questioner finally explained that walking with God should be "at a slow pace."

So why draw attention to this? When God went looking for Adam and Eve in Genesis 3:8, he was walking in the cool of the day. The image is that of God ambling around the garden interacting with Adam and Eve. In the same way, following Jesus is not a race but a gentle walk where we can grow in our knowledge of him and in our obedience to his commands.

When we first become followers of Jesus, we may be very enthusiastic and seek to race ahead of ourselves and of God, trying to amass head knowledge of him rather than slowly and steadily building our relationship with him. This is a generalisation as everyone's experience will be different. But we do need to take our time and allow the Holy Spirit to lead us as we become more aware of our position as beloved citizens of the kingdom, complete with our faults, which God will deal with as he prompts us and as we let him.

This has been my own experience to a large degree. In my early days as a Christian, I was very enthusiastic and constantly seeking to know more. As time has passed, God has gradually brought things to my attention. I am still a work in progress complete with faults and failings, but I recognise that in Jesus I am loved and forgiven as I strive to serve him in the context he has put me.

Study 5 - Kingdom Fundamental Health Check

Biblical Support Section

- What is your response to the suggestion that the biggest challenge from Jesus to you personally is to follow him?

Our Context Section

- In your cultural context, what does following Jesus mean, and how is it regarded in wider society?
- In Scripture's call to follow Jesus, are you surprised that he wants to take your burdens upon himself? Please explain your answer.
- Of the difficulties listed in the "Our Context" section, are there any you need to address, either in terms of seeking healing related to negative experiences or ongoing situations you face?
- Alternatively, do you need to be set free from behaviours resulting from past experiences that are not God-honouring?

If you are working through this material with a group, you may not want to respond publicly to these questions. But do consider what God may be prompting you to do. You can pray about it and perhaps already have. But you may also benefit from talking to a Christian counsellor (if this is available and affordable), your pastor/minister, or a good and trusted disciple. Keep in mind that Jesus never turned away anyone seeking his help, and he will not do so now either.

Kingdom Fundamental Application Section

- How is your walk with Jesus/God?
- What are the easiest and hardest things about following Jesus?
- Is Jesus calling you to do something that you have not yet said yes to? If so, is there a reason you have put this off?
- Is there someone you could share this with to seek their input, advice, and prayer support?

The Following Studies

While not the spoken words of Jesus, further reading on the implications of living out our role as a follower of Jesus can be found in Ephesians 4 and 5. Also, in the subsequent four studies we will be looking at four Kingdom Practices stemming from Jesus's commands that correspond to the Kingdom Fundamental to Follow Jesus:

- Submit to Jesus's Lordship.
- Pursue Holiness (Integrity/Purity).

- Live out Kingdom Values.
- Exercise Discernment.

Study 5 - Possible Action

Is the Holy Spirit prompting you to do something that would help you follow Jesus more closely? Why not write this down in the form of a prayer and record the date in the outlined text box provided (or your notebook/journal).

Health Warning

Remember that you should not respond to this Kingdom Fundamental in a legalistic way. It is much more about serving God as part of our love for him because of our salvation in Jesus. We will become more like Jesus the more we allow the Holy Spirit to lead and guide us day by day, and God will get the glory.

My Response/Prayer and Date

Space For You To Record Responses To Questions, Make Notes, Etc.

Study 5 - Follow Jesus

Study 5 - Follow Jesus

Study 5 - Memorising the Structure

Can you fill in the blank boxes without looking at the figure displayed at the beginning of this study?

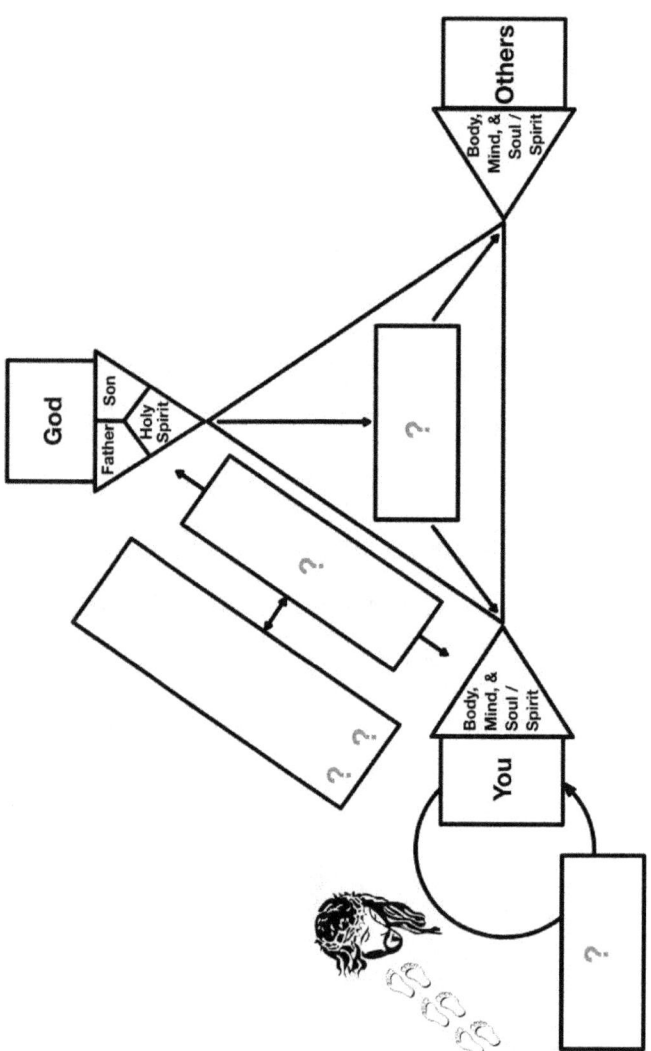

Study 6 - Submit to Jesus's Lordship - (KP3)
Subtitle: The Process of Coming to Jesus and Accepting Him as Saviour and Lord of Our Lives Moving Forward

Submit: To yield oneself to the authority or will of another.

Lordship: The authority or power of a lord.

Study 6 - Introduction

We have now considered the Kingdom Fundamental to Follow Jesus under an overall message to "teach them to obey all that I have commanded you." In this study we are going to consider the first Kingdom Practice that correlates to Follow Jesus, which is the challenge to Submit to Jesus's Lordship.

Figure 9 presents this first Kingdom Practice as a subset of our response to Jesus's invitation to follow him. As with nearly every study in this book, it also shows that the Bible is our primary reference together with the indwelling support and prompting of the Holy Spirit.

Figure 9 - Kingdom Practice 3 - to Submit to Jesus's Lordship

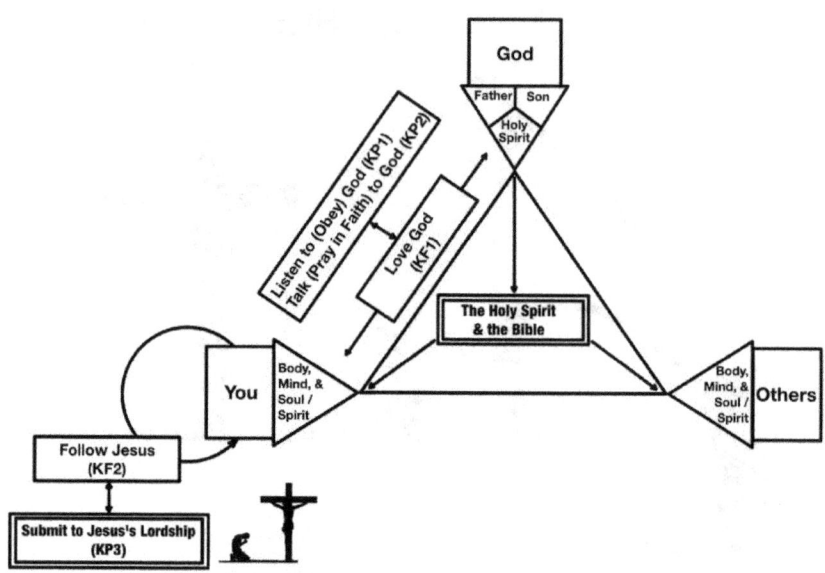

Study 6 - Biblical Support for This Kingdom Practice

A prerequisite to becoming a disciple of Jesus is that we come under his lordship by submitting to his God-given authority:

> That power is the same as the mighty strength he exerted when he [God] raised Christ from the dead and seated him at his right hand in the heavenly realms, far above all rule and authority, power and dominion, and every name that is invoked, not only in the present age but also in the one to come. (Ephesians 1:19b-21, NIV)

We cannot be a true disciple without doing this.

Many people who have attended church for years may have become "Christianised". This means they have adopted patterns of worship and practice that to all intents and purpose suggest they are Jesus's disciples, yet they have not formally repented and confessed Jesus as their personal Saviour and Lord. This is fundamentally important and an area where the church in its broadest global sense has not been diligent.

In submitting to Jesus's lordship, let us consider eight Kingdom Behaviours that his commands encompass. Collectively, these help to show us whether we are truly his disciples and part of God's kingdom:

- Choose the narrow way that leads to life.

- Receive the kingdom of God like a child.

- Believe in Jesus.
- Repent of our sins.
- Be born again.
- Take Jesus's yoke and learn from him.
- Seek first the kingdom of God.
- Come to Jesus.

In this study we will take a look at each in turn (see Appendix 2 or the *All That I Have Commanded You* book, Chapter 3.1, for a complete set of scriptures).

6.1 - Choose the Narrow Way That Leads to Life

Jesus tells us that he is the way, the truth, and the life and that the only way into the kingdom of God is through him:

> Jesus answered, "I am the way and the truth and the life. No one comes to the Father except through me." (John 14:6, NIV)

> Enter through the narrow gate. For the gate is wide and the road is broad that leads to destruction, and there are many who go through it. How narrow is the gate and difficult the road that leads to life, and few find it. (Matthew 7:13-14)

6.2 - Receive the Kingdom of God like a Child

Jesus explains that we must be child-like (trusting simply) in our approach to coming into the kingdom. We cannot intellectualise it or approach it on our own terms:

> I assure you: Whoever does not welcome the kingdom of God like a little child will never enter it. (Mark 10:15. Luke 18:17)

6.3 - Believe in Jesus

Jesus encourages us to believe in him:

> Your heart must not be troubled. Believe in God; believe also in Me. (John 14:1)

6.4 - Repent of Our Sins

We must repent if we are to receive the benefits of Jesus's sacrifice, including forgiveness for our sins and the promise of eternal life beginning now:

> From then on Jesus began to preach, "Repent, because the kingdom of heaven has come near." (Matthew 4:17)

6.5 - Be Born Again

Only by accepting Jesus as our Saviour can our spiritual life commence as we receive the Holy Spirit and begin a relationship with God and Jesus:

Do not be amazed that I told you that you must be born again. (John 3:7)

6.6 - Take Jesus's Yoke and Learn from Him

When we come to Jesus and trust in him for all things, the challenges we have will be made more bearable, though this is not a promise that all challenges will go away:

> All of you, take up My yoke and learn from Me, because I am gentle and humble in heart, and you will find rest for yourselves. For My yoke is easy and My burden is light. (Matthew 11:29-30)

In this context we should think of a yoke for a pair of oxen. Jesus will take the leading position, and we will take the other. He takes the strain and the main part of the burden as we walk alongside in submission to him.

6.7 - Seek First the Kingdom of God

When we put the increase of God's kingdom ahead of everything else, God will then supply all our needs for life:

> Consider how the wildflowers grow: They don't labour or spin thread. Yet I tell you, not even Solomon in all his splendour was adorned like one of these! If that's how God clothes the grass, which is in the field today and is thrown into the furnace tomorrow, how much more will He do for you –you of little faith? Don't keep striving for what you should eat and what you should drink, and don't be anxious. For the Gentile world eagerly seeks all these things, and your Father knows that you need them. But seek His kingdom, and these things will be provided for you. (Luke 12:27-31)

6.8 - Come to Jesus

When we choose to follow Jesus, we begin our spiritual life in him. We also receive the gift of the Holy Spirit, who as we allow him will help us to love God and show Jesus's love to others "from the inside out."

> On the last and most important day of the festival, Jesus stood up and cried out, "If anyone is thirsty, he should come to Me and drink! The one who believes in Me, as the Scripture has said, will have streams of living water flow from deep within him." He said this about the Spirit. Those who believed in Jesus were going to receive the Spirit, for the Spirit had not yet been received because Jesus had not yet been glorified. (John 7:37-39)

Study 6 - Our Context

In applying this Kingdom Practice to our lives today, we can find an excellent illustration of submitting to God in Jesus in the parable Jesus himself told of the Prodigal Son. The son is living in the context of a father who is happy to provide for his family. But the son wants to benefit by sharing in his father's wealth while simultaneously throwing off his father's authority and going his own way:

> There was a man who had two sons. The younger one said to his father, "Father, give me my share of the estate." So he divided his property between them. Not long after that, the younger son got together all he had, set off for a distant country and there squandered his wealth in wild living. After he had spent everything, there was a severe famine in that whole country, and he began to be in need. So he went and hired himself out to a citizen of that country, who sent him to his fields to feed pigs. He longed to fill his stomach with the pods that the pigs were eating, but no one gave him anything.
>
> When he came to his senses, he said, "How many of my father's hired servants have food to spare, and here I am starving to death! I will set out and go back to my father and say to him: Father, I have sinned against heaven and against you. I am no longer worthy to be called your son; make me like one of your hired servants." So he got up and went to his father.
>
> But while he was still a long way off, his father saw him and was filled with compassion for him; he ran to his son, threw his arms around him and kissed him.
>
> The son said to him, "Father, I have sinned against heaven and against you. I am no longer worthy to be called your son."
>
> But the father said to his servants, "Quick! Bring the best robe and put it on him. Put a ring on his finger and sandals on his feet. Bring the fattened calf and kill it. Let's have a feast and celebrate. For this son of mine was dead and is alive again; he was lost and is found." So they began to celebrate.
>
> Meanwhile, the older son was in the field. When he came near the house, he heard music and dancing. So he called one of the servants and asked him what was going on. "Your brother has come," he replied, "and your father has killed the fattened calf because he has him back safe and sound."
>
> The older brother became angry and refused to go in. So his father went out and pleaded with him. But he answered his father, "Look! All these years I've been slaving for you and never disobeyed your orders. Yet you never gave me even a young goat so I could celebrate with my friends. But when this son of yours who has squandered your property with prostitutes comes home, you kill the fattened calf for him!"
>
> "My son," the father said, "you are always with me, and everything I have is yours. But we had to celebrate and be glad, because this brother of yours was dead and is alive again; he was lost and is found." (Luke 15:11-32, NIV)

Before we come into submission to Jesus, we are like the Prodigal Son, wanting to live our lives our way. Like the father in the parable, God loves us and wants the best for us. We need to recognise that we must come to Jesus in repentance and under his lordship. Just as the father rejoiced upon his son's return, Jesus tells us in Luke 15:7:

> I tell you, in the same way, there will be more joy in heaven over one sinner who repents than over 99 righteous people who don't need repentance. (See also Luke 15:10)

It can be difficult for people to submit to government and other authorities. We all like to be in control of our own lives and destinies. In practice, however, we are frequently at the mercy of others, whether undergoing some job interview or needing help from someone, and we begin to realise that we cannot manage all circumstances to suit our wants or even our needs. In some Eastern cultures, making decisions is vested in the group or community (family, work, club, etc.), so the ability to make a personal choice is reduced because of cultural peer pressure.

Pride is a difficult attitude to overcome. Yet Jesus says that we need to become like little children to enter his kingdom:

> And he said: "Truly I tell you, unless you change and become like little children, you will never enter the kingdom of heaven." (Matthew 18:3; NIV)

This requires us to understand that we can't earn our salvation. Instead, we should accept and depend on what God has done for us in Jesus. In coming to Jesus and accepting him as our only Saviour, we will be responding to the prompting and work of the Holy Spirit, either in the short term or over a period of months or years. People can help us to know about Jesus and how to become his disciples, but no one can make the decision for us. It is ours alone. The outline below characterises the typical process of becoming disciples:

Understand that no one can come to God on their own merits.

> As it is written: There is no one righteous, not even one. There is no one who understands; there is no one who seeks God. All have turned away; all alike have become useless. There is no one who does what is good, not even one. (Romans 3:10–12)

Recognise that your condition of sinfulness separates you from God.

> For all have sinned and fall short of the glory of God. (Romans 3:23)

Know the penalty for sin.

> For the wages of sin is death, but the gift of God is eternal life in Christ Jesus our Lord. (Romans 6:23)

Believe that God sent Jesus to die in your place.

But God proves His own love for us in that while we were still sinners, Christ died for us. (Romans 5:8)

Repent of (turn away from) your sins.

Therefore, having overlooked the times of ignorance, God now commands all people everywhere to repent, because He has set a day when He is going to judge the world in righteousness by the Man He has appointed. He has provided proof of this to everyone by raising Him from the dead. (Acts 17:30-31)

Receive Jesus as your Saviour and Lord.

If you confess with your mouth, "Jesus is Lord," and believe in your heart that God raised Him from the dead, you will be saved. One believes with the heart, resulting in righteousness, and one confesses with the mouth, resulting in salvation. (Romans 10:9-10)

Accept peace with God.

Therefore, since we have been declared righteous by faith, we have peace with God through our Lord Jesus Christ. (Romans 5:1)

Therefore, no condemnation now exists for those in Christ Jesus, because the Spirit's law of life in Christ Jesus has set you free from the law of sin and of death. (Romans 8:1-2)

Each of us comes to faith in a unique way, so it is not possible to describe a single model or pattern for this. God is sovereign and will work through his Holy Spirit, whether directly, via his disciples, and/or other means.

A study by the American National Association of Evangelicals (USA) in 2015 found that 63% of believers accepted Christ between the ages of four and fourteen (known as the 4-14 Window), while an additional 34% accepted Christ between the ages of fifteen and twenty-nine. More globally, the International Bible Society found that 85% of Christians accepted Christ between the ages of four and fourteen while a further 10% did so between the ages of fifteen and thirty. The Barna Group (www.barna.com) found that only 6% of adult Christians made their decision to follow God over the age of eighteen which means that 94% made decisions as children that follow them throughout their life. In addition, the Barna Group's research has also revealed that:

- A person's moral foundations are generally in place by the time they reach the age of nine.

- Fundamental perspectives on truth, integrity, meaning, justice, morality, and ethics are formed quite early in life.

- A majority of Americans make a lasting determination about the personal significance of Christ's death and resurrection by age twelve.

This research makes clear that focusing on children's ministry is of great importance for people to make a personal decision to submit to Jesus's lordship.

Study 6 - Kingdom Practice Application

Jesus as Our Example

Matthew 3 provides an account of the baptism of Jesus. Here we have an example of Jesus submitting to this act of repentance and symbolic forgiveness of sins even though the Bible tells us that Jesus was without sin:

> God made him who had no sin to be sin for us, so that in him we might become the righteousness of God. (2 Corinthians 5:21, NIV)

In undergoing the sacrament of baptism administered by John the Baptist, Jesus chose to identify with humankind's sinfulness, thereby setting us an example and demonstrating he did not consider himself above the process. In fact, in Matthew 3:15 Jesus states that his baptism was to "fulfil all righteousness." This in turn echoes back to Isaiah 53, which describes Jesus's life mission, in particular verse 11, which speaks of "the righteous one" making many righteous (see the New Living or the International Standard Versions).

In the "Jesus as Our Example" section of Study 3, we looked at some passages from the Gospel of Matthew that demonstrate how Jesus was obedient to the Father's will. These were in the garden of Gethsemane and upon his arrest when he refrained from calling upon an angel army. These acts of obedience indicate submission to the Father's will. Jesus's submission was total even to the point of his approaching death, where he became sin for our sake. He was separated from his Father for the first time in eternity (at least in terms of his physical part of the God-man being sacrificed to pay the sins of mankind). There are theological questions about whether it was possible for him to be separated spiritually since the Trinity is three in one, but that is not an investigation we are making here:

> About three in the afternoon Jesus cried out in a loud voice, "Eli, Eli, lema sabachthani?" (which means "My God, my God, why have you forsaken me?") (Matthew 27:46, NIV. Mark 15:34)

The apostle Paul explicitly describes Jesus's motivations and submission (referenced as humility in the passage below):

> In your relationships with one another, have the same mind-set as Christ Jesus: Who, being in very nature God, did not consider equality with God something to be used to his own advantage; rather, he made himself nothing by taking the very nature of a servant, being made in human likeness. And being found in appearance as a man, he humbled himself by becoming obedient to death— even death on a cross! Therefore God exalted him to the highest place and gave him the name that is above every name, that

at the name of Jesus every knee should bow, in heaven and on earth and under the earth, and every tongue acknowledge that Jesus Christ is Lord, to the glory of God the Father. (Philippians 2:5-11, NIV)

As ever, Jesus is our prime example of someone being submissive to God's will. God the Father and Jesus (the Word) had eternally co-existed until the point of Jesus's death on the cross. The pain of that separation must have been unbearable, as shown when Jesus cries out (see references above from Matthew 27:46, Mark 15:34). Even then, Jesus had the assurance that God would resurrect him from the dead (Matthew 12:39-40, Isaiah 53, Psalm 22).

Some Brief Personal Reflections on Submitting to Jesus

I grew up as the son of a minister in both Presbyterian and United Reformed churches in the UK, so I was pretty familiar with Bible accounts (often mistakenly called stories), including the life and ministry of Jesus. But in my early teen years, my faith seemed to evaporate. I could not see how Christ's death on the cross could be a victory. From my perspective at that time, it seemed more of a failure. It was not until after I was married, when I began attending church again, that I came to understand how important Christ's resurrection is because it demonstrates his victory over sin and death.

During my mid-to-late teens and beyond, I occasionally had nightmares involving Christianity. Waking up in the middle of the night, I would expect some sort of Damascus Road experience (Acts 9). This never did happen, but I had every expectation of becoming a Christian someday. Just not yet!

When I was first married, my wife Mary-Anne and I didn't attend church unless my parents were staying with us. I found that I liked the minister at the church we visited with my parents, and Mary-Anne and I began attending regularly. We also started communicant classes (to be confirmed as believing church members). My experience of being trained as an engineer allowed me to understand the Bible and Gospel accounts from a logical perspective. What I lacked was personal faith.

I was twenty-eight years old when I finally did come to Christ, partly through a friend who had been my best man at my wedding and his wife. They visited us one weekend. On the Saturday evening, we discussed a whole range of topics Mary-Anne and I did not think the Bible covered. Each time, my friend and his wife were able to answer with relevant references.

The next morning at church, many of these same topics came up during our regular Sunday service. That evening we accompanied my best man and his wife to a nearby Elim Pentecostal church they'd wanted to visit. During the service, other topics we'd discussed were brought up. To my logical mind, this seemed a bit too unlikely to be a coincidence. When I mentioned this, my friend's wife asked if I'd been praying. I responded that I'd only started that week. She replied that as I was not stupid, if I'd started praying, then I had clearly already made a decision to follow Jesus.

The following week, which was Easter Sunday 1987, I went ahead with the confirmation service. That was really the point when I put my trust in God and Jesus as my Saviour and Lord. It really was a step of faith, and several years later in 1993, my wife and I were both baptised as well. My parents were both alive to see this happen, so it was a great occasion for them as they had prayed for this throughout my life.

Study 6 - Kingdom Practice Health Check
Biblical Support Section
- What do you understand about the need to submit to Jesus? What does it mean for you?

Our Context Section
- In your cultural context, what does submitting to Jesus mean?
- How did the Lord bring you into a relationship with him? Was it a dramatic experience, a slow realisation over time, or something else? If you are studying this material in a group, please share your testimony briefly if the others don't already know it.
- What are your views on the steps in becoming a follower of Jesus outlined in the "Our Context" section? Are they reasonable? Is there anything missing?

Kingdom Practice Application Section
- Have you accepted (submitted to) Jesus as Saviour by repenting from your previous lifestyle?
- Have you made Jesus Lord of your life? How is this different from accepting him as Saviour? We need Jesus to be both our Saviour and our Lord. If you have not reached this stage yet, you might consider seeking out disciples of Jesus you know and trust to help you with questions you may have.
- Have you been baptised as a believer? If not, is there something preventing you from doing this?[33] Salvation is not

---

[33] I recognise that some Christian traditions support and practise infant baptism followed by a confirmation once the believer is old enough. If you are from

dependent upon believers' baptism, but baptism is an outward sign and witness to others that you have obeyed Jesus's command.

- Do those who are close to you know of your decision to follow Jesus? This may depend upon your cultural context as in some places this can be dangerous, thus caution and discernment may be necessary.
- Does the way you conduct yourself at work, at leisure, and at home reflect that Jesus is in control of your life? In other words, throughout your day, do you endeavour to reflect Jesus' character (love, mercy, forgiveness, generosity etc.)?

Study 6 - Possible Action

Is there something you feel you are being prompted to undertake in relation to your submitting to Jesus's lordship? Consider writing it down and recording the date in the outlined text box provided (or your journal/notebook).

Health Warning

Remember that you should not respond to this Kingdom Practice in a legalistic way. It is much more about serving God as part of our love for him because of our salvation in Jesus. We will become more like Jesus the more we allow the Holy Spirit to lead and guide us day by day, and God will get the glory.

that background, you can still consider whether believer's baptism is something to which you would like to submit.

My Response/Prayer and Date

Space For You To Record Responses To Questions, Make Notes, Etc.

Study 6 - Submit to Jesus's Lordship

Study 6 - Submit to Jesus's Lordship

Study 6 - Memorising the Structure

Can you fill in the blank boxes without looking at the figure displayed at the beginning of this study?

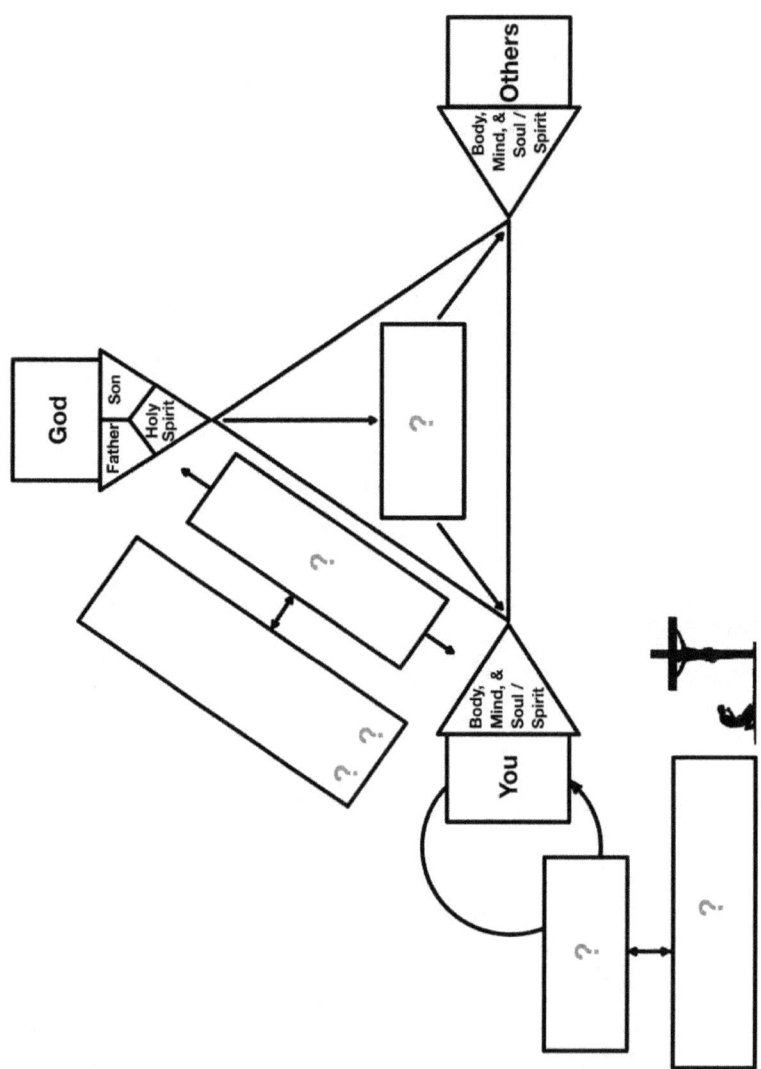

Study 7 - Pursue Holiness (Integrity/Purity) - (KP4)

Subtitle: Followers Are Already Set Apart as Holy and We Need to Rely on the Holy Spirit to Help Us Live Lives Worthy of Jesus's Calling.

Pursue: To follow and try to catch or capture (someone or something) for usually a long distance or time.

Holiness: The quality or state of being holy.

Holy: Devoted entirely to the deity or the work of the deity.

Integrity: Conduct that conforms to an accepted standard of right and wrong. Devotion to telling the truth. Faithfulness to high moral standards.

Purity: Lack of guilt or evil thoughts.

Study 7 - Introduction

In this study we will consider the second Kingdom Practice correlating to the Kingdom Fundamental to Follow Jesus, which is to Pursue Holiness (Integrity/Purity).

Figure 10 shows that the need to pursue holiness is one element of the task of following Jesus. It is one where we have to make choices day by day about what we do and how we do them. It is about our response to God as he seeks to transform our attitudes and our character.

Figure 10 - Kingdom Practice 4 - to Pursue Holiness (Integrity/Purity)

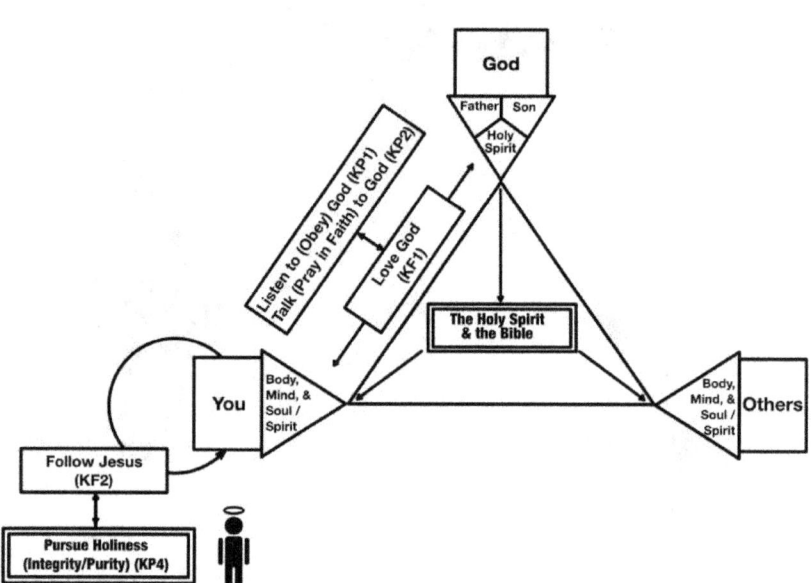

Study 7 - Biblical Support for This Kingdom Practice

In the Old Testament, God's covenant with the Israelites included the following provisions:

> Now if you obey me fully and keep my covenant, then out of all nations you will be my treasured possession. Although the whole earth is mine, you will be for me a kingdom of priests and a holy nation. These are the words you are to speak to the Israelites. (Exodus 19:5-6, NIV)

God's vision for the Israelites was that by being set apart as a holy nation of priests they would act as intermediaries in bringing other nations and people groups into a relationship with God. In the Temple of Solomon, there was specific provision of an outer court where non-Jews were able to worship God. This was the area where Jesus famously overturned the moneychangers' tables and scattered sacrificial offerings being peddled for sale to worshippers (Matthew 21:12, Mark 11:15, John 2:15).

As Jesus's disciples, we are also to lead holy lives as best we can, assisted by the Holy Spirit. This includes being set apart in the service of God and Jesus as well as the need to be holy, demonstrating integrity in all the things we do and say. Jesus's teachings and commands about this can be considered in terms of seven Kingdom Behaviours:

- Live with integrity.
- Address our own issues and faults before challenging others.
- Do not cause others to stumble.
- Do not take oaths (watch what you say).
- Store up treasures in heaven.
- Let our light shine before others.
- Rejoice, including when being persecuted.

The biblical justification for these topics are set out below (see Appendix 2 or the *All That I Have Commanded You* book, Chapter 3.2, for a complete set of scriptures).

7.1 - Live with Integrity

As followers of Jesus, we are to be consistent in what we think and say and more importantly in what we do, including the supporting Kingdom Behaviours that follow.

Be Perfect

Jesus challenges us to be perfect. This does not necessarily mean being without any fault or blemish as is a typical understanding of the term perfect, although it can be looked at that way. Other interpretations include the concept of completeness, maturity, consistency, and integrated. From such terms we can infer the need for integrity in terms of our thoughts and actions.

This command immediately follows Jesus's instruction to love our enemies. So one way in which Jesus is calling us here to be perfect may be in how we love others, including our enemies. As we seek to obey this command with the help of the Holy Spirit, we will need to remain humble and dependent upon him:

> Be perfect, therefore, as your heavenly Father is perfect. (Matthew 5:48)

Pursue Righteousness

Guided by the Holy Spirit, we should strive to be like Jesus in all our actions, whether we are alone or with others. His words below were said to the Jews to highlight that they were unable to live up to standards set by God. While they are not technically a command of Jesus to his followers, they highlight that earthly religious leaders should not be our standard for righteousness but Jesus himself:

> For I tell you, unless your righteousness surpasses that of the scribes and Pharisees, you will never enter the kingdom of heaven. (Matthew 5:20)

Pursue Purity of Thought

We must strive always to keep our thought life wholesome (see also the second part of 2 Corinthians 10:5). The reference below is again not strictly a command from Jesus, but Jesus is making clear the correlation between impurity of thought and sinful behaviour. (See also Matthew 5:27-28):

> Then He said, "What comes out of a person—that defiles him. For from within, out of people's hearts, come evil thoughts, sexual immoralities, thefts, murders, adulteries, greed, evil actions, deceit, promiscuity, stinginess, blasphemy, pride, and foolishness. All these evil things come from within and defile a person." (Mark 7:20-23)

7.2 - Address Our Own Issues and Faults before Challenging Others

Jesus requires us to examine and sort out our own hearts, behaviours, and attitudes before we consider rebuking or correcting a fellow brother or sister in God's family:

> Why do you look at the speck in your brother's eye, but don't notice the log in your own eye? Or how can you say to your brother, "Brother, let me take out the speck that is in your eye," when you yourself don't see the log in your eye? Hypocrite! First take the log out of your eye, and then you will see clearly to take out the speck in your brother's eye (Luke 6:41-42. See also Matthew 7:3-5).

7.3 - Do Not Cause Others to Stumble

The way in which we act, whether in private or in public, should not be a basis for leading someone else to do anything of which God would not approve:

> But whoever causes the downfall of one of these little ones[34] who believe in Me – it would be better for him if a heavy millstone were hung around his neck and he were drowned in the depths of the sea! Woe to the world because of offences. For offences must come, but woe to that man by whom the offence comes. (Matthew 18:6-7)

---

[34] This term "little ones" can refer to those who are new to or weak in faith, young, or lacking in knowledge and understanding.

7.4 - Do Not Take Oaths (Watch What You Say)

Oaths are not a very common legal process in the Western world these days. An exception is within the court system, where such are often administered to a witness prior to giving evidence in relation to the truth of the testimony they will give (e.g., "I solemnly swear to tell the truth, the whole truth, and nothing but the truth, so help me, God."). In principle, our honesty and integrity should be sufficient to demonstrate that we mean (or will do) what we say:

> Again, you have heard that it was said to our ancestors, You must not break your oath, but you must keep your oaths to the Lord. But I tell you, don't take an oath at all: either by heaven, because it is God's throne; or by the earth, because it is His footstool; or by Jerusalem, because it is the city of the great King. Neither should you swear by your head, because you cannot make a single hair white or black. But let your word "yes" be "yes," and your "no" be "no." Anything more than this is from the evil one. (Matthew 5:33-37)

7.5 - Store Up Treasures in Heaven

We should focus on our investment in God's kingdom rather than trying to build wealth for its own sake here on earth:

> Don't collect for yourselves treasures on earth, where moth and rust destroy and where thieves break in and steal. But collect for yourselves treasures in heaven, where neither moth nor rust destroys, and where thieves don't break in and steal. For where your treasure is, there your heart will be also. (Matthew 6:19-21, NIV. See also Luke 12:33-34)

7.6 - Let Our Light Shine before Others

Our conduct and witness to others should be blameless so that they can see we are really followers of Jesus:

> In the same way, let your light shine before men, so that they may see your good works and give glory to your Father in heaven. (Matthew 5:16)

7.7 – Rejoice, Including When Being Persecuted

Having an attitude of thankfulness and rejoicing even in the most difficult circumstances can only be a gift from God since we could not do this in our own strength:

> You are blessed when they insult and persecute you and falsely say every kind of evil against you because of Me. Be glad and rejoice, because your reward is great in heaven. For that is how they persecuted the prophets who were before you. (Matthew 5:11-12. See also Luke 6:22-23)

Study 7 - Our Context

So how does Jesus's instruction to be holy apply to us today? Perhaps his best illustration of the need for holiness in his disciples can be found in Matthew 5:13-16:

> You are the salt of the earth. But if the salt loses its saltiness, how can it be made salty again? It is no longer good for anything, except to be thrown out and trampled underfoot. You are the light of the world. A town built on a hill cannot be hidden. Neither do people light a lamp and put it under a bowl. Instead they put it on its stand, and it gives light to everyone in the house. In the same way, let your light shine before others, that they may see your good deeds and glorify your Father in heaven. (NIV)

Along with adding flavour, salt is an antiseptic and preservative. In fact, it is essential for life. We would all die without salt in our bodies. The term "salary" is actually derived from the Latin word for salt—*sal*—because salt was so valuable that it was often used to pay wages in Roman times. So what better analogy to describe the effect we should have as Jesus's disciples on those around us?

Similarly, we can all understand and visualise the importance of having light in a dark place. In a spiritual sense, light and darkness are in conflict with one another. The resurrection of Jesus is our guarantee that spiritual light has conquered spiritual darkness and that we have the victory and authority in him.

If we live our lives in a holy way, we have the assurance that we can overcome spiritual challenges through the power of the Holy Spirit within us:

> Everyone who believes that Jesus is the Christ is born of God, and everyone who loves the father loves his child as well. This is how we know that we love the children of God: by loving God and carrying out his commands. In fact, this is love for God: to keep his commands. And his commands are not burdensome, for everyone born of God overcomes the world. This is the victory that has overcome the world, even our faith. Who is it that overcomes the world? Only the one who believes that Jesus is the Son of God. (1 John 5:1-5, NIV)

The call to be holy is not new. As we saw at the beginning of this study, holiness was a part of the covenant God made with Israel in the Old Testament (Exodus 19:5-6). This meant being set apart from the other nations, but also living under a specific set of laws intended to set the Israelites apart and draw others to God. Unfortunately, the Israelites did not really carry this out. The challenge to live a holy life remains difficult to execute, just as it was for Israel. The difference for us as believers is that we have the indwelling Holy Spirit to help us overcome temptation.

This world holds many attractive things, and not all of them are right or wholesome for us as disciples. What attractions do you face that may be preventing you from being holy? Note that the aim here is not to lead us into self-condemnation, but to recognise that our society and culture is filled with things that are inappropriate for a disciple of Jesus:

> For the grace of God has appeared with salvation for all people, instructing us to deny godlessness and worldly lusts and to live in a sensible, righteous, and godly way in the present age, while we wait for the blessed hope and appearing of the glory of our great God and Saviour, Jesus Christ. He gave Himself for us to redeem us from all lawlessness and to cleanse for Himself a people for His own possession, eager to do good works. (Titus 2:11-14)

Although we are saved by grace, becoming a follower of Jesus does not mean we no longer have a sinful nature. As we grow in our relationship with the Father and Son through the Holy Spirit, we will be convicted of wrong thinking, attitudes, and desires. As we respond positively to these challenges, we will chip away more and more at our sinful nature. However, it will only be completely gone when we reach the heavenly kingdom.

Again, let us be clear that we are not capable of living as perfect a life as Jesus did. He lived, died, and rose again so we wouldn't have to be perfect to get to heaven. We will all fail at being perfect, but if we allow the Holy Spirit to help and lead us, we will grow to become more holy.

Study 7 - Kingdom Practice Application

Jesus as Our Example

Any number of biblical references state clearly that Jesus was without sin (was holy):

> God made him who had no sin to be sin for us, so that in him we might become the righteousness of God. (2 Corinthians 5:21, NIV)

> Therefore, since we have a great high priest who has ascended into heaven, Jesus the Son of God, let us hold firmly to the faith we profess. For we do not have a high priest who is unable to empathise with our weaknesses, but we have one who has been tempted in every way, just as we are – yet he did not sin. Let us then approach God's throne of grace with confidence, so that we may receive mercy and find grace to help us in our time of need. (Hebrews 4:14-16, NIV)

> He did not commit sin, and no deceit was found in His mouth. (1 Peter 2:22)

> You know that He was revealed so that He might take away sins, and there is no sin in Him. (1 John 3:5)

Jesus represents the pinnacle of human sinlessness. He lived a perfect life on earth, being both divine and human, and resisted all enticements to sin so that he could be an unblemished sacrificial lamb to take away our sin. He complied with and obeyed all the laws in the Old Testament so that we would not be required to do so. As we strive to live a life of holiness, the Holy Spirit assists us as we allow him by helping us in times of need.

Some Brief Personal Reflections on Pursuing Holiness

Personal holiness is something many believers struggle with putting into practice. As a disciple, I am only too aware of times when I know I haven't met the perfect standard (i.e., always!). Other times I fail and do not even realise it, though I'm sure those around me would have no problem recognising and pointing out my failings. But my failure to meet the highest standards doesn't mean that I should not seek to do better.

As a follower of Jesus, I am now a citizen of God's kingdom. Thus I'm already set apart from "the world", even while I live in it (see John 15:18-21, John 17:14-19). In other words, I am "holy" in the sense of the definition at the beginning of this study. But that holiness is my (our) position in relation to God. Our daily challenge is trying to live up to the standard of our position as holy in God. It's not about staying above some imaginary graph line with "sin" below and "holiness" above. That would be legalism. It is about being intentional in pursuing godly behaviour and practices.

Living with an attitude of integrity is one component of pursuing holiness. In addition to the definition given at the start of this session, integrity includes displaying consistency between what we say and what we do. I had a colleague who had once held an office at his local church, but was no longer active. One reason was the discrepancy he saw between Christian ideals and church teaching as he understood them and the actual behaviours and attitudes of other church members. He once confided that he could see I not only claimed to be a Christian but actually "lived it". I don't share this to impress anyone. But at least as far as he was concerned, something about the way I acted and responded to situations matched what I professed to be as a disciple of Jesus.

Outside of a courtroom, taking oaths in a literal sense is not really common these days in Western cultures. But the general principle includes being careful of what we say at all times. I can think of times when my sense of humour and a flippant remark has caused unintended offence. In my own life, this is still a work in progress as my sense of fun can sometimes get the better of me.

Persecution is becoming more widespread in a militant and less tolerant world and is not something any of us would deliberately seek out. But most people with whom I come into contact have responded positively to my faith and are supportive of me offering to pray for them if they are going through difficulties or health concerns. This is not a universal experience, of course. Jesus is explicit in forewarning that being challenged is part of the cost of being a disciple.

In terms of storing up treasures in heaven, this relates to the balance we maintain between putting the kingdom first and accumulating worldly wealth. In the consulting field where I've spent much of my career, there are relentless pressures, targets, and a strong ethos to seek promotion and increase salary and bonuses. All this comes at a price. Above all, a lack of quality time with family and time for rest and relaxation.

Many colleagues who reached the top levels of the company I worked for paid the penalty in terms pursuing wealth in broken marriages and all the challenges that generates. Some years into my career with my last employer, I recognised that the pain associated with the next level was not worth the gain in financial and personal responsibility terms. Especially since the gain itself was not guaranteed. Instead of seeking higher levels of seniority, I resolved instead to be content with the rewards for working hard for my clients.

The culture in some parts of the UK and in certain professions is to pursue the accumulation of wealth almost to the exclusion of everything else. I came to realise that this is at odds with Jesus's teaching that we cannot serve God and money. Striving after kingdom values felt more appropriate than solely pursuing personal gain. And yet as we have invested as a family in furthering God's kingdom (heavenly treasures), God has always provided generously for us.

Another way to think of this is seeking to adopt a simpler lifestyle as an objective, rather than one of accumulation. I'm not there yet. John Wesley is quoted as saying:

> "Earn all you can, give all you can, save all you can."[35]

---

[35] https://www.goodreads.com/author/quotes/151350.John_Wesley

Study 7 - Kingdom Practice Health Check
Biblical Support Section
- What does pursuing holiness mean for you?

Our Context Section
- In your cultural context, what is the wider societal view on the need to live a holy life?
- What does being salt and light mean to you?
- Are there worldly things that are dimming your light or reducing your saltiness? How might you change this?
- Is there a modern-day cultural equivalent of salt and light where you live? If so, what is it?
- If you are a disciple of Jesus, you are already set apart for holy use because you are a citizen of his kingdom here on earth. How does this knowledge of what you are compare with your lifestyle, attitudes, and behaviours?

Kingdom Practice Application Section
- Is there anything that might help you become more holy?

Again, we need to recognise that being salt and light to those around us is not about good works or earning credit with God, but an aspect of obedience. Ask the Holy Spirit to reveal to you any areas you need to reflect on moving forward. Bring these to God in prayer.

Study 7 - Possible Action
If you are being prompted in some way about your personal holiness, consider responding by asking the Holy Spirit to help you day by day, then write this down with the date in the outlined text box provided (or your journal/notebook).

Health Warning
Remember that you should not respond to this Kingdom Practice in a legalistic way. It is much more about serving God as part of our love for him because of our salvation in Jesus. We will become more like Jesus the more we allow the Holy Spirit to lead and guide us day by day, and God will get the glory.

My Response/Prayer and Date

Study 7 - Bribery and Corruption Exercise

In looking at the subject of integrity across your wider society, either in a group, couple, or as an individual, consider the following questions:

- ➤ How do you define corruption? What kind of acts do you think are corrupt?
- ➤ What is your understanding of corruption/bribery in your country/context?
- ➤ What do you think are the main causes of corruption/bribery in your country/context?
- ➤ What do you think are the consequences of corruption/bribery your country/context?
- ➤ In what way does your faith influence your attitude and response to each of the above questions?

Space For You To Record Responses To Questions, Make Notes, Etc.

Study 7 - Pursue Holiness (Integrity/Purity)

Study 7 - Pursue Holiness (Integrity/Purity)

Study 7 - Memorising the Structure

Can you fill in the blank boxes without looking at the figure displayed at the beginning of this study?

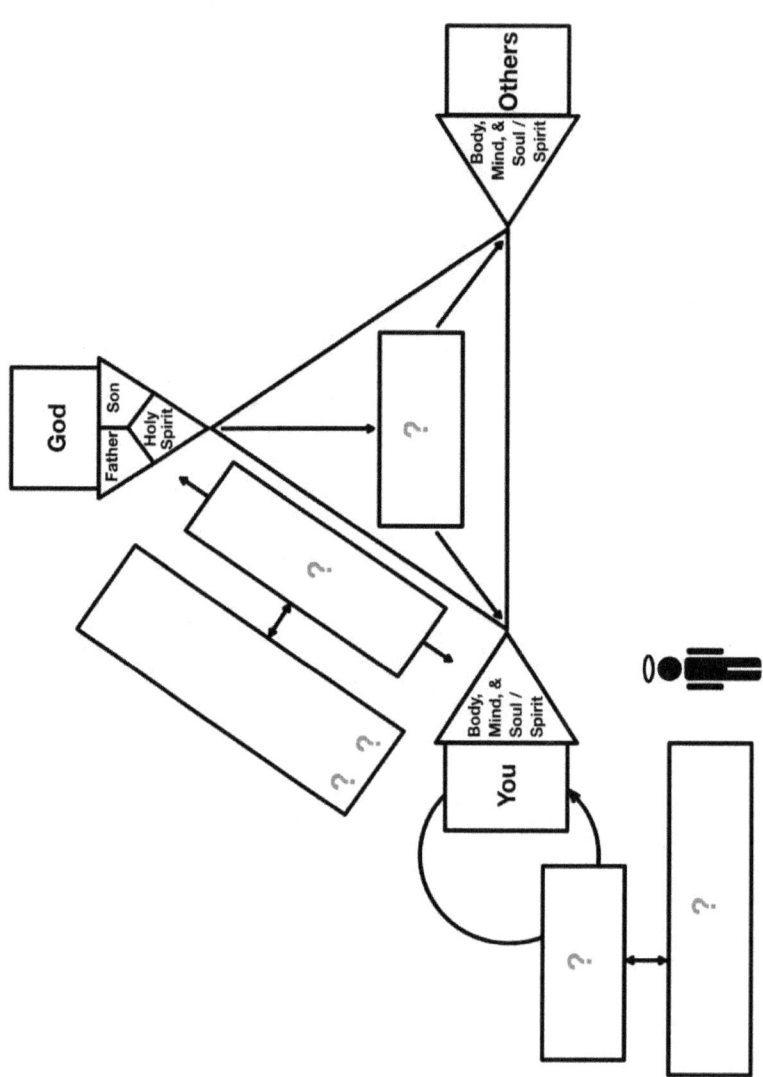

Study 8 - Live Out Kingdom Values - (KP5)
Subtitle: Understand What Living as a Citizen of God's Kingdom Implies

Live: To have a life rich in experience. To maintain oneself.

Value(s): Something (as a principle or quality) intrinsically valuable or desirable.

Study 8 - Introduction

In this study we are considering the third Kingdom Practice correlating to the Kingdom Fundamental to Follow Jesus, which is to Live Out Kingdom Values.

In a similar way to figures from studies 6 and 7, Figure 11 demonstrates that the need to live out kingdom values is a component of our response to follow Jesus. Once again, we are influenced by our reading of the Bible and the extent to which we permit the Holy Spirit to lead and change us.

Figure 11 - Kingdom Practice 5 - to Live Out Kingdom Values

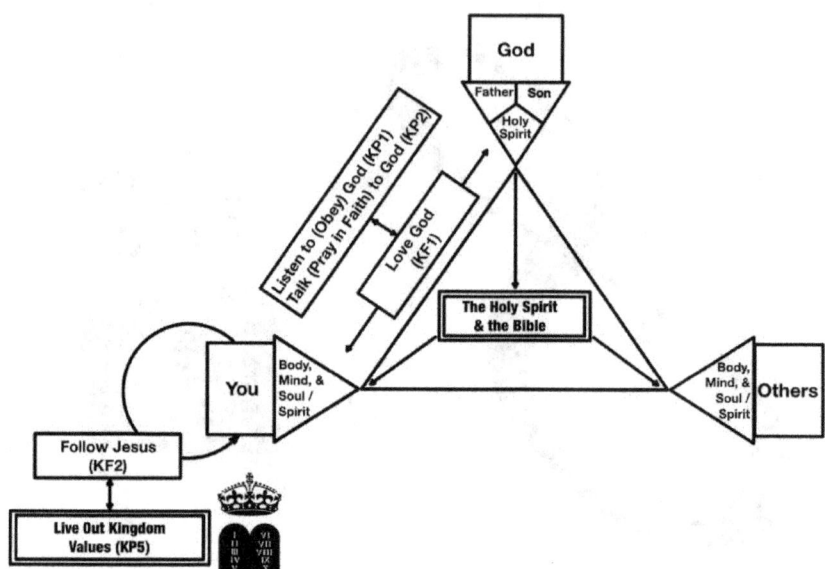

Study 8 - Biblical Support for This Kingdom Practice

Jesus's teachings were challenging to the perceived wisdom of the society in which he lived and often called for very different behavioural responses to those the religious leaders were teaching from the Old Testament. In many cases, Old Testament decrees were more restriction than permission, such as:

> Life for life, eye for eye, tooth for tooth. (Deuteronomy 19:21)

As laid down in Old Testament law, such a provision was intended, among other things, to restrict the extent of retribution with which the Israelites responded to an offence. In contrast, other surrounding people groups practised "revenge" on an escalatory level, which is why God warned the Israelites when giving them his law:

> Vengeance belongs to me; I will repay. (Deuteronomy 32:35)

The teachings of Jesus went even further, setting his disciples apart in inner attitudes as well as in outward behaviour and practices. There are seven areas of Jesus's teaching that can help us understand what it means to live out our lives within God's kingdom and differentiate us from non-believers:

- Live honourably.

- Practise giving, praying, and fasting.

- Practise justice, mercy, and faithfulness.
- Give to God what is God's and to authorities and others what is due to them.
- Trust in God's provision and peace.
- Celebrate the Lord's Supper,
- Be ready for Jesus's return/keep watch.

We will consider the basis for each of these subheadings in the Scripture references presented below (see Appendix 2 or the *All That I Have Commanded You* book, Chapter 3.3, for a complete set of scriptures).

8.1 - Live Honourably

In Studies 2 and 5, we considered briefly some of the Ten Commandments. In this study we will see that the remainder of the Ten Commandments (see Exodus 20, Deuteronomy 5) are addressed explicitly by Jesus in his own commands to his disciples. As disciples we should seek to comply with these commandments under the guidance of the Holy Spirit, both for our own right living and as they relate to our interactions with others. To fulfil Jesus's call to live honourably, we must practise these supporting Kingdom Behaviours:

Honour God's Law

Jesus makes it clear that he came to live fully by the law and that it still remains as a standard until the end of time. However, we are freed from the penalty for breaking the law because of Jesus's sacrifice:

> Don't assume that I came to destroy the Law or the Prophets. I did not come to destroy but to fulfil. For I assure you: Until heaven and earth pass away, not the smallest letter or one stroke of a letter will pass from the law until all things are accomplished. Therefore, whoever breaks one of the least of these commands and teaches people to do so will be called least in the kingdom of heaven. But whoever practises and teaches these commands will be called great in the kingdom of heaven. (Matthew 5:17-19)

> "Which ones?" he asked Him. Jesus answered: "Do not murder; do not commit adultery; do not steal; do not bear false witness; honour your father and your mother; and love your neighbour as yourself." (Matthew 19:18-19, Mark 10:19, Luke 18:20)

Honour Our Parents

We need to respect and honour our parents (note in Deuteronomy 5:16 that this commandment in particular includes a conditional promise from God for those who fulfil it). Naturally, this can be a particularly difficult command for those who have grown up with parents who were abusive or neglected them:

For God said: Honour your father and your mother; and, the one who speaks evil of father or mother must be put to death. (Matthew 15:4)

Do Not Covet (Guard Against Greed)

Jesus highlights that we should not desire to acquire or own many things, especially those that belong to others:

> Then he said to them, "Watch out! Be on your guard against all kinds of greed; [Some translations say "covetousness"] life does not consist in an abundance of possessions." (Luke 12:15, NIV)

Honour Marriage

We are to hold to our marriage vows if we have made them:

> So they are no longer two, but one flesh. Therefore, what God has joined together, man must not separate. (Matthew 19:6, Genesis 2:24)

Do Not Commit Adultery

Jesus makes it clear that we should not have extramarital relationships or a relationship with a married person if we are single. He also challenges us that adultery is not just a physical act, but is first conceived in the mind/heart as lustful thoughts. Consequently, we should aim to maintain mental purity by not allowing or cultivating such ideas (see 2 Corinthians 10:5 as highlighted in Study 7, Section 7.1 above and/or look at this hard-hitting sermon:[36]

> You have heard that it was said, Do not commit adultery. But I tell you, everyone who looks at a woman to lust for her has already committed adultery with her in his heart. (Matthew 5:27-28)

8.2 - Practise Giving, Praying, and Fasting

In Matthew 6:1-18, Jesus gives specific commands about how we are to give. This includes not broadcasting what we have done (see Study 13), praying in secret (see Study 4), and fasting in such a way that others will not notice:

---

[36] https://dextergaspard.org/2015/08/30/dont-commit-adultery/

Giving

Be careful not to practise your righteousness in front of people, to be seen by them. Otherwise, you will have no reward from your Father in heaven. So whenever you give to the poor, don't sound a trumpet before you, as the hypocrites do in the synagogues and on the streets, to be applauded by people. I assure you: They've got their reward! But when you give to the poor, don't let your left hand know what your right hand is doing, so that your giving may be in secret. And your Father who sees in secret will reward you.

Praying

Whenever you pray, you must not be like the hypocrites, because they love to pray standing in the synagogues and on the street corners to be seen by people. I assure you: They've got their reward! But when you pray, go into your private room, shut your door, and pray to your Father who is in secret. And your Father who sees in secret will reward you. When you pray, don't babble like the idolaters, since they imagine they'll be heard for their many words. Don't be like them, because your Father knows the things you need before you ask Him.

Therefore, you should pray like this: Our Father in heaven, Your name be honoured as holy. Your kingdom come. Your will be done on earth as it is in heaven. Give us today our daily bread. And forgive us our debts, as we also have forgiven our debtors. And do not bring us into temptation, but deliver us from the evil one [For Yours is the kingdom and the power and the glory forever. Amen]. 'For if you forgive people their wrongdoing, your heavenly Father will forgive you as well. But if you don't forgive people, your Father will not forgive your wrongdoing.

Fasting

Whenever you fast, don't be sad-faced like the hypocrites. For they make their faces unattractive so their fasting is obvious to people. I assure you: They've got their reward! But when you fast, put oil on your head, and wash your face, so that you don't show your fasting to people but to your Father who is in secret. And your Father who sees in secret will reward you.

8.3 - Practise Justice, Mercy, and Faithfulness

We are to behave in a way that is just and shows grace and mercy. We are also to be full of faith, which is as important as paying our tithes. Note that Jesus lived in a context where tithing was culturally expected. Views within church groups today differ on whether there is an ongoing requirement for Christians to pay tithes (see 2 Corinthians 9:7). Jesus himself neither reiterated the command to tithe nor explicitly dismissed it as no longer relevant:

> Woe to you, scribes and Pharisees, hypocrites! You pay a tenth of mint, dill, and cumin, yet you have neglected the more important matters of the law – justice, mercy, and faith. These things should have been done without neglecting the others. (Matthew 23:23)

8.4 - Give to God What is God's and to Authorities and Others What is Due to Them

As part of our duty to our government, we should pay our taxes (however unpalatable!), return to others anything that they have loaned to us (money or other things), and give to God what he asks of us:

> "Show Me the coin used for the tax." So they brought Him a denarius. "Whose image and inscription is this?" He asked them. "Caesar's," they said to Him. Then He said to them, "Therefore give back to Caesar the things that are Caesar's, and to God the things that are God's." (Matthew 22:19-21. See also Mark 12:17, Luke 20:25)

8.5 - Trust in God's Provision and Peace

Jesus offers each of us his peace, an inner peace that is different from peace as the world understands it and upon which we can draw when things become difficult:

> This is why I tell you: Don't worry about your life, what you will eat or what you will drink; or about your body, what you will wear. Isn't life more than food and the body more than clothing? Look at the birds of the sky: They don't sow or reap or gather into barns, yet your heavenly Father feeds them. Aren't you worth more than they? (Matthew 6:25-26)

8.6 - Celebrate the Lord's Supper

We are to regularly remember Jesus by celebrating the sacrament of the Lord's Supper, which he specifically instituted before his crucifixion:

> As they were eating, Jesus took bread, blessed and broke it, gave it to the disciples, and said, "Take and eat it; this is My body." Then He took a cup, and after giving thanks, He gave it to them and said, "Drink from it, all of you." (Matthew 26:26-27)

> Then He took a cup, and after giving thanks, He said, "Take this and share it among yourselves. For I tell you, from now on I will not drink of the fruit of the vine until the kingdom of God comes." And He took bread, gave thanks, broke it, gave it to them, and said, "This is My body, which is given for you. Do this in remembrance of Me". In the same way He also took the cup after supper and said, "This cup is the new covenant established by My blood; it is shed for you." (Luke 22:17-20)

8.7 - Be Ready for Jesus's Return/Keep Watch

The Bible tells us that the end of the age "will come like a thief" (2 Peter 3:10), so we are to be ready for Jesus's return. There are many theories and interpretations about the signs of the times and what and when this will happen. However, the Bible says:

> Now concerning that day or hour no one knows –neither the angels in heaven nor the Son –except the Father. Watch! Be alert! For you don't know when the time is coming. It is like a man on a journey, who left his house, gave authority to his slaves, gave each one his work, and commanded the doorkeeper to be alert. Therefore be alert, since you don't know when the master of the house is coming –whether in the evening or at midnight or at the crowing of the rooster or early in the morning. Otherwise, he might come suddenly and find you sleeping. And what I say to you, I say to everyone: Be alert. (Mark 13:32-37. See also Luke 12:35-40)

Study 8 - Our Context

Jesus is not recorded as sharing a parable that indicates how we should be living the Christian life today. But in a very real sense, all the Kingdom Fundamentals and Kingdom Practices identified in this book are things we should be exhibiting in greater measure as we develop spiritually along our journey with him:

> How happy is the man who does not follow the advice of the wicked or take the path of sinners or join a group of mockers! Instead, his delight is in the Lord's instruction, and he meditates on it day and night. He is like a tree planted beside streams of water that bears its fruit in season and whose leaf does not wither. Whatever he does prospers. The wicked are not like this; instead, they are like chaff that the wind blows away. (Psalm 1:1-4)

So what is the law of the Lord in our modern world context? What should we today be meditating on day and night? How should we put this law into practice?

Of 613 identifiable laws set out in the Old Testament, 365 are negative things to be abstained from and 248 are positive things to practice.[37] The law of the Lord set out in the Old Testament can be broken down into three principal groups:

---

[37] See http://www.jewfaq.org/613.htm

Ceremonial laws:
- Offering sacrifices.
- Observing feasts and holy days.

Dietary laws:
- Not eating pork, rabbit, and horse products.
- Not eating reptiles, insects, or amphibians.
- Not eating sea animals without fins or scales (shellfish/crustaceans).
- Eating meat killed in a kosher way (the Muslim equivalent is called halal).
- Processes surrounding the ritual cleaning of food utensils.

Moral laws:
- Not stealing.
- Not coveting.
- Not committing adultery.
- Not bearing false witness/lying.
- Etc.

If we fail to keep the ceremonial or dietary laws, this doesn't have any impact upon other people. We could argue that at the cross when Jesus fulfilled the law through his sacrificial death, the responsibility to comply with all the ceremonial and dietary elements of the Old Testament law was removed. In terms of sacrificial laws, we have Jesus as the final sacrifice for sins (Romans 6:10, Hebrews 10:10), which puts an end to the need for any other sacrifice. As to ceremonial laws, scripture passages like Romans 14:5-6 indicate there is no requirement for Christians to celebrate particular feasts or holy days. As to dietary regulations, we have the vision of Peter (Acts 10:9-22; 11:1-18), which makes clear Christians are not bound by Old Testament dietary restrictions.

In contrast, if we do not keep a moral law, this will almost always have a negative impact on someone else and/or us. God will never ask us to do something that is contrary to his instructions in terms of moral laws. That said, we cannot keep moral laws in our own strength. We need the power of the Holy Spirit to:

Assist us in prayer.
> In the same way the Spirit also joins to help in our weakness, because we do not know what to pray for as we should, but the Spirit Himself intercedes for us with unspoken groanings. (Romans 8:26)

Lead us into all truth.

As we study and learn the Scriptures, we will become more like Jesus.

> When the Spirit of truth comes, He will guide you into all the truth. For He will not speak on His own, but He will speak whatever He hears. He will also declare to you what is to come. (John 16:13)

Be with us as we share fellowship with other believers.

> For where two or three are gathered together in My name, I am there among them. (Matthew 18:20)

Witness to others of Jesus.

We are to share the gospel as the Holy Spirit presents us with opportunities.

> But you will receive power when the Holy Spirit has come on you, and you will be My witnesses in Jerusalem, in all Judea and Samaria, and to the ends of the earth. (Acts 1:8)

Help stop us from giving in to temptation.

> No temptation has overtaken you except what is common to humanity. God is faithful, and He will not allow you to be tempted beyond what you are able, but with the temptation He will also provide a way of escape so that you are able to bear it. (1 Corinthians 10:13)

Practising each of these will help us "abide in Christ" (see Study 4 and John 15 reference below). Indeed, the two "greatest commandments" and the Great Commission sum up what the law of the Lord is for us as disciples of Jesus.

Jesus said in Matthew 5:17:

> Don't assume that I came to destroy the Law or the Prophets. I did not come to destroy but to fulfil.

James 2:10 adds:

> For whoever keeps the whole law and yet stumbles at just one point is guilty of breaking all of it (NIV).

As disciples, we understand that Jesus fulfilled all Old Testament laws so that we can be forgiven for having broken God's law. This is why on the cross Jesus exclaimed, "It is finished" (John 19:30). He lived the perfect life by keeping the Ten Commandments, obeying the rules and regulations of the Torah (the first five books of the Bible), as well as civil law and all the sacrificial, ceremonial, and moral laws on our behalf.

By accepting Jesus as our Saviour and Lord, we recognise that he paid the price for our sins, including our failures to uphold Old Testament commands. We do not have to keep any of these laws in order to be saved or to retain our salvation. However, Jesus also tells us:

> Remain [some translations say "abide"] in Me, and I in you. Just as a branch is unable to produce fruit by itself unless it remains on the vine, so neither can you unless you remain in Me. I am the vine; you are the branches. The one who remains in Me and I in him produces much fruit, because you can do nothing without Me. (John 15:4-5)

In other words, we need to remain connected to Jesus. We do this through Bible study, our prayer lives, and as we respond to circumstances. We are also to walk, be led by, and live by the Holy Spirit:

> For the entire law is fulfilled in one statement: Love your neighbour as yourself. But if you bite and devour one another, watch out, or you will be consumed by one another. I say then, walk by the Spirit and you will not carry out the desire of the flesh. For the flesh desires what is against the Spirit, and the Spirit desires what is against the flesh; these are opposed to each other, so that you don't do what you want. But if you are led by the Spirit, you are not under the law. (Galatians 5:14-18)

The law that applies to disciples now is not the law as set out in the Old Testament, whether ceremonial, dietary, or moral. That was a law no one except Jesus was ever able to keep blamelessly. Rather, we follow the law of Christ, which is really an amplified and extended version of the moral laws already laid down in the Old Testament. This law of Christ is not a specific list of rules and regulations we must comply with to obtain or retain our salvation. Our faith in Jesus has set us free from such constraints. But this doesn't mean we can just live as we please as Galatians 5:19-21 illustrates:

> Now the works of the flesh are obvious: sexual immorality, moral impurity, promiscuity, idolatry, sorcery, hatreds, strife, jealousy, outbursts of anger, selfish ambitions, dissensions, factions, envy, drunkenness, carousing, and anything similar. I tell you about these things in advance –as I told you before –that those who practise such things will not inherit the kingdom of God.

Rather, it is the application of the law of love that needs to be part of every aspect of our lives, as the same passage goes on to illustrate:

> But the fruit of the Spirit is love, joy, peace, patience, kindness, goodness, faithfulness, gentleness, self-control. Against such things there is no law. Now those who belong to Christ Jesus have crucified the flesh with its passions and desires. Since we live by the Spirit, we must also follow the Spirit. We must not become conceited, provoking one another, envying one another. (Galatians 5:22-26)

Another way to phrase this is that we have been freed by the gospel from compliance to the Old Testament law. But as we now "work out our salvation" (Philippians 2:12), we can look back to Old Testament law as a pointer to those things we should be doing to please God. This is not in a "salvation through works" sense, but in terms of a life motivated by our gratitude to God for the grace he extends to us in Jesus. This is demonstrated through our love and service for God, to others, and for his glory.[38]

This is what we are called to meditate on day and night and put into practice in terms of our own obedience.

Study 8 - Kingdom Practice Application

Jesus as Our Example

As we discussed in Study 7, Jesus lived a sinless life. In practice, this means that he fully lived out kingdom values as highlighted in Section 8.1 above. In the John 10 passage below, we can see that Jesus explicitly states that his disciples will have life in abundance (fullness). This is, of course, dependent upon us remaining in a right relationship with Jesus and living a life of obedience (living righteously).

> So Jesus said again, "I assure you: I am the door of the sheep. All who came before Me are thieves and robbers, but the sheep didn't listen to them. I am the door. If anyone enters by Me, he will be saved and will come in and go out and find pasture. A thief comes only to steal and to kill and to destroy. I have come so that they may have life and have it in abundance." (John 10:7-10)

While we may not have much insight into Jesus's everyday life, we know that his relationship with the Father was deeper than any other person's in history. The Father had given Jesus a task to do, which was to redeem all of creation and to introduce God as Father and his kingdom in a different way than had been previously revealed in the Old Testament. His relationship with the Father, underpinned by prayer, was key to Jesus's effective communication with others, a communication that restored people physically, mentally, spiritually, and socially (e.g., Jesus's healing of lepers so they could be restored to their families and communities). This in turn resulted in disciples and followers.

We may easily fall into the trap of thinking that life in abundance is measured or determined by our wealth or power. Jesus sets the example by showing that life lived out by serving others can be the most fulfilling:

> But seek first the kingdom of God and His righteousness, and all these things will be provided for you. (Matthew 6:33)

---

[38] See Chapter 10 of *Galatians For You* - Tim Keller - The Good Book Company 2013.

Jesus is not recorded as having owned anything apart from his clothing (Luke 23:34, John 19:23-24). He trusted God for his daily food, clothing, health, a place to sleep, as well as for the power and words to heal and minister. During his earthly ministry, Jesus lived life to the full by living and working as his Father wanted, and as we saw in Study 2 (see also Matthew 3:16-17; 17:5) he gained his Father's unqualified approval. God in turn supplied his daily needs.

Some Brief Personal Reflections on Living Out Kingdom Values

The subsections 8.1 to 8.8 above illustrate the breadth of what it means to live as a disciple of Jesus in our daily personal lives. The sub-point "Living Honourably" encompasses six of the Ten Commandments that focus on how we should relate to and treat others. I try my best to live within these guidelines day by day, so let me share my perspective on just some of these topics.

Stealing

Growing up in a Christian household with a minister as my father, I was always taught to be honest. Consequently, I had a pretty well-tuned conscience from an early age. However, on one occasion when I was about twelve years old, I put a fifty-pence piece that wasn't mine in my back pocket. Living with the guilt of my action caused me enough personal grief and angst to instil in me a life lesson I continue to apply. I have never taken anything from a shop without paying for it nor conducted any dodgy deals when buying and selling things. After I became a Christian, I was even more scrupulous in my attention to detail, particularly when preparing and submitting expense claims to my employers.

Coveting

Coveting things has been more of a challenge from time to time. But as I get older, I've come to realise that things of beauty typically carry a hidden price tag as well as an obvious one. For example, we have had our fair share of vehicles over the years, some grander than others, although we've sought to reduce our "carbon footprint" in more recent purchases. It has become a standard family joke when we see someone driving a luxury vehicle to say, "Do you think he/she is happy driving that ****?" Indeed, the answer may be yes. But hiding behind the ornamental exterior are the costs of insurance, servicing, spare parts, security provisions, threat of criminal damage or theft, never mind the costs of repayment and depreciation. So I am much happier in our modest family car that gets us from A to B without drawing attention to itself.

Adultery

I have kept my marriage vows and try to love my wife and family as best I can. However, I would be lying to suggest I have never looked lustfully at another woman (see Matthew 5:27-30) since the day Mary-Anne and I were married over thirty years ago. We all have God-given drives and desires, and most of us have likely fallen short at some point in channelling these in the right way. Which as far as the Bible is concerned means within the context of marriage. Or if we are single, sublimating those drives into positive activities and actions vs. pursuing any unhealthy course of behaviour.[39]

The easy accessibility of pornography on the internet presents challenges for Christian men and women of all ages, including teens. Viewing such things has negative implications not only for upholding and living out kingdom values but also for our personal holiness. I have not visited such websites, although even with strong parental controls set on our home computer, I have on a few occasions seen images that are inappropriate for a Christian to view. If you need more information and help on this subject, try a website like *www.fightthenewdrug.org*.[40]

We cannot always control what appears in front of our eyes, but we do have a choice as to what we do subsequently. Some have described it in this way: "The first look is not sinful, but the second one is." As with any sin of thought, word, or action, this should be confessed so that we can be forgiven and re-establish our confidence before God (1 John 3:21). We must then seek stronger input and restraining power from the Holy Spirit to resist future temptations that may come along.

Bearing False Witness

We may not have opportunity these days to bear false witness in a legal sense unless we are in court ourselves giving evidence. But gossip is, unfortunately, a very common form of false witness. Increasingly, I have realised that even sharing information that may be relatively common knowledge could be construed as gossip. My aim is to be truthful in my dealings with everyone,

---

[39] https://www.barna.com/research/porn-in-the-digital-age-new-research-reveals-10-trends/
[40] http://fightthenewdrug.org/about/

provided that I am not betraying a confidence or where speaking truthfully would cause distress. In the latter case, I will simply refuse to answer.

Rendering and Giving

I am more than happy to pay our taxes to the government and our tithes to God, primarily because these help provide respectively for the services we receive from the government and for the furtherance of God's kingdom. I want to pay the right taxes, not more and not less, by claiming the permitted allowances. Thankfully, I live in a nation where I can be reasonably sure the assessments of what is due will be carried out fairly and correctly. Our family position is that we consider a tithe to be the minimum level for us to give for the furtherance of God's kingdom.

Fasting

I would not claim to be someone who regularly fasts. However, desperate times call for desperate measures, and where there are clear concerns on an issue (for example, a friend needs prayer for healing), I have fasted to help me focus on prayer and seek God's power to be directed into that situation. More recently in preparation for a ministry trip to India, I made a deliberate decision to fast and pray in the lead-up to the trip, primarily because spiritual warfare is much more visible and prevalent where I was travelling, and I needed God's protection.

Denying Self

Denying myself is also something I have struggled with, especially when I was working in a career where my free time was much more limited than now. Striking a balance between living for God, family, work, and self is not always easy. But we need to keep in mind that taking up our cross and following Jesus does not entail a daily life of 100% ministry. It also includes time for meeting personal needs, including rest and relaxation, as well as taking time to be with and love others. This balance will vary by life's seasons and the context in which God has placed us.

Study 8 - Kingdom Practice Health Check

Biblical Support Section

> ➤ What does living out a kingdom lifestyle mean for you?

Our Context Section

> ➤ In your cultural context, what is the perception of the moral laws of the Bible? Do people live by them?

> ➤ Are these moral laws held in high regard by those with whom you come into contact? If not, why might that be? Let's

recognise that many of the sins of the world are just as common in the church body as outside it, as various scandals and revelations of cover-ups in recent years have highlighted.

As we've discussed, the Holy Spirit helps us to live out a life consistent with God's moral teaching by:

- Assisting us in prayer (Romans 8:26).
- Leading us into all truth as we study and learn the Scriptures (John 16:13).
- Being with us as we share fellowship with other believers (Matthew 18:20).
- Helping us witness to others of Jesus as we are given opportunity (Acts 1:8).
- Helping us resist giving in to temptation (1 Corinthians 10:13).

➢ How do you feel about each of these five points? Is anything missing you feel should be added?

Kingdom Practice Application Section

➢ The call to live a life of obedience in the kingdom is difficult intellectually, emotionally, and practically. What about spiritually? Is that different, and should it be easier since we can call on the Holy Spirit to assist us?

➢ Is there something that would help you align your life better with living as God in Christ would have you do?

➢ What are the real challenges you are facing?

➢ How might you begin to address them?

Study 8 - Possible Action

Ask the Holy Spirit to reveal to you things you should work on, and consider how you will respond as he guides and directs. Why not write down anything you feel prompted to do as well as the date in the outlined text box provided (or your journal/notebook).

Health Warning

Remember that you should not respond to this Kingdom Practice in a legalistic way. It is much more about serving God as part of our love for him because of our salvation in Jesus. We will become more like Jesus the more we allow the Holy Spirit to lead and guide us day by day, and God will get the glory.

My Response/Prayer and Date

Space For You To Record Responses To Questions, Make Notes, Etc.

Study 8 - Live Out Kingdom Values

Study 8 - Live Out Kingdom Values

Study 8 - Memorising the Structure

Can you fill in the blank boxes without looking at the figure displayed at the beginning of this study?

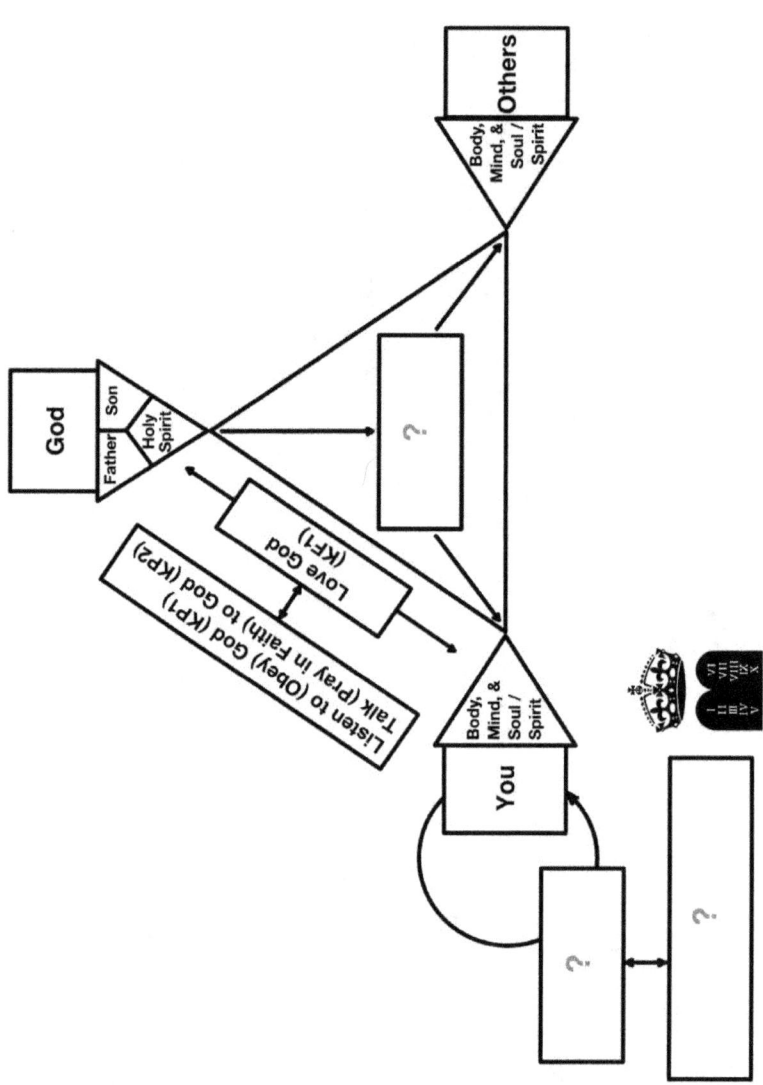

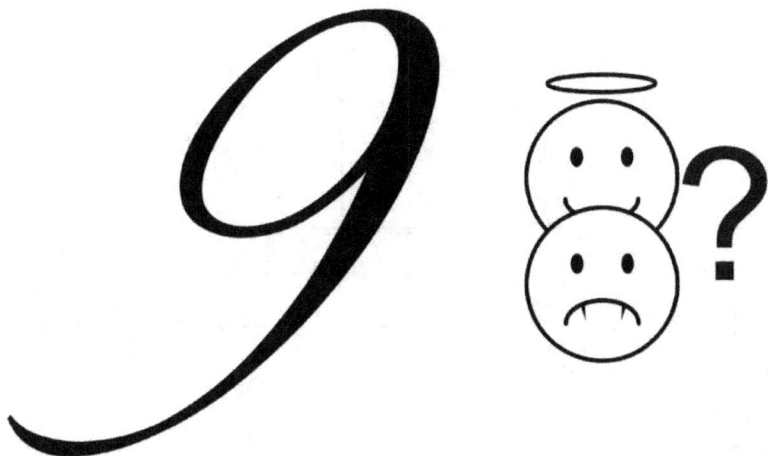

Study 9 - Exercise Discernment - (KP6)

Subtitle: We Need to Test What We Read and Learn from Others and Determine Whether Situations We Face Have a Spiritual Dimension

Exercise: Something that is done or practised to develop a particular skill.

Discernment: The quality of being able to grasp and comprehend what is obscure.

Study 9 - Introduction

This study investigates the fourth Kingdom Practice that correlates to the Kingdom Fundamental to Follow Jesus, which is to Exercise Discernment. Exercising discernment is another component of our response to the call to follow Jesus. It is illustrated in Figure 12 and shows again the importance of the Holy Spirit and the Bible as key influencing factors.

Figure 12 - The Kingdom Practice 6 - to Exercise Discernment

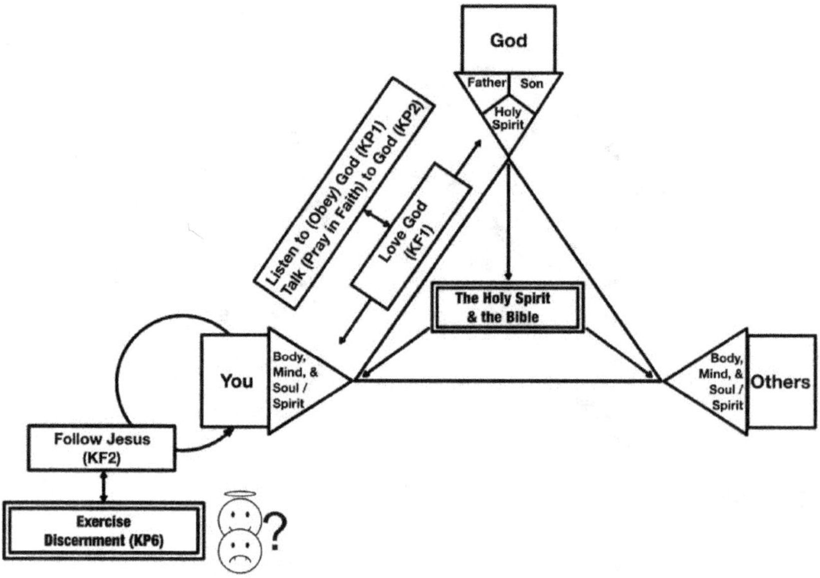

Study 9 - Biblical Support for This Kingdom Practice

To be better disciples, we must also exercise discernment. This includes being careful what we share about the kingdom and with whom. It also involves thinking more deeply about the true source of things around us. For example, we should be seeking to recognise where God is at work and give him the glory. In other contexts, things we may observe may not actually be from God, so we need to listen to the Holy Spirit's prompting in order to discern the source of what we are witnessing. Another facet of discernment is for us to seek out and determine where God is at work in the world around us and how he may be inviting us to join him in ministering to others (in service–see Study 12). Also, in a larger sense, we need to discern what God wants us to be doing with our lives (role, job, vocation etc.).

Jesus addresses this important aspect of a disciple's life in what can be summarised as five behaviours:

- Guard against falsehood.
- Do not be deceived.
- Be wise as serpents and innocent as doves.
- Do not throw our pearls to pigs.
- Do not blaspheme against the Holy Spirit.

Let's consider each of these behaviours in turn by looking at the teachings of Jesus himself (see Appendix 2 or the *All That I Have Commanded You* book, Chapter 3.4, for a complete set of scriptures).

9.1 - Guard against Falsehood

As followers of Jesus, we are warned that we should test whether we are being misled by our spiritual leaders. How they live will be a true indicator of where their hearts really lie, as these supporting Kingdom Behaviours indicate.

Beware of False Teaching.

We need to check that those who teach and disciple us are being true to God's Word:

> Why is it you don't understand that when I told you, "Beware of the yeast of the Pharisees and Sadducees," it wasn't about bread? Then they understood that He did not tell them to beware of the yeast in bread, but of the teaching of the Pharisees and Sadducees. (Matthew 16:11-12. See also Matthew 16:6)

Beware of False Prophets.

Similarly, we should be checking whether those who claim to be God's messengers truly are. We can do this by looking at their fruit and seeing if their lives are consistent with what they say:

> Beware of false prophets who come to you in sheep's clothing but inwardly are ravaging wolves. You'll recognise them by their fruit. Are grapes gathered from thorn bushes or figs from thistles? In the same way, every good tree produces good fruit, but a bad tree produces bad fruit. A good tree can't produce bad fruit; neither can a bad tree produce good fruit. Every tree that doesn't produce good fruit is cut down and thrown into the fire. So you'll recognise them by their fruit. (Matthew 7:15-20)

9.2 - Do Not Be Deceived

The Bible tells us how Jesus will return (1 Thessalonians 4:13-18). This means that any alternative message in contradiction of Scripture is false, and we are being deceived if we believe it. If what we are being told does not conform with the Scriptures and their reasonable interpretation, then it should be scrutinised very closely:

> If anyone tells you then, "Look, here is the Messiah!" or, "Over here!" do not believe it! False messiahs and false prophets will arise and perform great signs and wonders to lead astray, if possible, even the elect. Take note: I have told you in advance. So if they tell you, "Look, He's in the wilderness!" don't go out; "Look, He's in the inner rooms!" do not believe it. For as the lightning comes from the east and flashes as far as the west, so will be the coming of the Son of Man. Wherever the carcass is, there the vultures will gather.

(Matthew 24:23-28. See also Matthew 24:4-5, Mark 13:5-9 and Mark 13:20-23)

9.3 - Be as Wise as Serpents and Innocent as Doves

Jesus expects us to use our ingenuity and shrewdness when dealing with non-believers, but in a way that is not sinful or dishonouring to him or the gospel message:

> Look, I'm sending you out like sheep among wolves. Therefore be as shrewd as serpents and as harmless as doves. (Matthew 10:16)

9.4 - Do Not Throw Our Pearls to Pigs

This warning is specifically not to share the gospel and things of God with those who are strongly antagonistic or likely to be potentially violent upon hearing the message (e.g., an angry crowd):

> Don't give what is holy to dogs or toss your pearls before pigs, or they will trample them with their feet, turn, and tear you to pieces. (Matthew 7:6)

9.5 - Do Not Blaspheme against the Holy Spirit

We are specifically warned that we should not defame the Holy Spirit or attribute the work of the Holy Spirit to any other power. We must therefore be discerning to ensure that we can recognise fully when God is at work. We have the Holy Spirit within us to bear witness to us when this is the case, but only if we choose to listen to him:

> "But whoever blasphemes against the Holy Spirit never has forgiveness, but is guilty of an eternal sin" – because they were saying, "He has an unclean spirit." (Mark 3:29-30. See also Luke 12:10)]

Study 9 - Our Context

Things of this world are transient. Some are beneficial, while others can have short or long-term negative effects on our emotional, mental, physical, social, and spiritual wellbeing. We need to seek the Lord to help us make sound judgements and discern the right way forward, not only in the big decisions that present themselves from time to time, but also in the everyday choices we make as we go about life.

Discernment in relation to kingdom teaching

Jesus warns us specifically that people will try to deceive us, most commonly for their own gain. We should be watchful and look at the lifestyles and fruit of those in leadership, particularly in the Christian context (see the Matthew 7 reference in 9.1 above).

In terms of teaching within the church, we should be like the Berean believers who studied the Scriptures to check that what they were being told was correct (Acts 17:11). If there is an issue to consider closely, then we might benefit from studying the Scriptures with others so as to understand their perspectives. For some thorny topics, there may be a wide range of views that appear irreconcilable. This is where we need to show some of the grace that God has shown us rather than always seeking to impose our own perspective (even if we believe we are right!). In practice, this is a form of submission, or as the apostle Paul taught, "considering others to be better than ourselves" (Philippians 2:3-4).

Spiritual Discernment

Perhaps even more important is the need to recognise that there is a spiritual battle going on around us:

> For our struggle is not against flesh and blood, but against the rulers, against the authorities, against the powers of this dark world and against the spiritual forces of evil in the heavenly realms. (Ephesians 6:12, NIV)

In Western cultures in particular, we have let our educational system, science, medicine, and our culture rationalise away any spiritual dimension to some of the problems and challenges that people face, playing down even its existence. We have largely become blind to these spiritual forces. Consequently, because we do not recognise or acknowledge them, they can operate unchallenged. Together with materialism and the relative comfort of our current society, this militates against a need to seek out Jesus as a solution to our problems and to put our dependence and trust wholly in him.

In contrast, there is a much greater awareness of spiritual forces at work in many parts of Africa, Asia, Latin America, and elsewhere. Many religions incorporate animistic[41] components or are explicitly animistic. This can have a real impact on the lives of people in communities where these things are practised. In certain cultures, there is widespread knowledge and fear of the spirit world, so discernment of these spiritual forces is especially important there. Missionaries from more secular, non-spiritual cultures in particular who find themselves serving in animistic societies will need sound cultural orientation training to understand what might be happening around them.

Many people are also searching for spiritual meaning. These days they have the opportunity to pursue a wide range of spiritual paths that may be inappropriate. Examples include New Age thinking, paganism, Tarot

---

[41] Animism - the belief that all natural things, such as plants, animals, rocks, and thunder, have spirits and can influence human events - https://dictionary.cambridge.org/dictionary/english/animism

reading, horoscopes, Ouija boards, spiritism, divination, and other religions. Such lead them to ignore the Bible and the unique claims of Jesus.

As followers of Jesus, we live in the world but are part of a heavenly kingdom. However, many of us live in a context where we are constantly bombarded with worldly marketing messages about things we must have that will fulfil us and help us to keep up with or stay ahead of our neighbours. Other social and cultural messages explicitly or implicitly target some of our basic physical, mental, and emotional desires. People taken in by these may end up getting into debt, various forms of addiction, or all sorts of other consequent difficulties. Not all of this can be attributed to spiritual forces, but such forces do underlie many things that can lead us into different forms of bondage that will detract from our relationship with God.

It is clear from Scripture that Jesus understood the very real nature of spiritual forces, although he himself had complete authority over them. The religious people of Jesus's time even tried to dismiss his ministry by suggesting that he was working in league with demonic forces:

> Jesus knew their thoughts and said to them: "Any kingdom divided against itself will be ruined, and a house divided against itself will fall. If Satan is divided against himself, how can his kingdom stand? I say this because you claim that I drive out demons by Beelzebul. Now if I drive out demons by Beelzebul, by whom do your disciples drive them out? So then, they will be your judges. But if I drive out demons by the finger of God, then the kingdom of God has come upon you. When a strong man, fully armed, guards his own house, his possessions are safe. But when someone stronger attacks and overpowers him, he takes away the armour in which the man trusted and divides up his plunder. Whoever is not with me is against me, and whoever does not gather with me scatters. When an impure spirit comes out of a person, it goes through arid places seeking rest and does not find it. Then it says, "I will return to the house I left." When it arrives, it finds the house swept clean and put in order. Then it goes and takes seven other spirits more wicked than itself, and they go in and live there. And the final condition of that person is worse than the first." (Luke 11:17-26, NIV)

So in looking at the subject of discernment, one important focus should be upon the spiritual rather than the physical realm, although this will depend upon the situation. In effect, Jesus has given each of his followers spiritual "keys" to his kingdom. This includes his instruction to share the gospel with others and disciple them. As mentioned in the earlier analogy of casting pearls before pigs (Matthew 7:6), sharing this knowledge in all its richness with those who would trample it underfoot would not be right. We are called to discern just who and where our audience is, and this is achieved through listening to the prompting of the Holy Spirit.

That said, people cannot respond until they have heard, so we are also to:

> Preach the word; be prepared in season and out of season; correct, rebuke and encourage—with great patience and careful instruction. (2 Timothy 4:2, NIV)

Some will respond positively, and these are the people in whom we should invest our time. Others will reject the message and possibly reject us too. In which case, we do not have to continue trying to share with them as Jesus himself acknowledged:

> If any place does not welcome you and people refuse to listen to you, when you leave there, shake the dust off your feet as a testimony against them. (Mark 6:11. See also Matthew 10:14, Luke 9:5)

Discernment about our role

We also need to discern what God is saying to us about his plans for us and what we are to do with and during our lives. As we have already seen, this can vary according to circumstances and different seasons. Such discernment should include not only bigger decisions about our career or vocation but also smaller interactions with others where we can see and become involved with God at work. It is important for us to establish what God wants us to do for the kingdom as that is where the greatest blessing is likely to be. Anything we do that is outside his plan puts us at a disadvantage in the sense that his will and ours are not in full alignment.

Sometimes it may take years for a vision or desire that we have to come to reality. This may be because God needs us to develop the skills and capabilities necessary to undertake the task he has for us. At other times, it may be immediately apparent what God wants us to do, whether a simple action or as part of his long-term plan.

So how do we really come to an understanding of what God wants from us? As with other areas of life, we need to:

- Practice hearing God's voice so we can know when and what he is speaking to us (see Study 1 for teaching about the Holy Spirit and Study 3 for Jesus's commands about listening to God).

- Learn from and apply Bible teaching in our fellowship, in study groups, Bible notes, and our private reading of the Bible.

- Recognise when a Bible text may come up time and again as God tries to attract our attention.

- Understand our own gifts, talents, and desires and how they can be used in God's service.

- Respond to a quickening in our spirit about an issue, vocation, or opportunity for service.

- Seek guidance from and listen to others - family, members of our fellowship, friends and colleagues, etc., always making sure such guidance is consistent with the Bible and teachings of Jesus.

Once we have done these things, then we can have some stronger sense of what God is calling us to do (both day to day and more broadly) and commit to move forward based upon his leading and timing.

Study 9 - Kingdom Practice Application

Jesus as Our Example

Discernment in relation to kingdom teaching

We understand that Jesus revealed the true nature of God. He did so to those who listened to his preaching, in his teaching to the disciples, and in some conversations with others we see recorded in the Gospels. He warned specifically against false teaching, false prophets, and human deception. So we need to be discerning in listening to and acting upon the preaching and advice of others. We need to check that what is being said is consistent with the Bible, that any references used have not been taken out of context, and that any suggested application to today's world or daily life is in keeping with Scripture teaching as a whole.

In particular, we must look at the fruit of those proclaiming themselves as spiritual leaders. What sort of lifestyle do they have? Is it consistent with Jesus's teaching and the Kingdom Practices presented in these studies?

We are told that everything in creation, visible and invisible, was created through Jesus (the Word). As he lived out his life of ministry, Jesus was able to demonstrate his power:

- Over the wind and waves of Galilee (Matthew 8:23-27, Mark 4:35-41, Luke 8:22-25).

- Over death through the resurrection of a number of individuals such as Lazarus (John 11:38-44) and Jairus's daughter (Mark 5:21-43, Luke 8:40-56).

- By creating food and drink, including turning water into wine (John 2:1-11), feeding four thousand (Mark 8:1-13, Matthew 15:29-39), and feeding five thousand (Mark 6:30-44, Matthew 14:13-21).

- To heal broken and infirm bodies (Matthew 9:1-8, Luke 6:6-11).

- To cleanse people from evil spirits (Luke 4:31-37; 9:37-43).

We are also told that Jesus knew people's thoughts, such as when the Pharisees were thinking he was in league with Beelzebub (Luke 11:17) and the passage below from John 2:24-25:

> But Jesus would not entrust himself to them, for he knew all people. He did not need any testimony about mankind, for he knew what was in each person. (NIV)

In our interactions with others, we need to be discerning about what to share with them and when. Being too bold in sharing the good news of the gospel may have a negative impact if we have not invested enough in the relationship first, prayed about the process of sharing, and listened to the Holy Spirit.

Spiritual Discernment

In the context of spiritual discernment, Jesus was able to order any demonic forces to leave a demon-possessed person by direct command. On one occasion, he actually entered into a dialogue with a demonic spirit:

> "What is your name?" He asked him. "My name is Legion," he answered Him, "because we are many." (Mark 5:9; see also Luke 8:30-31)

We will not cover this topic in depth here, but a comprehensive consideration can be found in such books as *War on the Saints* by Jesse Penn-Lewis and Evan Roberts.

So how might we understand the warning not to blaspheme against the Holy Spirit?

In effect, this means neither recognising God at work nor giving him the glory, attributing instead the outcome of God's working to other forces. This is what the Pharisees did in accusing Jesus of being in league with Satan/demons.[42] In doing so, they were explicitly rejecting Jesus, God, and the Holy Spirit.

Let me hasten to add here that if we as Christians feel we have misattributed God being at work or perhaps have not even been spiritually aware to recognise the working of the Holy Spirit, this does not imply we are guilty of blasphemy, therefore beyond forgiveness. Unintentional ignorance or error is completely different from a deliberate and total rejection of God. Nor does God expect us to be spiritually perfect or mature overnight. Consequently, in such instances we should not come under condemnation or feel there is no forgiveness for us:

---

[42] We should note that there are different interpretations concerning what "blaspheming against the Holy Spirit" means in today's context, so not all will understand this in the way described here.

> Therefore, there is now no condemnation for those who are in Christ Jesus. (Romans 8:1, NIV)

> For I am convinced that neither death nor life, neither angels nor demons, neither the present nor the future, nor any powers, neither height nor depth, nor anything else in all creation, will be able to separate us from the love of God that is in Christ Jesus our Lord. (Romans 8:38-39, NIV)

> If we claim to be without sin, we deceive ourselves and the truth is not in us. If we confess our sins, he is faithful and just and will forgive us our sins and purify us from all unrighteousness. If we claim we have not sinned, we make him out to be a liar and his word is not in us. (1 John 1:8-10, NIV)

Discernment as to our role

There are no specific commands from Jesus about discernment in the context of finding out what God wants us to do for a job or a vocation (though as we have seen in these studies, plenty is said in terms of living out a life of Christian witness). This is why we have the gift of the Person of the Holy Spirit within us (Study 1) and the Kingdom Practice of listening to (obeying) God as we considered in Study 3.

We read in John 5 that Jesus was effectively living under the direction of his father:

> Jesus gave them this answer: "Very truly I tell you, the Son can do nothing by himself; he can do only what he sees his Father doing, because whatever the Father does the Son also does. For the Father loves the Son and shows him all he does. Yes, and he will show him even greater works than these, so that you will be amazed. (John 5:19-20, NIV)

Sometimes God will appear to be silent on a matter. In these situations, this may be because God does not want us to change direction since we are already exactly where he wants us to be as part of his wider plan. Or it may be that God is waiting to reveal something to us later. Although this can be frustrating, if we are truly dependent upon God, then we should continue doing the last thing to which we believe he has led us until we hear differently from him.

Other times it may be very clear what God wants from us, but this may be something that we are not looking forward to or we perceive as difficult. God equips the called rather than always calling the equipped, so we must battle our own will in order to obey God when we discern that he needs us to get involved in something that in our own strength we'd rather not.

Some Brief Personal Reflections on Discernment

Discernment in relation to kingdom teaching

I count myself fortunate that most, if not all, of the teaching I have received in church, study groups, and conferences has been wholesome and biblically sound. As I have become more and more familiar with the nature and character of Jesus, and Scripture more generally, I believe that I am better placed to determine whether the material I'm being taught is consistent with Christian living. Only on rare occasions have I felt that a message I've heard preached was partially in error, and in these cases I simply don't take that particular teaching to heart.

In a similar way, some Christian books can introduce ideas that are not scriptural. We have to be careful we are not seduced by messages that on their face seem appealing but are taking us in a direction that we should not pursue.

Spiritual Discernment

In Study 6, I explained that during my teen years before I became a Christian I had "lost" my faith in God and Jesus. Strangely, I can remember being more afraid during that period of other spiritual forces, which in many respects seemed more real. I recall when some friends wanted to use an Ouija board. To their amazement, I resolutely refused to take part as I knew in my heart that this was wrong. Perhaps it was the protection of my parents praying for me that prevented me from getting involved, but I was keenly aware that spiritual forces were at work, all the more unusual as I had not accepted Christ at that time.

On another occasion many years ago, someone came to our house seeking help regarding a bad spiritual experience in a holiday home the family owned and were scheduled to visit again. My wife and I were very young Christians at that time, and all we felt that we could do was to pray the Lord's Prayer with this person. Now I have a much better understanding of the reality of Christ's victory and that he has total authority over these things. We did not get any explicit feedback following this family's return, and the subject has never been mentioned by them again, so we do not know the real outcome. However, this serves to show that there are spiritual forces we cannot rationalise adequately that can affect those around us.

While I was on a ministry trip in India in late 2017, it became clear to me that there is a much greater emphasis placed upon the spirit world in that country. Many new Christians have come out of a Hindu background where there are many "gods" to be worshipped, revered, and appeased. Helping new Christians break free from lingering influences from "spiritual forces of evil" (Ephesians 6:12) can take some time. Anything negative or untoward that happened was routinely viewed by the Christians that I met as a spiritual attack.

Whether this was always actually the case, I was not really able to determine. However, I was asked on a number of occasions to pray for cleansing and healing for people who were affected by spiritual forces. In a small number of instances, I had a real sense while praying for these people that the Holy Spirit was at work. On other occasions I did not, though whether this was because the latter instances were not spiritual in nature, I do not know.

One lady I was asked to pray with began to shake quite violently while I was laying hands on her head and shoulder to the point where I kept my eyes open to ensure I was not to be the recipient of a violent assault. After some minutes, she became much more subdued and ultimately at peace. My interpretation is that God was at work within her as I prayed and that she experienced some degree of alleviation from her situation. Because of the language barrier, it was not possible to determine the outcome explicitly, but the woman's facial responses and gestures suggested that she had benefitted from the time of prayer.

Discernment in regard to our own role

About six weeks after I retired from my consulting career, I received a letter from a mission organisation that we had been supporting for over ten years, thanking us for our monthly giving. Included in this letter was a request for me to pray about two posts within the organisation that needed to be filled here in the UK.

My wife Mary-Anne and I had previously gone to Japan on holiday, but she hadn't overly enjoyed her time there. So my suggestion that we spend three to six months in short-term ministry in Japan once I retired had become a long running joke in my church house group. They routinely teased Mary-Anne as to whether God had told her yet that he was calling her to go to Japan!

While these two job opportunities didn't involve going to Japan, I wondered whether God was prompting me to volunteer in a mission's capacity within UK. The thought was a bit of a surprise since I had only just retired. I called the mission organisation's UK office about these opportunities, one of which was to become part of their London Team. I began praying about whether this was God's calling. I also talked it over with members of our house group. Increasingly, I sensed that God was calling me to become involved with this ministry. I began the application process, believing that if God wanted this to happen he would bring about the right outcome. I eventually met with organisational leadership, went through an interview process, and the volunteer appointment was confirmed.

Study 9 - Kingdom Practice Health Check

Biblical Support Section
- What does exercising discernment mean for you?

Our Context Section
- To what extent do you question the truth of Bible teaching you receive?
- How can you be sure that you are being "fed" spiritually in a wholesome way and not being misled?
- What is your cultural context in spiritual terms? Are people in your culture aware or unaware of spiritual forces around them?
- In Matthew 28:18, Jesus told his disciples, "All authority has been given to me in heaven and on earth." How does the fact that Jesus has full authority give you confidence in his power over every circumstance?

Kingdom Practice Application Section
- How sensitive are your spiritual antennae?
- Recall any situation where you found that sharing something of the kingdom led to a strong adverse reaction. Is there any way you might have dealt with it differently?
- When you face major life decisions, in what way do you involve God in determining what you should do?

Study 9 - Possible Action
Is there anything in this study that might help you respond to difficult situations in the future? What role could prayer play in this? What might help you be more discerning? Consider writing this down and dating it in the outlined text box provided (or your journal/notebook).

Health Warning
Remember that you should not respond to this Kingdom Practice in a legalistic way. It is much more about serving God as part of our love for him because of our salvation in Jesus. We will become more like Jesus the more we allow the Holy Spirit to lead and guide us day by day, and God will get the glory.

My Response/Prayer and Date

Space For You To Record Responses To Questions, Make Notes, Etc.

Study 9 - Exercise Discernment

Study 9 - Exercise Discernment

Study 9 - Memorising the Structure

Can you fill in the blank boxes without looking at the figure displayed at the beginning of this study?

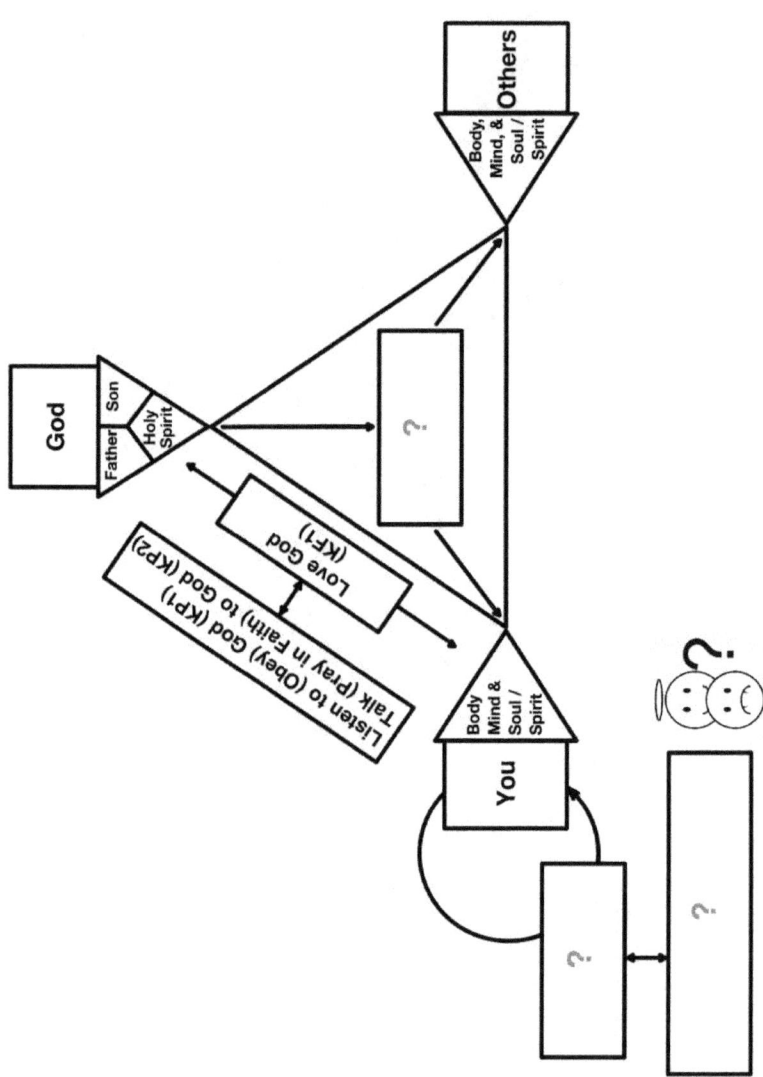

Study 10 - Love Your Neighbour as Yourself - (KF3)
Subtitle: Have a Positive Attitude towards Those with Whom We Come into Contact

Love:

> Love is patient, love is kind. It does not envy, it does not boast, it is not proud. It does not dishonour others, it is not self-seeking, it is not easily angered, it keeps no record of wrongs. Love does not delight in evil but rejoices with the truth. It always protects, always trusts, always hopes, always perseveres (1 Corinthians 13:4–7, NIV).

Neighbour: Any person in need of one's help or kindness (after biblical use); https://en.oxforddictionaries.com/

Study 10 - Introduction

We now move on to the last of the three Kingdom Fundamentals that we have been considering under the overarching direction to "teach them to obey all that I have commanded you." In this study and the next three, we will be considering the requirement to Love Your Neighbour as Yourself and its supporting Kingdom Practices.

Figure 13 demonstrates that we have considered the Kingdom Fundamentals to Love God and Follow Jesus with their supporting Kingdom Practices (Studies 2 to 4 and 5 to 9 respectively) while showing the final Kingdom Fundamental to Love Your Neighbour as Yourself. Again, we see that the Bible and the Holy Spirit are important elements to help us do this well. We also recognise that some people we interact with will already have a developing relationship with God in Jesus, while others will hopefully come into such a relationship through our influence, the influence of others, and most importantly through the work of the Holy Spirit.

Figure 13 - Kingdom Fundamental 3 - to Love Your Neighbour as Yourself

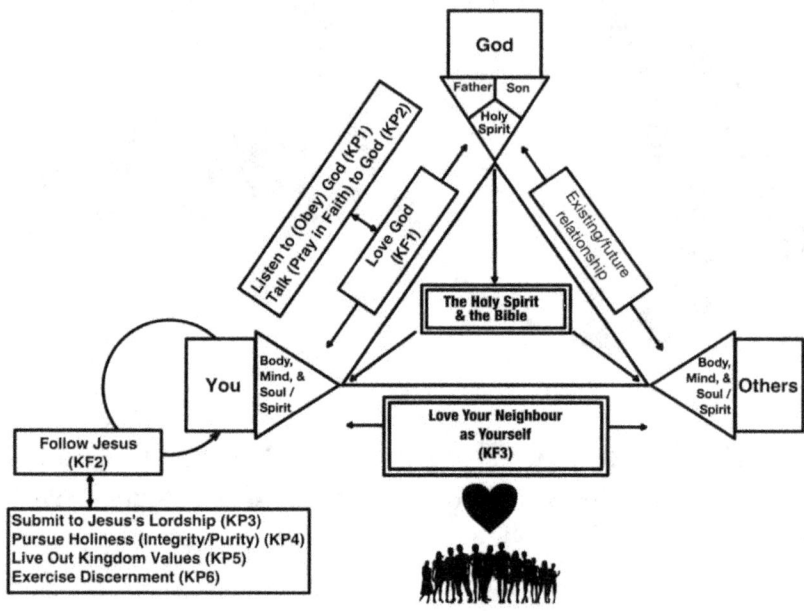

Study 10 - Biblical Support for This Kingdom Fundamental

We addressed the first of the two "greatest commandments" in Study 2. We will now look at the second as stated by Jesus in Mark 12:31:

> The second is: Love your neighbour as yourself. There is no other command greater than these. (See also Matthew 22:39)

The context for the discussion in this passage was that the Pharisees, teachers of the law, and government officials (Herodians) were trying to trick or trap Jesus through his own words. In responding that they should love their neighbour as themselves, he was perhaps challenging them to reach out to the poor, disabled, tax collectors, prostitutes, disadvantaged, and the sinful. These religious leaders saw themselves as righteous but were in truth far from it.

If we look back to the Old Testament, we can see that Jesus was quoting from Leviticus 19:18 when he instructed that we should "love your neighbour as yourself." This was one of many instructions in Leviticus 19 on how the people of Israel should love others, including their families, the disabled, employees, foreigners (minorities) living in the land, and so on.

Later on in the New Testament, the apostle Paul separately reiterates the command to love your neighbour as yourself in two of his epistles (Galatians 5:13-14, Romans 13:8-10), specifically in Romans 13:10:

> Love does no wrong to a neighbour. Love, therefore, is the fulfilment of the law.

The Bible tells us that we are made in God's image (Genesis 1:27). This includes having free will as well as the right to make choices about our lives and how we live them. Jesus teaches that we should love all people with whom we come into contact, even those who mistreat us, are annoying, provocative, or even violent towards us. Our natural tendency is to react negatively against such attitudes and behaviours. But loving those who don't love us should be a specific characteristic of all Jesus's disciples.

This approach—i.e., trying to respond in a godly, positive way to conflict or any oppression to which we may be subjected—was countercultural in Jesus's time and still is for us today. It is clear that for some this will represent a real and ongoing challenge, particularly if they are in relationships with people who are abusive or controlling. However, Paul warned his own disciple in 2 Timothy 3:1-5 that this would be a common problem in the future:

> But know this: Difficult times will come in the last days. For people will be lovers of self, lovers of money, boastful, proud, blasphemers, disobedient to parents, ungrateful, unholy, unloving, irreconcilable, slanderers, without self-control, brutal, without love for what is good, traitors, reckless, conceited, lovers of pleasure rather than lovers of God, holding to the form of godliness but denying its power. Avoid these people!

Would you say that description fits with what you see around you in society today?

Specific scriptures relating to loving others have been grouped under two subheadings below (the complete set can be found in Appendix 2 or the *All That I Have Commanded You* book, Chapter 4).

10.1 - Love One Another

One very specific command from Jesus is for us to love our fellow followers of him:

> I give you a new command: Love one another. Just as I have loved you, you must also love one another. By this all people will know that you are My disciples, if you have love for one another. (John 13:34-35)

Jesus called this a "new" commandment because he was instructing his disciples at the time and all subsequent disciples that we should love our fellow disciples as he loves us. In other words, he has an explicit expectation that we will show love for our fellow disciples over and above our love for other people:

> Therefore, as we have opportunity, let us do good to all people, especially to those who belong to the family of believers. (Galatians 6:10, NIV)

While this is simply one particular instance of loving your neighbour as yourself, Jesus singles it out as a specific requirement for his followers:

> This is what I command you: Love one another. (John 15:17)

10.2 - Love Your Enemies

He also commanded us to love our enemies, a challenge that is countercultural regardless of where we live:

> But I say to you who listen: Love your enemies, do what is good to those who hate you, bless those who curse you, pray for those who mistreat you. If anyone hits you on the cheek, offer the other also. And if anyone takes away your coat, don't hold back your shirt either. (Luke 6:27-29. See also Matthew 5:44).

Study 10 - Our Context

The parable Jesus told about the Good Samaritan most clearly illustrates the challenges of loving others. He told the parable in the context of the actual two "greatest commandments" we are discussing, specifically in response to a legal expert who wanted to know just who was this neighbour he was supposed to love as himself (Luke 10:25-29). Jesus told this parable to answer that question:

> In reply Jesus said: "A man was going down from Jerusalem to Jericho, when he was attacked by robbers. They stripped him of his clothes, beat him and went away, leaving him half dead. A priest happened to be going down the same road, and when he saw the man, he passed by on the other side. So too, a Levite, when he came to the place and saw him, passed by on the other side. But a Samaritan, as he travelled, came where the man was; and when he saw him, he took pity on him. He went to him and bandaged his wounds, pouring on oil and wine. Then he put the man on his own donkey, brought him to an inn and took care of him. The next day he took out two denarii and gave them to the innkeeper. "Look after him," he said, "and when I return, I will reimburse you for any extra expense you may have." Which of these three do you think was a neighbour to the man who fell into the hands of robbers?". The expert in the law replied, "The one who had mercy on him." Jesus told him, "Go and do likewise." (Luke 10:30-37, NIV)

Loving Our Neighbours

In discipleship terms, we are encouraged to get along with others as best we can:

> If possible, on your part, live at peace with everyone. (Romans 12:18)

But more than that, we are to allow our hearts to be changed by God so that we can love them too. That means we should be prepared to love anyone, whether Christian or non-Christian, irrespective of their theology or religion, gender, educational background, age, or any other barriers which may exist. This is a serious calling and one which needs to be carefully worked out. Loving as God loves can be costly and tough for us, a process that can make us vulnerable but also give us softer hearts so that we mirror Jesus in all our encounters.

Jesus expects us to love and serve those who need our help, fellow Christians in particular, but also non-Christians and even our "enemies", whether real or imagined. One challenge of submitting to Jesus's lordship is that of adopting a servant heart, no matter where God has placed us. This includes within our family, work, fellowship, or leisure. While we may feel inadequate in our giftings, God gives each of us unique skills and capabilities. He created each of us to have a specific role or roles over different seasons of life, and part of our task is to discern what he wants us to do for him.

In the professional work context, there are a number of widely accepted psychological tools that can help us understand our preferences, aptitudes, and weaknesses in relation to our interactions with others. Two of the more popular ones are the Myers-Briggs Type Indicator (MBTI)[43] and Belbin Team Inventory[44]. These can be used to help team members understand themselves as well as their strengths, weaknesses, and preferences for working together. They can also help us discern our most appropriate role(s) within the body of Christ.

Look at your existing personal relationships, whether at home, work, clubs, societies, your worshipping community, or other places. Who do you find it difficult to get along with? Why might that be?

---

[43] http://www.myersbriggs.org/my-mbti-personality-type/mbti-basics/
[44] http://www.belbin.com

Some Considerations of the Phrase "... As Yourself."

We've already discussed that in quoting the second "greatest commandment" to love your neighbour as yourself, Jesus is not in any way calling upon us to focus on loving ourselves. On the contrary, the context perhaps assumes that we already love ourselves (i.e., put ourselves first) and so should treat our neighbour with the same consideration as we by nature treat ourselves.

Some though may be truly struggling with issues of low or no self-esteem, whether because of current or past circumstances. This may, in turn, complicate their ability to love others. We touched upon this briefly in Study 5, and if this remains relevant to you as a reader, please do take steps to share your inner concerns and turmoil with God in prayer and with a pastor or another brother or sister in Christ that you trust.

Far from Jesus calling us to love ourselves, we saw earlier in Section 5.5 that Jesus said of those wanting to be his disciples that each:

> Must deny himself, take up his cross, and follow Me. (Matthew 16:24)

When we come to Jesus as new followers, we may be carrying things around from our past that hold us back from our full potential in him. When we become part of his body here on earth, Jesus not only makes us right with God, but he also wants to move us forward from being focused on ourselves and our own problems/issues to focusing on the well-being of others. The church has many broken and hurting people, and as we allow the Holy Spirit to lead us and begin to invest in God's kingdom, we will mature to the point of ministering to others instead of simply being ministered to. Jesus says to us:

> A thief comes only to steal and to kill and to destroy. I have come that they may have life, and have it to the full. (John 10:10, NIV)

In other words, Jesus wants to transform us into effective disciples who will further extend his kingdom, whether with our next-door neighbour, in our local community, or even as a missionary to another people group, whether within our own nation or crossing borders to another country. This will take time, but Jesus can use our experiences and weaknesses as a means of reaching out to others.

Self-worth is a difficult subject, and many followers of Jesus continue to feel that they are inadequate and don't live up to Jesus's expectations of them or their own expectations of themselves. If we cannot value ourselves, does this impact our ability to love others as God has called us to do? It may do for some until they have been through a process of restoration and healing from their past experiences and mixed emotions. However, God can and does use us for his service just as we are, provided that we are willing.

We have free will to make decisions about our lives, our actions, and how we respond to events that affect or have affected us. In that sense, we are called to love, forgive, serve, and be generous to others in the way we would expect others (especially other disciples) to be to us, even if the love we demonstrate towards others is not returned. As God loves us unconditionally, so we are called to give this love to others selflessly (more in Studies 11 to 13).

All that said, from a practical perspective we do have a responsibility to ourselves, whether body, mind, and/or spirit. We cannot continually give out spiritually without receiving back spiritual refreshment from the Lord. Nor can we give constantly to others physically or mentally without taking time out to rest, relax, and recuperate. We are only given one body in this life, and we have a responsibility to look after ourselves, primarily so that we can be in good condition to reach out to and love others.

There are many things we can do to look after ourselves properly. This includes seeking healing and/or professional counselling if needed (Study 5) as well as forgiving others and ourselves (Study 12). But the following three broad actions are a good place to start.

Take care of our bodies.

As far as possible, we should aim to eat healthily, take regular exercise, and have appropriate amounts of rest. Inappropriate nutrition (including from eating disorders) and a lack of suitable exercise put stresses on our bodies that can lead to longer term health issues.[45] Of course we recognise that as followers of Jesus we may develop or have pre-existing health or other conditions that hinder us from caring for ourselves as much as we would like. But that doesn't mean we can't do our part to care properly for our bodies. While Jesus himself never specifically addressed this or the following issues, the apostle Paul reminds us that our bodies are the dwelling place of the Holy Spirit, so we should try to take care of ourselves

---

[45] http://www.something-fishy.org/dangers/dangers.php
http://apps.who.int/iris/bitstream/10665/42665/1/WHO_TRS_916.pdf?ua=1
https://www.britannica.com/science/nutritional-disease/Alcohol#toc247877
https://www.publications.parliament.uk/pa/cm201415/cmselect/cmhealth/845/845.pdf
http://www.nhs.uk/news/2012/07July/Pages/Lack-of-exercise-as-deadly-as-smoking.aspx
https://www.symptomfind.com/health/effects-of-physical-inactivity/
https://en.wikipedia.org/wiki/Sedentary_lifestyle

physically, mentally, and spiritually and not pollute ourselves by adopting unhealthy habits as far as this is possible for us:

> Don't you know that your body is a sanctuary of the Holy Spirit who is in you, whom you have from God? You are not your own. (1 Corinthians 6:19)

Feed and develop our minds.

Secondly as far as we are able, we should seek out knowledge, wisdom, and understanding of the physical, social, and spiritual world around us as well as how we should interact with God's creation. In particular, we have a responsibility to ourselves and our families to try and equip ourselves with sufficient skills and capabilities to earn a living. The Apostle Paul tells the Thessalonians:

> For even when we were with you, we gave you this rule: "The one who is unwilling to work shall not eat." (2 Thessalonians 3:10, NIV)

We are called to be "salt" and "light" in this as well as other contexts. Proverbs 3:13-15 highlights the benefits of developing our minds:

> Blessed are those who find wisdom, those who gain understanding, for she is more profitable than silver and yields better returns than gold. She is more precious than rubies; nothing you desire can compare with her. (NIV)

Protect and nourish our souls.

As we have already considered, we should read the Bible (Study 3), pray (Study 4), and share fellowship with other disciples. The early church followed this very pattern:

> They devoted themselves to the apostles' teaching and to fellowship, to the breaking of bread and to prayer. (Acts 2:42, NIV)

So we can conclude that spending time with God and other believers is also important to our well-being.

Getting adequate rest includes obeying the fourth of the Ten Commandments (see Exodus 20, Deuteronomy 5), where we are to keep the Sabbath holy. Jesus himself reflects upon its importance in Mark 2:27-28:

> Then He told them, "The Sabbath was made for man and not man for the Sabbath. Therefore, the Son of Man is Lord even of the Sabbath."

The Sabbath (most commonly celebrated on Sunday within Christian denominations/communities globally) is a day for us to worship, rest, and relax. Setting aside time for these things has benefits for our physical body, our mental wellbeing, and our souls, which is why it is so important for us.

Study 10 - Kingdom Fundamental Application
Jesus as Our Example

Jesus demonstrated God's love and purposes for others through his teaching, healing, and other miracles.

Jesus was often challenging and provocative when preaching, frequently in the context of the hypocrisy, pride, and religiosity of the religious leaders, who in turn felt threatened by Jesus's influence on the public. He is only recorded as getting "physical" on two occasions, both within the Temple precinct in Jerusalem, where people had created a market in the area set aside for the Gentiles to worship God (John 2:13-17, Matthew 21:12-13, Mark 11:15-18).

One description of Jesus's love for others can be found in Matthew 4:23-25.

> Jesus went throughout Galilee, teaching in their synagogues, proclaiming the good news of the kingdom, and healing every disease and sickness among the people. News about Him spread all over Syria, and people brought to Him all who were ill with various diseases, those suffering severe pain, the demon-possessed, those having seizures, and the paralysed; and he healed them. Large crowds from Galilee, the Decapolis, Jerusalem, Judea and the region across the Jordan followed Him. (NIV)

While people may think of Jesus as ministering primarily to the Jews, the Gospels contain numerous accounts where he also ministered to Gentiles. In Matthew 15, Jesus heals the daughter of a Canaanite woman. Similarly, he also healed the servant of a Roman centurion (Luke 7:1-10, Matthew 8:5-13). He spent time preaching in the Decapolis, a region with a predominantly Gentile population, including strong Greek influences. He had a lengthy exchange with a Samaritan woman at the town well (John 4) and preached to people from many regions beyond Israel (see Mark 3:7-8).

Towards the end of his ministry, Jesus outlines the following in John 10:14-18:

> I am the good shepherd; I know my sheep and my sheep know me – just as the Father knows me and I know the Father –and I lay down my life for the sheep. I have other sheep that are not of this sheep pen. I must bring them also. They too will listen to my voice, and there shall be one flock and one shepherd. The reason my Father loves me is that I lay down my life –only to take it up again. No one takes it from me, but I lay it down of my own accord. I have authority to lay it down and authority to take it up again. This command I received from my Father. (NIV)

This passage clarifies that Jesus's aim is for others beyond Israel to be added to God's kingdom. They are an outworking of the second "great commandment" as well as a partial fulfilling of God's promise to the patriarch Abraham, father of the Jewish people, in Genesis 12:2-3:

> I will make you into a great nation, and I will bless you; I will make your name great, and you will be a blessing. I will bless those who bless you, and whoever curses you I will curse; and all peoples on earth will be blessed through you. (NIV)

A direct descendant of Abraham, Jesus is the means through which all people groups can indeed be blessed through submission to his lordship (Study 6).

In one of Jesus's final commands (Acts 1:8), he charges his disciples to reach out to others, beginning in Jerusalem, Judea, Samaria, and to the ends of the earth. This command makes clear that God's love and salvation is for everyone.

In summary, Jesus highlights that all people are our neighbours and that we should love them as best we can, as illustrated by the parable of the Good Samaritan.

Jesus's Own Practise as to Caring for Himself and Others

No direct parables or teachings of Jesus are recorded in connection to "loving ourselves", since as we have seen this is not one of his commandments. But we do find application in Jesus's habits and daily life to our prior discussion about taking proper care of ourselves physically, mentally, and spiritually. The Gospels describe occasions when Jesus drew back from ministry to the multitudes to take a time-out, whether alone or with his own small team of disciples. In effect he was setting time aside for his own well-being and that of his team. This includes going off on his own to pray as well as sharing privately with his disciples and close supporters of his ministry (Mark 1:35-39, Luke 5:16, Luke 6:12).

The Gospels also speak of times when Jesus shared meals with others, either because he had been invited, had invited himself, or was fellowshipping with friends and disciples (Matthew 9:9-13, Luke 4:38-39, Luke 7:36-50, Luke 11:37-54, Luke 14:1-15).

Jesus also regularly attended the synagogue to worship God and frequently to teach as well. Worshipping God with other believers was important to Jesus and the pattern he followed throughout his life and ministry (Matthew 13:54, Mark 1:21, Mark 3:1, Mark 6:2, Luke 4:16, Luke 6:6, John 6:59, John 18:20).

Communal worship was also practised by Jesus's disciples and New Testament communities of believers all the way to the present day. This has implications for our personal walk as Jesus's disciples, our relationship with God in terms of receiving teaching and participating in corporate prayer and worship, as well as our fellowship with other believers.

While the Gospels give us only brief snapshots of Jesus's life outside of formal ministry, we never get a sense that he allowed himself to be overworked, stressed, or out of control of the situations in which he found himself. There are occasions when he became tired, but he was able to recognise this and draw back from ministry (examples include Matthew 8:24 and John 4:6).

Some Brief Personal Reflections on Loving Others

I have been fortunate that for most of my life I have been able to get on well with those with whom I have spent considerable amounts of time. This includes family, friends, work colleagues, social contexts, and elsewhere. As a teenager, I went into secondary education at a school where pupils had a wide range of backgrounds and capabilities, so I learned to be friends with many kinds of personalities. When I left at sixteen to become an engineering apprentice, I again worked, studied, and socialised with a broad group of people from a much wider geographic area and from various cultural backgrounds.

I then studied at a technical university that had many international students, which provided a much stronger cross-cultural dimension to living, socialising, and studying with them. Throughout all this time, I never really encountered any major confrontational issues. In my professional career, I was also able to form good working and social relationships with colleagues and clients, which made our office a pleasant place to be.

This is not to say I have never had disagreements along the way. In the first few years of our marriage, Mary-Anne and I were pretty tight for money, so I spent long hours commuting to and working for clients. We also struggled with lack of sleep once our son arrived. As might be expected, this resulted in stress and at times sharp words between my wife and me. Through it all, though, faith and the need to love each other were important components of our spiritual walk. We were also supported by good friends from our then house group and the love and discipling from our son's three godparents. After over thirty years together, I love my wife more now than when we were first married.

There will always be some people with whom we just do not gel, and I suppose the easy route I have taken from time to time has been not to really engage with them unless it became a necessity. I'm not sure whether this was really a failure to love them from Jesus's viewpoint. After all, Jesus did not call us to be close friends with everyone. We simply do not have the time or resources to do that.

However, there may be times where the Lord needs us to support those we don't know well. I remember a time when I corresponded with a prison inmate I had never met up to that point. When he was subsequently released, I met with him regularly over a period of time as he integrated back into life, fellowship and work.

Thoughts on Looking after Myself

In terms of looking after myself, keeping fit is important to me, not only to keep my physical body healthy and in good working order, but also for my own mental well-being and self-esteem. I also choose to follow a healthy eating regime and am currently lighter and fitter than I have been for much of my adult life. Some of my extended family has a tendency for being overweight, and I have tried to ensure I don't join them. While keeping fit and managing our diet isn't necessarily a guarantee of good health in the long term, professional and governmental health advice certainly supports pursuing such a lifestyle.

Rest and relaxation have been more of a challenge for me, as I had a demanding career that made considerable calls on my time. For many years, I had less sleep than is recommended for overall well-being. Transition to "retirement" has improved this, though I'm not sure those close to me would say that I relax more.

My professional career as a specialist consultant in transport is in the past now, and I no longer spend much time following the field that I worked in for many years. These days I try to keep abreast of current world issues, read mainly factual material, and focus on things related to helping me be more effective in my volunteering and church activities. I'm not a great television watcher except perhaps for wildlife and nature programmes.

In terms of my responsibility to God, I participate in church worship each week with fellow disciples and am part of the community there, supporting a number of activities. My house group is drawn from this community. We meet most weeks during the school term to study the Bible through a range of materials and have built up a deep level of trust and love for one another.

Study 10 - Kingdom Fundamental Health Check

Biblical Support Section

> ➢ What does loving others as yourself mean for you?

Our Context Section

> ➢ How does your cultural context influence the way you interact with your neighbours?
>
> ➢ If cultural barriers limit your ability to love your neighbours, how might they be broken down?

Part of the answer is the need to pray for them. If we try to put ourselves in their position, the Holy Spirit may give us insight into some of the challenges they are facing. Many have also found that when they pray for those to whom they react negatively or just dislike, their attitude towards those people changes as God through the Holy Spirit works within them (i.e., those who are praying).

Kingdom Fundamental Application Section

- ➢ Should we find it easier to get along with fellow believers than non-believers? What do you think?

- ➢ How do you see yourself, and how does this compare to how God sees you in Jesus?

- ➢ How do you look after yourself in body, mind, and spirit as well as those with whom you live or who are dependent upon you?

- ➢ Are there things you could do to serve your worshipping community or other people or to help others grow and develop as disciples?

- ➢ Are there any steps or actions you could take to love others more, particularly those who annoy you, frustrate you, or are rude or abusive?

Remember that no matter how you perceive others, they in turn may be facing challenges of which you are completely unaware, no matter how well you think you know the person. Regardless of outward appearances or seeming success, no one has a life completely free from worry or difficulty. And what one person considers inconsequential may be a huge burden to someone else.

If you are really having difficulties with someone, pray first of all. Then if possible, seek to bless them in some way. This may include a meeting on neutral ground or with a mutual friend to get a better understanding of them and to build rapport. For some readers it may take a long time (if ever) to get to such a stage, so this is not advice for everyone in every situation. But irrespective of this, you can pray to God about it and be led by the Holy Spirit within you, even if this does not lead to a resolution.

See for example Matthew 5:23-24:

> Therefore, if you are offering your gift at the altar and there remember that your brother or sister has something against you, leave your gift there in front of the altar. First go and be reconciled to them; then come and offer your gift. (NIV)

The Following Studies

In the next three studies, we will look at three Kingdom Practices drawn from an analysis of Jesus's commands that correlate to the Kingdom Fundamental to Love Your Neighbour as Yourself:

- Make Disciples.

- Forgive (Don't Judge) Others.

- Undertake Acts of Service/Generosity.

Study 10 - Possible Action

Consider writing down how you might love others more and make it a reality. Similarly, is there something you can do to look after yourself better? Again, consider writing this in the outlined text box provided (or in your journal/notebook).

Don't try to put too many changes in place at the same time. This is not a sprint but a long distance (life-long) race. Trying to do too much can result in failure and discouragement. Better to start small, which will make a positive outcome more achievable, then build upon this.

Health Warning

Remember that you should not respond to this Kingdom Fundamental in a legalistic way. It is much more about serving God as part of our love for him because of our salvation in Jesus. We will become more like Jesus the more we allow the Holy Spirit to lead and guide us day by day, and God will get the glory.

My Response/Prayer and Date

Space For You To Record Responses To Questions, Make Notes, Etc.

Study 10 - Love Your Neighbour as Yourself

Study 10 - Memorising the Structure

Can you fill in the blank boxes without looking at the figure displayed at the beginning of this study?

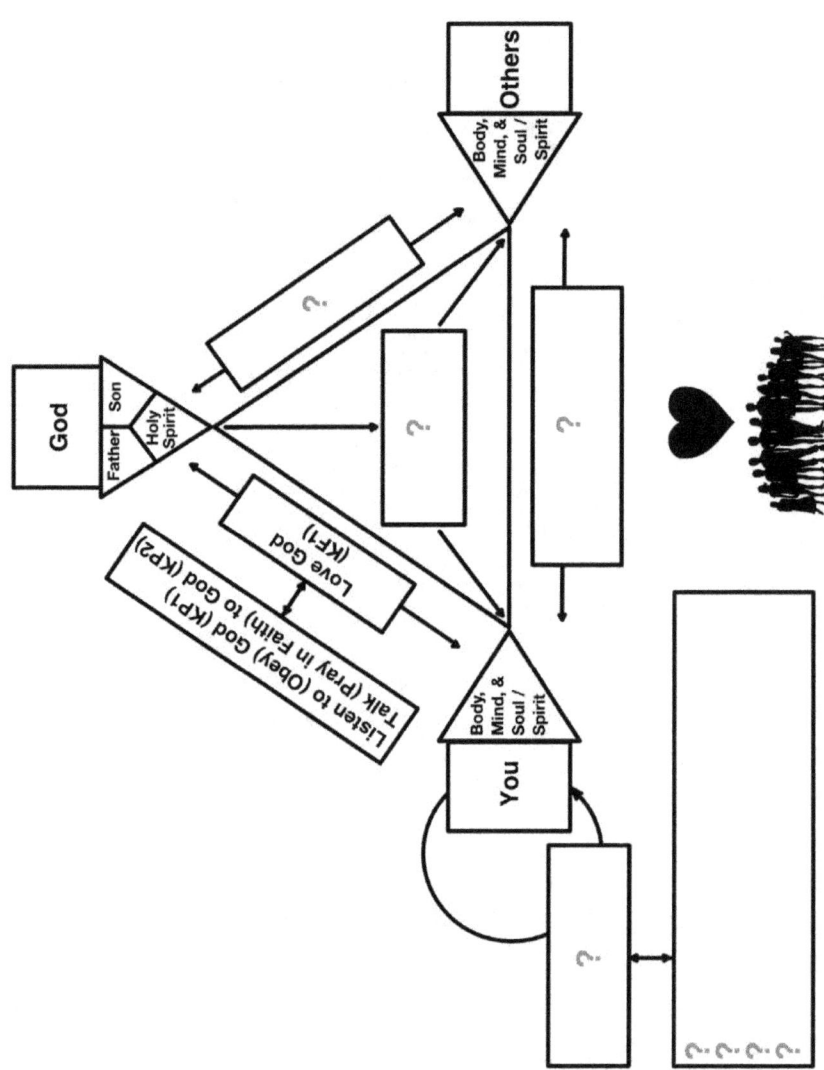

Study 11 - Make Disciples - (KP7)

Subtitle: All That We Do and Say Can Help Others Come to Know and Learn More about Jesus

Make: To cause to be or become. To produce as a result of action, effort, or behaviour with respect to something.

Disciple of Christ: A person who has repented of their sins, accepted Jesus as their personal Saviour and Lord, and who actively seeks to become more like Jesus. This occurs through applying and practising Jesus's teaching as recorded in the Bible and assisted by the leading and guidance of the indwelling person of the Holy Spirit (author's definition).

Study 11 - Introduction

In Study 11, we will consider the first Kingdom Practice that correlates to the Kingdom Fundamental to Love Your Neighbour as Yourself, which is to Make Disciples. This again comes under the overarching requirement to "teach them to obey all that I have commanded you."

Figure 14 also shows the third Kingdom Fundamental to Love Your Neighbour as Yourself together with the Kingdom Practice to Make Disciples. The Bible and the Holy Spirit remain as essential elements to help us do this.

Figure 14 - Kingdom Practice 7 - to Make Disciples

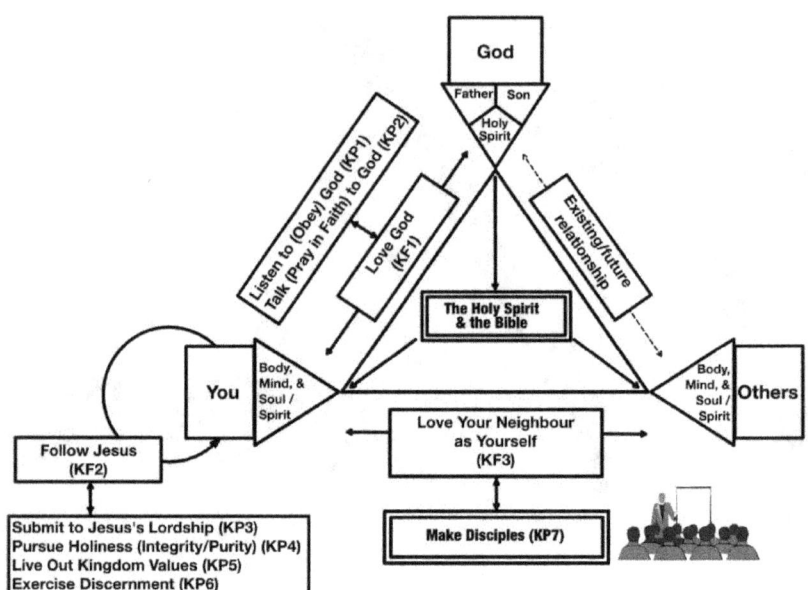

Study 11 - Biblical Support for This Kingdom Practice

One of Jesus's most important commands was that his disciples should make disciples of all peoples/nations. The purpose of this instruction was so that everyone would have the opportunity of a living relationship with God in Jesus as part of their lives here on earth. The challenges we face as disciples include:

- Biblical illiteracy within the church–i.e., Christians not understanding scriptural teaching in order to disciple others effectively.

- An increase in global population, making the task larger as each new generation reaches the point where they may be able to receive and respond to the gospel.

- Overcoming or circumventing legal barriers to the explicit proclamation of salvation in Jesus that exist in some countries.

- Spiritual, intellectual, secular, social, and emotional resistance to the message of the gospel.

In terms of this Kingdom Practice, Jesus commands us to undertake the following Kingdom Behaviours:

- Go, make, and baptise disciples.

- Teach disciples to obey Jesus.
- Feed Jesus's sheep.
- Preach to all nations, and then the end will come.
- Testify to others of Jesus.

The biblical underpinnings of these behaviours are presented below (see Appendix 2 or the *All That I Have Commanded You* book, Chapter 4.1, for a complete set of scriptures).

11.1 - Go, Make, and Baptise Disciples

Sharing our love of Jesus with others is a command to every follower of Jesus. This necessitates relying upon the Holy Spirit to convict others of their need for Jesus and to bring them to repentance:

> Go, therefore, and make disciples of all nations, baptising them in the name of the Father and of the Son and of the Holy Spirit. (Matthew 28:19)

While English translations of Matthew 28:19 may read as though "go" is the main verb in this verse, in the original language the only imperative command in the Great Commission is to "make disciples", while the other verbs—going, teaching, baptising—are participial (in essence, "as you are going, make disciples"). From Acts 1:8, we understand that Jesus expects his disciples to be witnesses "in Jerusalem" (our own community), "in Judea" (our own region), "in Samaria" (neighbouring countries), and "to the ends of the earth." We are not all called to travel abroad as missionaries. But in whatever situation God has placed us, we should be living for him. As we see people come to faith, we should also encourage them to be baptised, even as Jesus himself did as an act of obedience (Study 6).

11.2 - Teach Disciples to Obey Jesus

We are to train and instruct new and existing followers so that they grow in their faith and in the practice of Jesus's commands:

> Teaching them to observe everything I have commanded you. And remember, I am with you always, to the end of the age. (Matthew 28:20)

11.3 - Feed Jesus's Sheep

This is another way of describing the need to help others grow in their relationship with God in Jesus:

> When they had eaten breakfast, Jesus asked Simon Peter, "Simon, son of John, do you love Me more than these?" "Yes, Lord," he said to Him, "You know that I love You." "Feed My lambs," He told him. A second time He asked him, "Simon, son of John, do you love Me?" "Yes, Lord," he said to Him, "You know that I love You". "Shepherd My sheep," He told him. He asked him the third time, "Simon, son of

> John, do you love Me?" Peter was grieved that He asked him the third time, "Do you love Me?" He said, "Lord, You know everything! You know that I love You." "Feed My sheep," Jesus said. (John 21:15–17)

This text comes after Peter's three denials of Jesus that followed Jesus's arrest. In this encounter, we see Jesus lovingly restoring Peter as he still does for any repentant follower time and again, no matter what we have done or how greatly we have failed. To each of Peter's three denials, Jesus offered three corresponding encouragements to move Peter forward from his failure and guilt.

This passage begs several questions. Was the command to "feed my sheep" just for Peter, or are all of us called to help others in their discipleship? If we are disciples who are to make disciples, then shouldn't we be feeding Jesus's sheep too?

11.4 - Preach to All Nations and Then the End Will Come

Jesus's words below give assurance that once we have shared the gospel with all people groups and they have been given opportunity to respond, then Jesus will return:

> And this gospel of the kingdom shall be preached in all the world for a witness unto all nations; and then shall the end come. (Matthew 24:14, NIV)

11.5 - Testify of Jesus to Others

While the following text is not strictly a command, Jesus implies here that part of being his follower is testifying to others about him:

> When the Counsellor comes, the One I will send to you from the Father –the Spirit of truth who proceeds from the Father –He will testify about Me. You also will testify, because you have been with Me from the beginning. (John 15:26-27)

Study 11 - Our Context

In looking at Jesus's ministry, we find two instances where he sends out his followers to proclaim the kingdom of God. He first sent the twelve disciples in pairs (Matthew 10:5-15, Mark 6:7-12, Luke 9:1-6), then later seventy (or seventy-two) followers (Luke 10:1-17). In each case they are told not to take anything with them, but to depend on God to provide for their needs. In contrast, at the Last Supper Jesus tells the disciples to take a purse, a pack, and to buy a sword (Luke 22:35-37). Perhaps this was because he knew his death, resurrection, and ascension would be followed by a time of persecution for the disciples and other followers. It is not clear what this means for us today, except that perhaps a sword might not be high on our list as we seek to make disciples! Some mission organisations do not make a direct appeal for funds, while other make direct appeals. All are seeking the expansion of God's kingdom according to how God is leading them. For us too, we need to be prepared to share our faith when we have the opportunity.

The parable Jesus told of the Sower and the Seed best illustrates the task of making disciples:

> A farmer went out to sow his seed. As he was scattering the seed, some fell along the path; it was trampled on, and the birds ate it up. Some fell on rocky ground, and when it came up, the plants withered because they had no moisture. Other seed fell among thorns, which grew up with it and choked the plants. Still other seed fell on good soil. It came up and yielded a crop, a hundred times more than was sown. (Luke 8:5-7, NIV)

Jesus goes on to explain the meaning of this parable in Luke 8:11-15:

> This is the meaning of the parable: The seed is the word of God. Those along the path are the ones who hear, and then the devil comes and takes away the word from their hearts, so that they may not believe and be saved. Those on the rocky ground are the ones who receive the word with joy when they hear it, but they have no root. They believe for a while, but in the time of testing they fall away. The seed that fell among thorns stands for those who hear, but as they go on their way they are choked by life's worries, riches and pleasures, and they do not mature. But the seed on good soil stands for those with a noble and good heart, who hear the word, retain it, and by persevering produce a crop. (NIV. See also Matthew 13:1-23 and Mark 4:1-20)

The church's (i.e., our) primary role is to reach out to those who do not know Jesus and make disciples, then help those new disciples get to the stage where they themselves can in turn make more disciples. You may find it helpful to look at the Modified Engel Scale[46] as a way of visualising how people can move from no awareness of God through to being fully committed disciples of Jesus. You might like to consider too where you are on that scale.

We must recognise that we cannot make disciples in our own strength. It is God through the work of the Holy Spirit who moves people's hearts to be receptive to the gospel message. That said, we have a duty to share our faith as God gives us the opportunity. This includes being prepared to explain

---

[46] http://www.hazelden.org.uk/pt02/art_pt068_modified_engel_full.htm

how God the Father through the Holy Spirit brought us personally into submission to Jesus's lordship:

> But honour the Messiah as Lord in your hearts. Always be ready to give a defence to anyone who asks you for a reason for the hope that is in you. (1 Peter 3:15)

People are naturally observers of others. If they know we profess to be disciples of Jesus, they will be watching to see how we measure up to their perception of what a Christian should be. As we have already seen, the real truth is that we are saved by grace and not by works. We know we cannot meet God's standards, which is why Jesus came, died, and was resurrected for us to demonstrate his victory over sin and death itself.

Some non-believers seem to have the mistaken impression that Christians should never sin or do the wrong thing in their eyes. If (and when) we don't live up to that expectation, they use this as an excuse to reject our message and/or Jesus as they perceive us to be hypocritical. In biblical terms we are indeed saints. But that doesn't mean we never sin. The difference is that we have already been forgiven. We are called to be "salt" and "light" (Matthew 5:13 and Matthew 5:16; see Study 5). We are also called to make disciples and to teach them to obey what Jesus commanded. So our attitude, responses, and behaviours should be an example to others. In fact, whatever way we conduct ourselves will have a marked impact upon others, whether we are conscious of it or not. This was at the heart of the criticism of Christians attributed to Mahatma Gandhi, as we discussed in the introduction:

> "I like your Christ, I do not like your Christians. Your Christians are so unlike your Christ."

We should be capable of telling someone how to become a Christian, including the process of submitting to the lordship of Jesus. The method illustrated in Study 6 is one that can be used along with many others readily available in Christian resources. What is important is to have a logical sequence of steps you can share that present the essence of the gospel without misrepresentation or watering down its main message.

The process of making disciples is broader than simply leading someone to take the first step of accepting Jesus as their own Saviour and Lord. At that stage, they are new Christians who now need to understand more fully what the Scriptures say. They also need to begin learning and adopting the Kingdom Fundamentals, Kingdom Practices, and Kingdom Behaviours that are consistent with living out their new lives as followers of Jesus. This is a life-long journey for all of us, as God will lead us continuously through different experiences and challenges, developing our dependence upon him to meet our needs and as we reach out to others in service and in mission.

Equipping each disciple both spiritually and practically is the responsibility of the church. We can only do this in partnership, which is why we should join together in worship, prayer, study, teaching, and fellowship. The global church is one of the few organisations that does not exist for its own benefit. However, we need to understand that some Christian denominations have huge wealth and encourage the giving of money in what might be considered manipulative ways (not just the so-called prosperity gospel churches). This links back to our discussion of spiritual discernment in Study 9 and how we should allow God to guide our giving (Study 13).

Entering into a right relationship with the Father, Son, and Holy Spirit is only the start of becoming a member of the body of Christ, the community of believers on earth. As we develop and grow in our understanding of God's will for each of us as followers, we will begin to fulfil the purposes for which God made us as we allow the guidance of the Holy Spirit to lead us.

The activity of making disciples needs to be underpinned by prayer in both the short and long-term. We are also wholly dependent upon the Holy Spirit to work in the hearts of those to whom we are reaching out, since in our own strength there is nothing we can do that will make someone become a Christian. As we have already considered, the response to the call of Jesus to "follow me" is a decision no one can undertake in a meaningful way unless they are convicted of their need for a personal Saviour. Once they have done this, it is our collective responsibility to walk alongside these new believers and spend time helping them to become mature disciples.

Study 11 - Kingdom Practice Application

Jesus as Our Example

For the majority of his earthly ministry, Jesus travelled with a number of companions. These included the twelve men Jesus designated as apostles, which were drawn from a larger group of disciples, and a number of women who supported his work (Luke 8:1-3). Some of these disciples were explicitly chosen and called by Jesus:

> As Jesus was walking beside the Sea of Galilee, he saw two brothers, Simon called Peter and his brother Andrew. They were casting a net into the lake, for they were fishermen. "Come, follow me," Jesus said, "and I will send you out to fish for people." At once they left their nets and followed him. Going on from there, he saw two other brothers, James son of Zebedee and his brother John. They were in a boat with their father Zebedee, preparing their nets. Jesus called them, and immediately they left the boat and their father and followed him. (Matthew 4:18-22, NIV)

> One of those days Jesus went out to a mountainside to pray, and spent the night praying to God. When morning came, he called his disciples to him and chose twelve of them, whom he also designated apostles. (Luke 6:12-13, NIV)

This strategy was consistent with the practices of the Pharisees and other religious groups of the time, who had students or "disciples" living and travelling with them and learning first-hand from them. Jesus is often referred to as rabbi and teacher, and the disciples he selected would witness him at work and in his day-to-day life. Ultimately, they would be able to witness to who Jesus was after his finite earthly ministry had come to an end and he had returned to heaven. The twelve disciples also became increasingly familiar with the message of God's kingdom, the parables and their underlying meaning, as well as other teachings Jesus shared with the crowds that came to hear him (Matthew 13:10-11, Luke 8:9-10) to the point where Jesus was able to send them out to minister in his name.

> Jesus called his twelve disciples to him and gave them authority to drive out impure spirits and to heal every disease and sickness. These are the names of the twelve apostles: first, Simon (who is called Peter) and his brother Andrew; James son of Zebedee, and his brother John; Philip and Bartholomew; Thomas and Matthew the tax collector; James son of Alphaeus, and Thaddaeus; Simon the Zealot and Judas Iscariot, who betrayed him. (Matthew 10:1-4, NIV. See also Mark 3:2-4)

Later, a much larger group of disciples was appointed by Jesus to go ahead of his ministry team.

> After this the Lord appointed seventy-two others and sent them two by two ahead of him to every town and place where he was about to go. (Luke 10:1, NIV)

After his resurrection, Jesus commanded his disciples to "make disciples of all nations." As his disciples today, we are similarly commanded to make disciples. To accomplish this, we are to use whatever skills and capabilities God has given us, whether as part of our personalities, our training and profession, or as gifted through the Holy Spirit (1 Corinthians 12:1-11).

In selecting and investing time and effort in the daily training of his disciples (an apprenticeship, if you like), Jesus was able to develop a number of men to continue sharing the message of God's kingdom and salvation in Jesus. Christian tradition suggests that the majority of Jesus's disciples were martyred for their faith, which demonstrates the powerful impact witnessing Jesus's life, teaching, miracles, death, and resurrection had on them. Different sources do not always agree upon how specific disciples died, but there is common agreement that Simon Peter was crucified, James (son of Zebedee) was beheaded by Herod (Acts 12:2), and Paul was beheaded in

Rome. John is believed to have died of old age of natural causes after being held captive on Patmos.[47]

If Jesus had not in truth risen from the dead, it is unlikely these men would have been prepared to lay down their lives for a lie. Their willing martyrdom attests to the truthfulness of their testimony about what they had seen.

So in Jesus we see someone who led by example, living, talking, training, and walking alongside the apostles and a wider group of people, some who provided financial and other support. This was an interactive, ongoing teaching and learning process involving the investment of time and effort to educate, correct, and subsequently release his disciples into ministry on his behalf.

In the same way, discipling for us should focus on sharing our lives with others in an intentional manner. Not with large numbers of people but perhaps one-to-one or as a small group where specific teaching can be undertaken by consent and issues and concerns can be discussed in confidence. As those we journey with build their own faith and confidence, we can enable them to seek God's will for their lives (Studies 3 and 9) as they begin to minister to and disciple others.

Some Brief Personal Reflections on Making Disciples

I have never been in the position to actually lead someone through the process as they made a personal commitment to accept Jesus as Saviour and Lord. But in my life, work, and witness, I have talked with many people on aspects of faith and our condition with and without Christ. This includes as participant in an Alpha course, which is an evangelistic course that presents the basics of the Christian faith,[48] and in other contexts. Two other methods besides the Alpha Course for introducing people to the gospel are the "Christianity Explored" and "Two Ways to Live" courses.[49] There are probably many more.

Someone close to our family had not been receptive to discussing matters of faith for a number of personal reasons. In later stages of life, this person was

---

[47] http://www.christianity.com/church/church-history/timeline/1-300/whatever-happened-to-the-twelve-apostles-11629558.html & https://www.whatchristianswanttoknow.com/how-did-the-12-apostles-die-a-bible-study/
[48] "The Alpha Course" - http://uk.alpha.org
[49] "Christianity Explored" course - http://www.ceministries.org and separately "Two ways to live" course - http://www.matthiasmedia.com.au/2wtl/whatis2wtl.html

diagnosed with cancer and began deteriorating much faster than anyone expected. During their final weeks, I was able to give the person a copy of a booklet titled *Knowing God Personally*. We later learned that this family friend had read the book, discussed it with their spouse, and begun to pray. We don't know exactly what went on in this person's heart and mind in those final few days, but we trust we will see our friend one day when we arrive in heaven ourselves.

In order to better share the gospel when an opportunity presents itself, I personally have studied a method of communicating the big picture perspective of the missional message of the Bible in a clear way. One example of this method is described in the "Two Ways to Live"[50] approach.

At the time of writing, I am working for a mission organisation as a part-time volunteer, so most of those with whom I come into contact are already disciples of Jesus. I really enjoy this activity and find it rewarding and worthwhile to come alongside people who have an interest in missions. I provide them support through a range of activities. We are all called to fulfil different roles in the kingdom, and at least at this time when I am writing the material you are now reading, I believe this is where God has called me to be, however that may change in the future.

Over the years I have also been part of a number of house groups/study groups and have led courses and studies on a variety of biblical topics. This includes sharing and leading these teaching materials with two groups in the UK and two groups in India (at the time of writing). Each of these in their own way are examples of discipling–not in the one-to-one sense but working with small groups to share biblical truths that hopefully enable them (and me!) to be Christians who reflect Jesus better as a result.

Study 11 - Kingdom Practice Health Check

Biblical Support Section

- How have you responded to the challenge to make disciples?
- In what ways could you actively support mission work to other people whether locally or abroad?

Our Context Section

- In your cultural context, what is the wider view of making disciples? Is it considered to be a positive or a negative thing,

---

[50] http://www.matthiasmedia.com.au/2wtl/

and why might that be? Does it differ from life coaching and mentoring?

- Has any experience you may have had of sharing your relationship with God in Jesus resulted in the message being received like the different soil types in the parable of the sower? If so what were the results?

Kingdom Practice Application Section

- Have you ever had the opportunity to share the gospel with someone? If so, how did it feel, and what was their reaction?
- Have you investigated ways in which you might be able to outline the essence of the gospel story if God so prompted you? Perhaps moving forward you could consider doing this in a way that is natural for you.

For many of us, it is not easy to make ourselves vulnerable by sharing our faith. But if God has placed someone in particular on your heart, pray regularly for them to come to faith and wait for the right circumstances as well as the Holy Spirit's prompting to share your testimony with them. There are also a range of resources that can help you learn to share naturally the gospel story as well as your testimony. The Kingdom Practice Health Check material in Study 6 gives an outline of such an approach, or consult footnotes 48 and 49.

Study 11 - Possible Action

Is there something you might be able to do to help less mature disciples develop their relationship with Jesus? Perhaps you could write this down in the outlined text box provided (or your journal/notebook).

Health Warning

Remember that you should not respond to this Kingdom Practice in a legalistic way. It is much more about serving God as part of our love for him because of our salvation in Jesus. We will become more like Jesus the more we allow the Holy Spirit to lead and guide us day by day, and God will get the glory.

My Response/Prayer and Date

Space For You To Record Responses To Questions, Make Notes, Etc.

Study 11 - Make Disciples

Study 11 - Make Disciples

Study 11 - Memorising the Structure

Can you fill in the blank boxes without looking at the figure displayed at the beginning of this study?

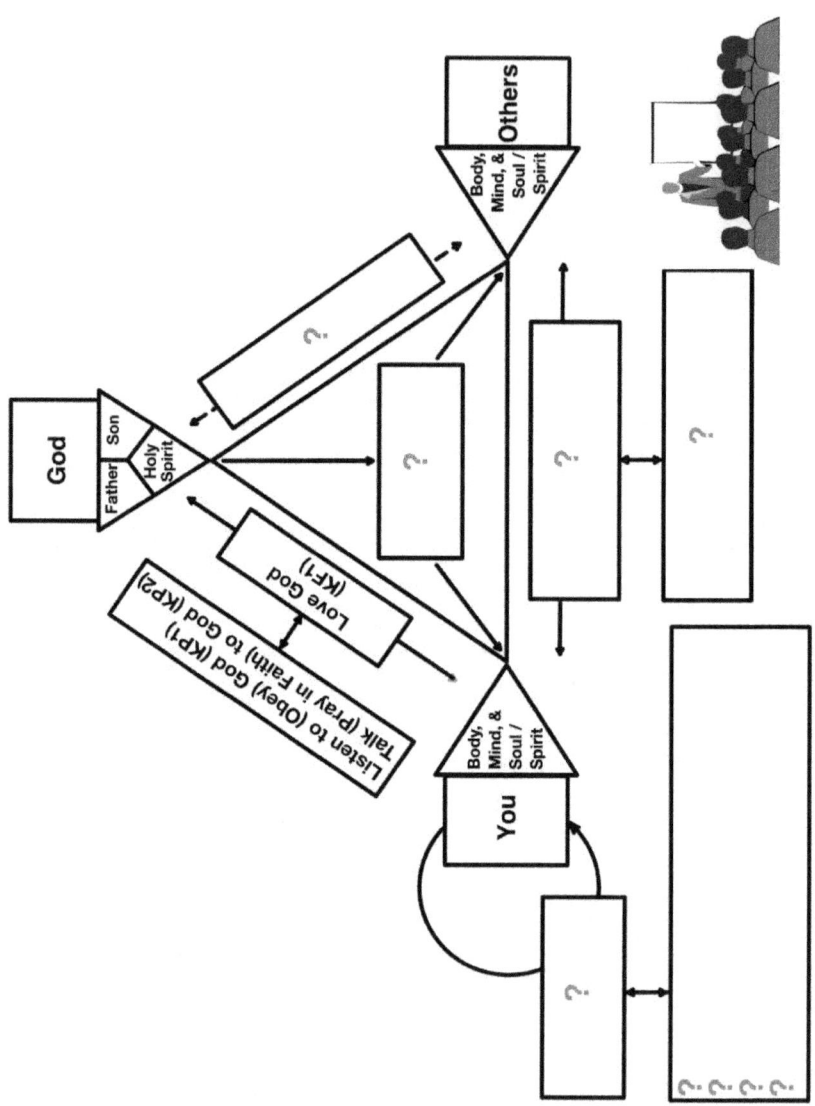

Study 12 - Forgive (Don't Judge) Others - (KP8)
Subtitle: We Must Forgive Others and Ourselves as Our Own Forgiveness from God is Dependent upon This

Forgive: To cease to feel resentment against (an offender). To give up resentment of or claim to requital for.

Judge: To form a negative opinion about. To form an estimate or evaluation of.

Study 12 - Introduction

In this study we will consider the second Kingdom Practice that correlates to the Kingdom Fundamental to Love Your Neighbour as Yourself, which is to Forgive (Don't Judge) Others. This again comes under the overarching requirement to "teach them to obey all that I have commanded you."

Figure 15 highlights the Kingdom Practice to Forgive (Don't Judge) Others as a component of the Kingdom Fundamental to Love Your Neighbour as Yourself. As with our previous studies, the Bible and the Holy Spirit remain as key elements to help us do this.

Figure 15 - Kingdom Practice 8 - to Forgive (Don't Judge) Others

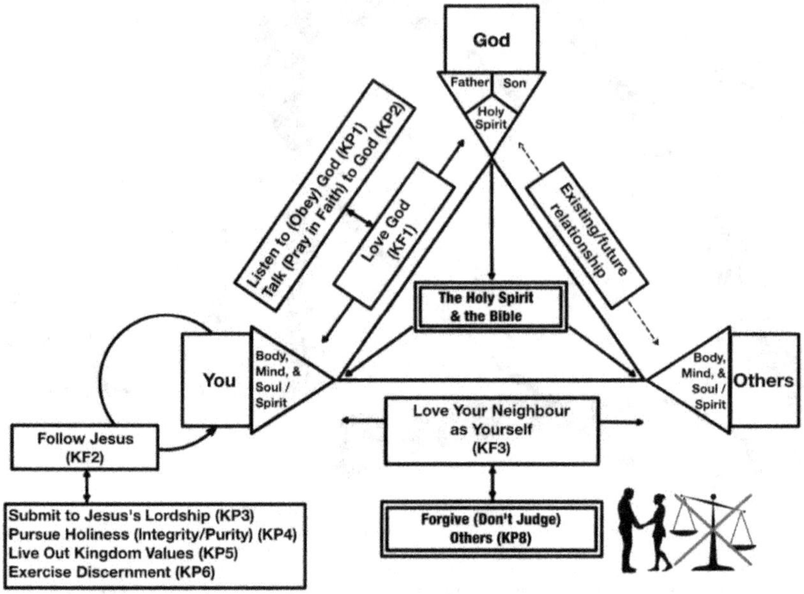

Study 12 - Biblical Support for This Kingdom Practice

Another big challenge for us as disciples is to forgive others as God has forgiven us in Jesus. In our human nature, we can be hurt physically, mentally, emotionally, and spiritually by the actions of others towards us, especially those people who are important to us. As we saw in Study 8, God set limits on retribution in the Old Testament. But Jesus's teaching requires us to go a step further, which is not to respond in a retaliatory like-for-like manner at all, but to forgive. We might characterise the commands of Jesus on this issue into five specific Kingdom Behaviours:

- Do not judge others.
- Do not despise little ones.
- Forgive without limit others who offend us.
- Be gracious.
- Correct other disciples (Christians).

We will consider the biblical support for each of these in the Scripture references presented below (see Appendix 2 or the *All That I Have Commanded You* book, Chapter 4.2, for a complete set of scriptures).

12.1 - Do Not Judge Others

Jesus tells that we must not judge other people. This applies especially to those outside God's kingdom (i.e., non-Christians) as they will generally not have any real understanding of what God wants from them in terms of the behaviours and practices we are considering in these studies. Because we are not perfect, we are not in a position to assess the behaviour of others (e.g., the account of the woman caught in adultery in John 8:3-11):

> Do not judge, so that you won't be judged. For with the judgement you use, you will be judged, and with the measure you use, it will be measured to you. (Matthew 7:1-2)

12.2 - Do Not Despise Little Ones

Essentially, Jesus is telling us not to look down on (be contemptuous of) those who are young, lacking in knowledge or understanding, or new to or weak in faith. Instead we should seek to build them up (see Study 11):

> See that you don't look down on one of these little ones, because I tell you that in heaven their angels continually view the face of My Father in heaven. (Matthew 18:10)

12.3 - Forgive without Limit Others Who Offend Us

We should continue forgiving when others ask us for forgiveness so that we will be forgiven ourselves:

> For if you forgive other people when they sin against you, your heavenly Father will also forgive you. But if you do not forgive others their sins, your Father will not forgive your sins. (Matthew 6:14-15, NIV)

> Then Peter came to Him and said, "Lord, how many times could my brother sin against me and I forgive him? As many as seven times?" "I tell you, not as many as seven," Jesus said to him, "but 70 times seven." (Matthew 18:21-22)

12.4 - Be Gracious

As followers of Jesus, we need to extend the grace we have received from God in Christ for the forgiveness of our sins to others who have wronged us. In terms of Jesus's commands, the following supporting Kingdom Behaviours tell us what he commands us to do:

Do Not Be Angry with Other Disciples.

We are to adopt an attitude of patience and perseverance with fellow believers, accepting their limitations and faults as we also have our own weaknesses:

> But I tell you that anyone who is angry with a brother or sister will be subject to judgment. Again, anyone who says to a brother or sister, 'Raca,' is answerable to the court. And anyone who says, 'You fool!' will be in danger of the fire of hell. (Matthew 5:22, NIV)

Be Reconciled to Those Who Have Offended Us.

If we hold something against another person, we need to release them in forgiveness so that we can be right before God:

> So if you are offering your gift on the altar, and there you remember that your brother has something against you, leave your gift there in front of the altar. First go and be reconciled with your brother, and then come and offer your gift. Reach a settlement quickly with your adversary while you're on the way with him, or your adversary will hand you over to the judge, the judge to the officer, and you will be thrown into prison. (Matthew 5:23-25. See also Luke 12:58-59).

12.5 - Correct Other Disciples (Christians)

Jesus gives explicit instructions for how to manage persistent sin and wrongdoing within his church. He provides an escalatory process for challenging and encouraging one of the fellowship to come into line with living righteously:

> If your brother sins against you, go and rebuke him in private. If he listens to you, you have won your brother. But if he won't listen, take one or two more with you, so that by the testimony of two or three witnesses every fact may be established. If he pays no attention to them, tell the church. But if he doesn't pay attention even to the church, let him be like an unbeliever and a tax collector to you. (Matthew 18:15-17)

Study 12 - Our Context

Jesus's teaching and commands essentially convey that we should forgive people without limit and we are not to count the number of times we do this for the same or different offences. In addition to the Matthew 18 reference in 12.3 above, that same chapter goes on to say in verses 23-35:

> Therefore, the kingdom of heaven is like a king who wanted to settle accounts with his servants. As he began the settlement, a man who owed him ten thousand bags of gold was brought to him. Since he was not able to pay, the master ordered that he and his wife and his children and all that he had be sold to repay the debt. "At this the servant fell on his knees before him. "Be patient with me," he begged, "and I will pay back everything." The servant's master took pity on him, cancelled the debt and let him go. "But when that servant went out, he found one of his fellow servants who owed him a hundred silver coins. He grabbed him and began to choke him. "Pay back what you owe me!" he demanded. His fellow servant fell to his knees and begged him, "Be patient with me, and I will pay it back." But he refused. Instead, he went off and had the man thrown into prison until he could pay the debt. When the other servants saw what had happened, they were outraged and went and told their master everything that had happened. Then the master called the

servant in. "You wicked servant," he said, "I cancelled all that debt of yours because you begged me to. Shouldn't you have had mercy on your fellow servant just as I had on you?" In anger his master handed him over to the jailers to be tortured, until he should pay back all he owed. This is how my heavenly Father will treat each of you unless you forgive your brother or sister from your heart. (NIV)

We should note that there is an implied contradiction between subsections 12.1 (judging) and 12.5 (correcting) above. Applying judgement, including engaging in gossip, could be interpreted as taking a stance against someone else's lifestyle choices or circumstances.

It is difficult to find the right balance between being non-judgemental and correcting someone whose actions are not consistent with biblical living without permanently damaging a relationship. This calls for discernment, immense sensitivity, and a willingness to listen and support. The church should have a documented disciplinary procedure just as it should have procedures for safeguarding children and vulnerable adults. It should also be prepared to call out harmful or abusive behaviours where these are observed or come to the attention of those in the fellowship. In some circumstances, those in a position of leadership within our worshipping community should address issues where a church member's behaviour is damaging to their closest relationships, the fellowship, the community's witness, or brings the gospel into disrepute.

On the other hand, we should not expect those who aren't Jesus's disciples to agree with and conform to our beliefs and values (1 Corinthians 5:12). We should, however, be prepared to speak up for our perspective as part of a rational, constructive debate, but not in a way that explicitly sets out to cause offence or inflame the situation.

Are you holding on to someone's offence against you or against others you care about? You may have suffered and still be suffering considerable pain, anxiety, or distress because of this, and it is potentially very difficult for you to come to the point of considering that forgiveness is even possible. But being able to start the process of forgiving will in turn release healing for these past hurts–not necessarily total healing as those hurts may continue, but they will reduce in severity as time and healing progresses.

If you are a follower of Jesus, then you already understand that God has forgiven your sins for all time because of your faith in Jesus as your Saviour and Lord (see Hebrews 10:1-13). However hurt you have been, the challenge remains that you allow God to lead you along the path to the point where forgiveness of others is possible, no matter how long that takes.

Maybe the issue is that you cannot forgive yourself for something you yourself have done. The difficulty we have sometimes is firstly believing the truth that we are already forgiven and secondly applying it to ourselves. You might like to consider the reference here about forgiving yourself.[51]

Forgiving can be very tough for us, perhaps in some circumstances one of the most challenging of Jesus's commands to obey. Depending upon people's experiences, it may be a lengthy, difficult, and painful process. But as Jesus commands it, we can be assured of his help and healing (through the Holy Spirit) in our brokenness as we seek to be obedient.

But let be clear what forgiveness isn't:[52]

- Pretending the injury or offence doesn't matter.
- That it means ceasing to hurt.
- That it means forgetting.
- That it means pretending that any relationship is going to be the same as before the offence.

Remember that there are no scales of sin as far as God is concerned. Sin is sin, whether we consider it a minor misdemeanour or something major like murder. God is holy and cannot tolerate any sin at all. But God can forgive everything you have ever done wrong if you have accepted Jesus.

This does not mean we can necessarily steer clear of the consequences of our sins. For example, even if God forgives a repentant thief for the act of sinning, he may still have to live with the trauma of a court case and the penalty of his crime.

We also need to recognise that becoming a disciple of Jesus does not mean that as believers we will never sin. We are all imperfect and will regularly need to ask for forgiveness from God and those we have wronged. But the important point here is that we are forgiven. As far as our spiritual status is concerned, we are saints and co-heirs with Christ:

> We always thank God, the Father of our Lord Jesus Christ, when we pray for you, for we have heard of your faith in Christ Jesus and of the love you have for all the saints [God's people]. (Colossians 1:3-4)

---

[51] https://www.allaboutgod.com/forgiving-yourself.htm
[52] Richard J Foster's Study Guide for Celebration of Discipline – Harper Collins.

> And if children, also heirs – heirs of God and co-heirs with Christ – seeing that we suffer with Him so that we may also be glorified with Him. (Romans 8:17)

As forgiven saints and co-heirs with Christ, we must also forgive others. This is not a matter of willpower or doing this in our own strength. It is a choice we make of extending the grace we have received from God to others through the power of the Holy Spirit. This is both a decision and a process as we dispense mercy and grace towards the person who has wronged us (whether they realise it or not), and it may take some time to truly feel forgiveness from the heart. An analogy might be the application of a dressing to a wound. This would need to be changed regularly until the injury is fully healed, and just how long this will take would depend on the extent of the injury.

A number of issues are currently topics of debate and dispute within the church around the world. Even a casual look on social media and the internet shows how polarised people are to the point of not really debating constructively but simply insulting each other's positions. Each side becomes more entrenched, which presents a poor witness both to fellow believers and non-believers. More grace is required from each of us!

Study 12 - Kingdom Practice Application

Jesus as Our Example

In Scripture we find a number of examples where Jesus openly forgave people brought to him. At his crucifixion, he not only asked God to forgive those nailing him to the cross but also pardoned one of the criminals crucified with him. There is no biblical account where he denied forgiveness to a repentant sinner. Let us look at three specific references where Jesus forgives:

> Two other men, both criminals, were also led out with him to be executed. When they came to the place called the Skull, they crucified him there, along with the criminals – one on his right, the other on his left. Jesus said, "Father, forgive them, for they do not know what they are doing." And they divided up his clothes by casting lots. (Luke 23:32-34, NIV)

> Jesus stepped into a boat, crossed over and came to his own town. Some men brought to him a paralysed man, lying on a mat. When Jesus saw their faith, he said to the man, "Take heart, son; your sins are forgiven." At this, some of the teachers of the law said to themselves, "This fellow is blaspheming!" Knowing their thoughts, Jesus said, "Why do you entertain evil thoughts in your hearts? Which is easier: to say, "Your sins are forgiven," or to say, "Get up and walk?" But I want you to know that the Son of Man has authority on earth to forgive sins." So he said to the paralysed man, "Get up, take your mat and go home." Then the man got up and went home.

> When the crowd saw this, they were filled with awe; and they praised God, who had given such authority to man. (Matthew 9:1-8, NIV)
>
> At dawn he appeared again in the temple courts, where all the people gathered around him, and he sat down to teach them. The teachers of the law and the Pharisees brought in a woman caught in adultery. They made her stand before the group and said to Jesus, "Teacher, this woman was caught in the act of adultery. In the Law Moses commanded us to stone such women. Now what do you say?" They were using this question as a trap, in order to have a basis for accusing him. But Jesus bent down and started to write on the ground with his finger. When they kept on questioning him, he straightened up and said to them, "Let any one of you who is without sin be the first to throw a stone at her." Again he stooped down and wrote on the ground. At this, those who heard began to go away one at a time, the older ones first, until only Jesus was left, with the woman still standing there. Jesus straightened up and asked her, "Woman, where are they? Has no one condemned you?" "No one, sir," she said. "Then neither do I condemn you," Jesus declared. "Go now and leave your life of sin." (John 8:2-11, NIV)

Each of these instances is different in context. Jesus offered forgiveness to those responsible for putting him to death, a person whose sins had led to a debilitating condition (though it isn't clear if the man was paralysed specifically because of sin), and someone caught in adultery.

Those who were involved in putting to death the sinless son of God without a legitimate charge, fair trial, or formal conviction might expect to receive their own just punishment from God in the fullness of time. But against any normal expectation, Jesus explicitly asks God to forgive them because they don't understand the full gravity of what they are doing. Note that in terms of proper justice there needs to be either an acquittal or a conviction followed by an appropriate penalty. If there is conviction without the penalty, then justice is not served. Similarly, if a penalty is issued without a conviction, then justice still has not been delivered.

In the healing of the lame man, Jesus draws attention to how there is no real difference between having the power to forgive sins and the power to miraculously heal a paralysed man. So while we don't have the power to heal (although God through the Holy Spirit could heal someone because of our intervention in a situation) or to forgive sins (only God can do that), we do have the power to forgive others what wrongs they do to us (or to forgive ourselves).

With the woman caught in adultery, all the accusers slipped away one by one because they realised that they were not perfect and hence not qualified to carry out the guilty sentence against her. Ironically, Jesus was the only person in the crowd who was without sin and therefore the only one with the right to stone her. Instead, he shows forgiveness and mercy in not condemning her. Even more importantly, he tells her not to sin again (and in doing so may have set her free from the person with whom she was in the adulterous relationship). It may be worth noting that Jewish teaching treated married men and women differently in respect to guilt concerning adultery, since married men were not prohibited from engaging in sexual relations with unmarried women.[53] So Jesus perhaps understood that the woman was already a victim as equality before the law did not exist.

When we have been treated badly by others, we may feel a sense of anger, resentment, or injustice. If we do not let these go through forgiveness, they can lead to ongoing hurt beyond any physical injury or mental or spiritual harm. This pain, if we nurse it, can become deep-seated within us so that when it comes to mind we get a knot in our stomach, adrenaline and anger rise, and we re-live the experience(s) as well as our feelings of resentment towards those who have hurt us. For some, this can impact our longer-term health, a point recognised by both the medical field and the church.[54] Only by seeking to let go of the injury and ill-treatment done to us can we begin to release the grip of the ongoing consequences of unforgiveness. We may need to revisit the decision to forgive time and again until we come to the point where healing really starts and that knot in the stomach begins to subside.

Within the worship fellowships to which we belong, we are required as followers of Jesus to forgive without limit (see Matthew 18:21-22). But we must not confuse the action of forgiving offences against us with being tolerant of sin. Tolerance is continuing to allow something to occur that is inconsistent with our beliefs and practices. God does not tolerate sin. This is why he can only accept us through our submission to Jesus as our Saviour and Lord (see Habakkuk 1:13, 1 Corinthians 5:1, Revelation 2:20). We may have to tolerate different attitudes, behaviours, and standards in society, but within the church we should be seeking to bring all who are members of our

---

[53] https://www.myjewishlearning.com/article/adultery/

[54] https://www.hopkinsmedicine.org/health/healthy_aging/healthy_connections/forgiveness-your-health-depends-on-it
https://www.theravive.com/today/post/the-negative-effects-of-unforgiveness-on-mental-health-0001467.aspx
https://www.ministrymagazine.org/archive/2017/01/The-role-of-forgiveness-in-the-recovery-of-physical-and-mental-health1
https://iblp.org/questions/what-consequences-occur-when-i-dont-forgive-offender

congregations into alignment with biblical principles.[55] That said, even here we must recognise there may be differences of opinion across different denominations and even within them.

By and large, enforcing church discipline is ultimately the responsibility of those in leadership, although we all have a part to play. And to our shame, sadly, some parts of the worldwide church have extended forgiveness to their own while then allowing perpetrators to be in situations where they can continue to abuse or cause offence. This is not only clearly wrong but shows disregard for those who have been impacted, denying them both justice and restitution.

Each believing community should have a set of core beliefs to which those accepted into membership have agreed. In parallel, the church's procedures should have clearly defined mechanisms for censuring members who are disobeying God's moral law. Jesus himself articulates what should be done in these circumstances as we saw in Matthew 18:15-17 above.

Some Brief Personal Reflections on Forgiveness and Not Judging

I count myself fortunate that I cannot recall being seriously wronged, offended, or defamed in a manner that led to great difficulties in forgiving others. In the more recent past, I was attacked by two men on my way home one evening. Taking me completely unawares, the two men knocked me to the ground, then stole my wallet and ran off. I called the police, and eventually an ambulance arrived. The paramedics checked that I was not concussed, as my head had banged the ground and I was developing a rather impressive black eye.

Despite my injuries, financial loss, and broken spectacles, I did not really feel anger towards the men and basically forgave them that same evening. But though I had forgiven them, I found myself over the following weeks replaying the events in my mind and wondering how I might have reacted differently or defended myself. I recognised that the outcome for me against two men could have been much worse, so in many respects I was thankful that I had not fought back. The two individuals were subsequently identified (not by me as I had not really seen them since it was dark), arrested, found guilty, and sentenced.

---

[55] https://bible.org/article/dealing-sinning-christians-overview-church-discipline-matthew-1815-17-1-corinthians-51-13 and
https://www.crossway.org/articles/10-things-you-should-know-about-church-discipline/

Forgiveness is a decision of the will (mind). It is also a process. It takes time to really let go of a hurt or wrong done to us or alternatively by us in terms of forgiving ourselves. Any anger or resentment that is fresh and raw to begin with will fade over time as we permit it. Remember Jesus says in Matthew 5:44:

> But I tell you, love your enemies and pray for those who persecute you.

It is sometimes difficult to forgive, but unless we release ourselves or others through forgiveness, we will remain a prisoner to the issue or incident.

In terms of not judging, I recall a situation where I was introduced to a Christian family with three children, one in the mid-teens and two early school-age or less. The couple was serving in ministry, and I subsequently discovered that they had been married for only nine or ten years. My mind immediately began wondering about the circumstances of the eldest child, since he was well above that age. I wasn't explicitly judging but rather was making assumptions. Upon further discussion, I learned that the eldest child had been adopted by the couple. This is just one illustration of how my overactive reasoning could jump to a conclusion not based upon the truth.

Study 12 - Kingdom Practice Health Check

If you are doing this in a study group and short on time, consider undertaking the Confidential Forgiveness Exercise that immediately follows the material below before considering these questions.

Biblical Support Section

- What does the practice of forgiveness mean for you?

Our Context Section

- In your cultural context, how do people respond to hurt or injustice? Is forgiveness a priority or not even something to be considered? Consider why this might be.

- What is your perspective on our need to be continuously forgiving of others while at the same time not be tolerant of sin within the church?

- The call to not be judgemental is focused on those outside the church. Under what circumstances is it necessary or appropriate to judge other members of our worshipping community? See 1 Corinthians 5:9-13 for some ideas.

Kingdom Practice Application Section
- ➢ If you are able, describe how forgiving someone has changed your attitude towards them or the event/events.
- ➢ Is there someone you need to forgive, including yourself?

If you are carrying any unforgiveness around with you, ask God to help release you from its grip. The person or people you are upset by may have no idea they have wronged you in the first place. In which case your grief, anger, or turmoil is just wasted energy. Maybe they would not consider or even admit that they have done anything wrong, but this does not mean you should not forgive them from your heart. Indeed, this is Jesus's command to us in subsection 12.3 above.

If you are in an ongoing abusive or violent situation where your wellbeing and that of any dependants is threatened, you should seriously consider seeking a safer environment, however difficult that might be. Forgiveness should still to be our longer-term aim, but physical and mental wellbeing are very important concerns that need to be protected. In such circumstances, external help from suitably qualified and motivated people should be sought to help provide for your protection.

Let's recognise that this is not easy, particularly where you have been badly impacted by others. Amazing grace is not just for us and our sin. It is also for us to apply in our interactions with others. This does not mean we have to be best friends with those who have wronged us, but it does mean we should not be carrying around anger, resentment, or guilt towards them or ourselves.

As we saw above in Matthew 6:15, Jesus warns us that we must forgive others, otherwise there will be consequences for us in being forgiven.

Study 12 - Possible Action

Consider writing down the name(s) of those whom you need to forgive (including yourself if applicable) somewhere, together with a date from which you will seek to actively forgive them/yourself. You could use the provided text box or choose a safer place. This does not mean the offence will necessarily be forgotten, just that you will not let past events have a hold over you moving forward. You can also do this as part of this session's Forgiveness Exercise.

You might also wish to consider whether there is any service or person (pastor, elder, counsellor, fellow disciple etc.) to whom you might be able to turn for support during this process.

Health Warning

Remember that you should not respond to this Kingdom Practice in a legalistic way. It is much more about serving God as part of our love for him because of our salvation in Jesus. We will become more like Jesus the more we allow the Holy Spirit to lead and guide us day by day, and God will get the glory.

My Response/Prayer and Date

Study 12 - Confidential Forgiveness Exercise

If you are in a group:

If you are working through this material as part of a group, the leader should have read the preparatory information in Appendix 3 in advance of undertaking this study.

This exercise is to help every reader/participant address any ongoing unforgiveness in their life in a confidential manner so that this issue is between them and God alone.

- Each participant should be given a piece of water-soluble paper by the leader.

- The leader should pray on the group's behalf, inviting the Holy Spirit to speak to each person about anything for which they need to forgive one or more people or forgive themselves. This could be something obvious or something hidden — whether from the distant past or perhaps a more recent issue or concern.

- Group members should then sit quietly, thinking, listening to the Holy Spirit, and praying.

- When all are ready, each participant should write on their paper something along the following lines: "From this day (date) forward, I will forgive XXXX for YYYY and allow God to restore me."

- Group members should then fold their paper.

- The group can then be led in prayer again, after which each person is invited forward to place their paper in a bowl of water for dissolution (or a paper shredder or flame, safely, of course, for the latter!).

- The leader might then give each person a predetermined "token" as an ongoing reminder of what they have done/committed to do.

- Once all group members have come forward, the leader can again lead in prayer, the group might sing a hymn of praise, or some other appropriate choice(s) to close the session.

If you are studying alone:

Follow a similar process to that outlined above.

- Pray for the Holy Spirit to reveal anything to you for which you need to forgive yourself or others. The issue may be obvious and already known to you or something that the Holy Spirit reveals.

- As with group session above, write this down: "From this day (date) forward, I will forgive XXXX for YYYY and allow God to restore me."

- Pray this through, then when you are ready, destroy the paper by dissolving, shredding, cutting, or burning it safely.
- Consider choosing something modest as a token to remind you of your commitment.
- Set your mind to carry through this process of forgiveness through the power of the Holy Spirit.

Space For You To Record Responses To Questions, Make Notes, Etc.

Study 12 - Forgive (Don't Judge) Others

Study 12 - Forgive (Don't Judge) Others

Study 12 - Memorising the Structure

Can you fill in the blank boxes without looking at the figure displayed at the beginning of this study?

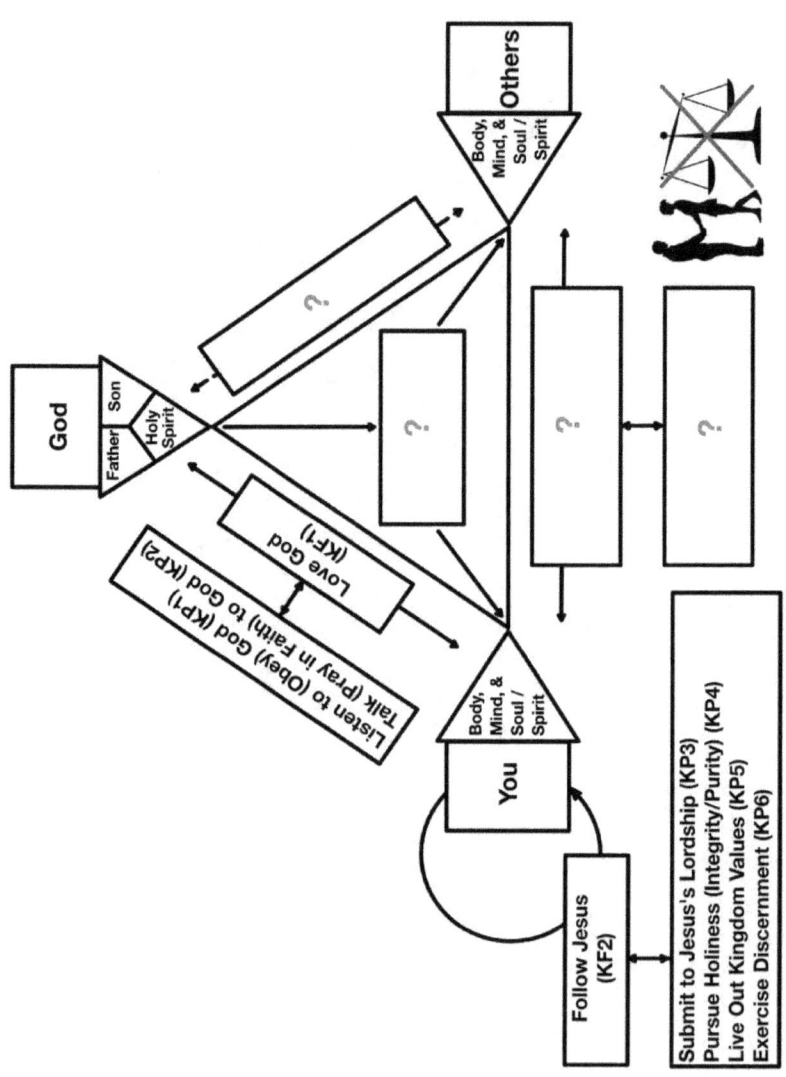

Study 13 - Undertake Acts of Service/Generosity - (KP9)

Subtitle: Be Prepared to Step Out in Faith to Serve Others Wherever and However We Are Called by God

Undertake: To put oneself under obligation to perform.

Service: A helpful act. Contribution to the welfare of others.

Generosity: An act of unselfish giving. Willingness to give or to share.

Study 13 - Introduction

In this penultimate study, we will consider the final Kingdom Practice that correlates to the Kingdom Fundamental to Love Your Neighbour as Yourself, which is to Undertake Acts of Service and Generosity. As with the previous studies, these all fit under the main message of "teach them to obey all that I have commanded you."

We see in Figure 16 that as part of loving our neighbours we are commanded to serve them and to be generous. As we have seen throughout this book, we will be influenced only to the extent to which we allow the Bible and the Holy Spirit to do so.

Figure 16 - Kingdom Practice 9 - to Undertake Acts of Service/Generosity

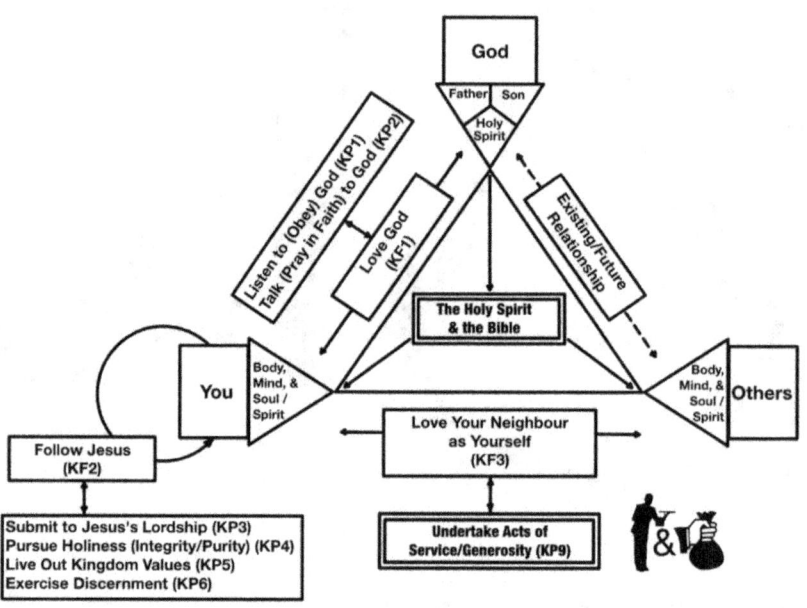

Study 13 - Biblical Support for This Kingdom Practice

A longstanding expectation of disciples of Jesus is that they are prepared to reach out to others in service. Similarly, there is an expectation that we will give freely of our wealth for the benefit of our neighbours—locally, nationally, and internationally. Jesus draws out six specific areas where we are to serve and be generous to others:

- Lead by being a servant of others.
- Wash the feet of others.
- Do unto others as we would have them do unto us.
- Do more than is expected from us even when this is difficult.
- Provide for those who cannot repay us.
- Give generously for the benefit of others, and we will be rewarded.

Detailed biblical support for these principles is laid out below (see Appendix 2 or the *All That I Have Commanded You* book, Chapter 4.3, for a complete set of scriptures).

Study 13 - Undertake Acts of Service/Generosity

13.1 - Lead by Being a Servant of Others

As followers of Jesus, we shouldn't adopt the world's accepted method of seeking power and authority as the mark of leadership. Instead, we are to lead by offering ourselves in service to those around us:

> It must not be like that among you. On the contrary, whoever wants to become great among you must be your servant, and whoever wants to be first among you must be your slave; just as the Son of Man did not come to be served, but to serve, and to give His life –a ransom for many. (Matthew 20:26-28. See also Mark 10:44-45)

13.2 - Wash the Feet of Others

Although not a common practice these days in industrialized nations, the process of foot washing is effectively saying that we should be prepared to serve others, even when this might be unpleasant or humbling for us:

> So if I, your Lord and Teacher, have washed your feet, you also ought to wash one another's feet. (John 13:14)

13.3 - Do unto Others as We Would Have Them Do to Us

We should adopt a mind-set that seeks to relate to others in a God-honouring way, treating them how we would like to be treated:

> Therefore, whatever you want others to do for you, do also the same for them –this is the Law and the Prophets. (Matthew 7:12. See also Luke 6:31)

13.4 - Do More than Is Expected from Us Even When This Is Difficult

Jesus uses examples from the Old Testament and life under Roman occupation to illustrate that, as his disciples, we should exceed the expectations of those around us, being especially generous with our time, resources (e.g., money), and energy:

> You have heard that it was said, An eye for an eye and a tooth for a tooth. But I tell you, don't resist an evildoer. On the contrary, if anyone slaps you on your right cheek, turn the other to him also. As for the one who wants to sue you and take away your shirt, let him have your coat as well. And if anyone forces you to go one mile, go with him two. (Matthew 5:38-41)

13.5 - Provide for Those Who Cannot Repay Us

Jesus wants us to use our worldly wealth to bless those who have no means to return the favour, i.e., the underprivileged and weakest in society:

> He also said to the one who had invited Him, "When you give a lunch or a dinner, don't invite your friends, your brothers, your relatives, or your rich neighbours, because they might invite you back, and you would be repaid. On the contrary, when you host a banquet, invite those who are poor, maimed, lame, or blind. And you will be blessed,

because they cannot repay you; for you will be repaid at the resurrection of the righteous." (Luke 14:12-14)

13.6 - Give Generously for the Benefit of Others and We Will Be Rewarded

This command to give generously is so that we can share those things with which God has blessed us with others, not with the ulterior motive of receiving even more back (the erroneous prosperity gospel):

> Give, and it will be given to you; a good measure – pressed down, shaken together, and running over – will be poured into your lap. For with the measure you use, it will be measured back to you. (Luke 6:38)

> Give to everyone who asks you, and from one who takes your things, don't ask for them back. (Luke 6:30)

In Matthew 25:31-46, Jesus speaks about the final judgement, describing the separation of the dead as a shepherd separating sheep from the goats. Acts of service in terms of feeding the hungry, giving drinks to the thirsty, inviting in strangers, clothing the naked, looking after the sick, and visiting those in prison are brought to our attention. These all reflect things that as God's followers we can be doing as part of our service to others. We should consider whether God is prompting us to do any of these things, either on a one-time basis or more intentionally. However, in terms of Jesus's teaching, these are not formally commands from him in the same sense that we have been considering in these studies. I say this, not to absolve us from any responsibility to do these things, but to highlight the reason why these elements have not been formally incorporated into the breakdown this analysis has considered.

Study 13 - Our Context

Jesus has some specific teaching to show how we should be helping and serving others:

> So when you give to the needy, do not announce it with trumpets, as the hypocrites do in the synagogues and on the streets, to be honoured by others. Truly I tell you, they have received their reward in full. But when you give to the needy, do not let your left hand know what your right hand is doing, so that your giving may be in secret. Then your Father, who sees what is done in secret, will reward you. (Matthew 6:2-4, NIV. See also Luke 14:12-14)

New Testament scriptures remind us that God has things for us to do as Jesus's disciples:

> For we are His creation, created in Christ Jesus for good works, which God prepared ahead of time so that we should walk in them. (Ephesians 2:10)

Service to the fellowship we belong to or the community we are part of is an expectation that runs throughout much of the New Testament. It should be something we do willingly out of our love and thanks to God for Jesus. Service ought to be something that aligns with our skills and giftings wherever possible but not necessarily so.

However for some, the expectations of others and from ourselves may lead to inappropriate prioritisation of service, contributing in turn to stress, guilt, and diverting time away from other things that are also important. Maybe we have the view that we earn "heavenly points" by doing things for God. This is an erroneous understanding.

Our response to the gift of salvation through Jesus Christ should naturally be to do things for God. But this should not arise out of intimidation, pressure, or a misplaced sense of duty. Rather, it should be based upon God's leading, which comes through the prompting of the Holy Spirit, reading the Bible, and receiving constructive input from others.

As disciples we do need to find our role in the body of Christ, i.e., the community of believers we worship with locally as well as around the world. This will depend in part on the skills and giftings God gives us. We may already know what these are. If not, we can work with others to identify where and how best we can serve.

However, this must be alongside our other priorities of developing our love for God in Jesus, following Jesus, loving others, and looking after ourselves and those who are our responsibility (spouse, children, parents, etc.).

Let us also remember that living as "salt" and "light" is itself a key element of our witness to others that can be a form of service over and above our duty as a family member, friend, colleague, or employee.

Study 13 - Kingdom Practice Application

Jesus as Our Example

Jesus tells us that he did not come to be served but to serve:

> For even the Son of Man did not come to be served, but to serve, and to give His life, a ransom for many. (Mark 10:45, NIV)

In his three years of ministry, Jesus focused on service, teaching, healing, deliverance, and the ultimate form of generosity, giving up his own life. Some examples of Jesus serving others include:

Service

> Jesus answered, "I did tell you, but you do not believe. The works I do in my Father's name testify about me, but you do not believe because you are not my sheep. My sheep listen to my voice; I know them, and they follow me. I give them eternal life, and they shall never perish; no one will snatch them out of my hand." (John 10:25–28, NIV)

Study 13 - Undertake Acts of Service/Generosity

When he had finished washing their feet, he put on his clothes and returned to his place. "Do you understand what I have done for you?" he asked them. "You call me "Teacher" and "Lord," and rightly so, for that is what I am. Now that I, your Lord and Teacher, have washed your feet, you also should wash one another's feet. I have set you an example that you should do as I have done for you. Very truly I tell you, no servant is greater than his master, nor is a messenger greater than the one who sent him. Now that you know these things, you will be blessed if you do them." (John 13:12-17, NIV)

Teaching

When Jesus had finished saying these things, the crowds were amazed at his teaching, because he taught as one who had authority, and not as their teachers of the law. (Matthew 7:28-29, NIV)

Healing

As Jesus went on from there, two blind men followed him, calling out, "Have mercy on us, Son of David!" When he had gone indoors, the blind men came to him, and he asked them, "Do you believe that I am able to do this?" "Yes, Lord," they replied. Then he touched their eyes and said, "According to your faith let it be done to you"; and their sight was restored. Jesus warned them sternly, "See that no one knows about this". But they went out and spread the news about him all over that region. (Matthew 9:27-31, NIV)

And when the men of that place recognised Jesus, they sent word to all the surrounding country. People brought all their sick to him and begged him to let the sick just touch the edge of his cloak, and all who touched it were healed. (Matthew 14:35-36, NIV)

Deliverance

When evening came, many who were demon-possessed were brought to him, and he drove out the spirits with a word and healed all the sick. This was to fulfil what was spoken through the prophet Isaiah: "He took up our infirmities and bore our diseases." (Matthew 8:16-17, NIV)

When he saw Jesus from a distance, he ran and fell on his knees in front of him. He shouted at the top of his voice, "What do you want with me, Jesus, Son of the Most High God? In God's name don't torture me!" For Jesus had said to him, "Come out of this man, you impure spirit!" Then Jesus asked him, "What is your name?" "My name is Legion," he replied, "for we are many." And he begged Jesus again and again not to send them out of the area. A large herd of pigs was feeding on the nearby hillside. The demons begged Jesus, "Send us among the pigs; allow us to go into them." He gave them permission, and the impure spirits came out and went into the pigs.

> The herd, about two thousand in number, rushed down the steep bank into the lake and were drowned. (Mark 5:6-13, NIV)

Generosity/Provision

See the Matthew 6:2-4 passage above on giving without letting your left hand know what your right hand gives. Also:

> As evening approached, the disciples came to him and said, "This is a remote place, and it's already getting late. Send the crowds away, so they can go to the villages and buy themselves some food." Jesus replied, "They do not need to go away. You give them something to eat." "We have here only five loaves of bread and two fish," they answered. "Bring them here to me," he said. And he directed the people to sit down on the grass. Taking the five loaves and the two fish and looking up to heaven, he gave thanks and broke the loaves. Then he gave them to the disciples, and the disciples gave them to the people. They all ate and were satisfied, and the disciples picked up twelve basketfuls of broken pieces that were left over. The number of those who ate was about five thousand men, besides women and children. (Matthew 14:15-21, NIV)

Laying down his own life

> Who, being in very nature God, did not consider equality with God something to be used to his own advantage; rather, he made himself nothing by taking the very nature of a servant, being made in human likeness. And being found in appearance as a man, he humbled himself by becoming obedient to death – even death on a cross! (Philippians 2:6-8, NIV)

When it comes to Jesus's ultimate generosity in giving his own life, this is an example Christians are still called to follow today. While estimates vary widely and up-to-date information is limited,[56] many believers around the world continue to be martyred for their faith and allegiance to Jesus. This should be a sobering reminder that even today followers of Jesus must be like the first apostles, ready to die for the Saviour who died for them. After eighteen centuries the words of early church leader Tertullian remain valid: "The blood of the martyrs is the seed of the church."[57]

---

[56] http://www.gordonconwell.edu/ockenga/research/documents/csgc_Christian_martyrs.pdf

[57] https://www.azquotes.com/author/14541-Tertullian

Some Brief Personal Reflections on Acts of Service and Generosity

During my very busy professional career, I often encountered uncertainties about when I could be available for regular service in God's kingdom. Some years after coming to personal faith, I was ordained as an elder in the fellowship where we then worshipped. At that time our son was very young, and I was often abroad, sometimes worked weekends, as well as a long regular work day. Due to my commute into London, I would leave home weekdays at 6:30 and not return until around 19:30 in the evening. The group of church members assigned to my oversight were largely pensioners, many of them in assisted-living accommodation, which made visiting them after I came home from work difficult for both sides. Consequently, I felt I was letting them down in not being able to see them on a schedule more convenient to them.

When we moved to another worship fellowship, my wife and I became involved in children's ministry. For over twenty years, we led a team that shared these responsibilities during the school term. I found this more satisfying than my elder duties as we could commit ourselves to attending church, preparing, and then delivering sound Bible teaching to these youngsters.

During this time I also became involved with our fellowship's Worldwide Missions Team. More recently, I have taken on the leadership of that group. We focus on those who have gone out from the church in some form of missions capacity (both short and long term) and strive to raise the profile of particular ministries through:

- Prayer breakfasts.
- Ethnic food nights and other activities.
- Specific mission-themed services.
- Special mid-year and Christmas missions appeals.

Following my retirement from paid employment, God led me to serve as a volunteer representative with a missions organisation, supporting the promotion of mission work within London and the South East of England. This has been a fulfilling role for me as it fits with having a heart for people and for the wider sharing of the gospel.

In relation to giving, after we first became disciples Mary-Anne and I were constantly prompted by God to tithe. We were very tight for finances at the time due to high mortgage costs of the home we were buying. When I changed jobs in the late 1980s, my salary increase enabled us to take the step forward to begin tithing. Our son came along shortly afterwards. We found it difficult to continue tithing as my wife had given up paid work to look after him. I eventually had to sell my motorcycle to prevent us from going into the red. Since then, we have never been in arrears with the bank, and God has ensured that we have always had enough. Apart from our mortgage and occasional purchases on interest-free credit, we have always practised saving up for what we wanted rather than a "buy now, pay later" philosophy.

The point here is that God has provided for all our needs and enabled us to invest further in his kingdom over and above our tithes when we have felt that God was prompting us to do this. He has been faithful to our obedience to Scripture, and we have never been short of the things we needed. Please do not interpret this as in any way supporting a "prosperity gospel" theology but rather my thankful recognition of God's generous provision over the last thirty-plus years.

Related to this theme of generosity, when I am walking in London or elsewhere, from time to time I will come across a homeless person who is understandably begging. There has been much in the UK press about this situation, and the general advice is that people should give through recognised charities rather than directly to the individual. In fact, press reports have been made of criminal groups placing individuals on the street to beg, taking advantage of people's good nature and generosity to defraud the public. This presents a challenge and dilemma to me and to other followers of Jesus about what to do when we are confronted with such situations. While I do not give to every such homeless person I pass, from time to time if God prompts me to do so, I will offer them something to eat or drink rather than money.

Recently, I was pushing my young grandson in his pram around my home town when I saw a gentleman sitting on the pavement with a few possessions around him. He was not begging, but I did not want to engage with him because of my grandson. Seated in his pram, my grandson was almost at the man's eye level, and as we went past, he put out his tiny arm and waved at the man. This was a very humbling experience for me, as it demonstrated how free from prejudice my young grandson was and that my attitude and heart were not necessarily in the right place at that time. It really spoke to me about how I might compare to the Parable of the Samaritan we discussed in Study 10 and how I should respond to such encounters moving forward.

Study 13 - Kingdom Practice Health Check

Biblical Support Section
- What does undertaking acts of service or being generous mean for you?

Our Context Section
- In your cultural context, what is the general attitude of society to caring and providing for others, particularly those who are vulnerable?
- Does it need to change, and if so, how might you be a part of that process?
- When you are involved in serving others, do you keep this between you and the Lord, or are you prone to "blowing your own trumpet" about it?
- Similarly, when you are giving to the work of the kingdom or even to secular initiatives, do you keep this quiet so that only God (and perhaps those with whom you have shared responsibilities, such as a spouse) really knows? If not, why is that?

Kingdom Practice Application Section
- Have you found your role in the worshipping community you are part of? If so, does it reflect your passions, concerns, and gifting? Are you encouraged to share your skills and abilities in your fellowship/church?
- If not, is there something that you feel God is calling you to do? Beyond praying about it, is there someone you trust whom you could approach to help you discern whether this is the right thing?

Look at how you divide your time. Depending upon the flexibility (free time) you have, consider the amount you devote to kingdom activities. If your time commitment to job and family is high, is there any way you can reschedule and change priorities to create a greater margin for serving others? Also we need to be sure that the tasks and roles in our fellowship are not falling upon the few but are undertaken by the many for the benefit of everyone. As well as committing to the effective use of our time serving others, we should also discern how to be generous with our skills and giftings for the benefit of the kingdom, not necessarily all to our own church but to support other things that God is doing through others.

In our giving, many Christians understand that our minimum responsibility to God is to provide a tithe of our income to further the work of extending his kingdom. We should also seek God's guidance on where specifically our giving should be directed, whether to support the programme of the community in which we worship, missionary agencies, disaster relief, child sponsorship, etc. There is no shortage of things to which we can give, and God loves a cheerful giver. Indeed, as far as is possible for us, we should always try to share more of what God has given us than a tithe since all we have comes from God and remains his.

While we may think of tithing as related solely to our finances, we can also "tithe" of our time and our talents (skills) for kingdom purposes.

- ➢ It can be very difficult to be financially generous when money is tight. If this is your experience, your time and skills can still be an offering that God will love. You are still a crucial part of the body of Christ. Is there a skill you have that you can share with others?
- ➢ What are your priorities? Are they aligned with God's kingdom? If not, what might you need to do to change this?

Study 13 - Possible Action

Is there anything you could do to be of greater service to others (both those already in the kingdom or outside it) and/or be more generous with your time, talents, and money? Consider writing down anything you sense about this in the outlined text box provided (or in your journal/notebook) and how you might respond to any challenges.

Health Warning

Remember that you should not respond to this Kingdom Practice in a legalistic way. It is much more about serving God as part of our love for him because of our salvation in Jesus. We will become more like Jesus the more we allow the Holy Spirit to lead and guide us day by day, and God will get the glory.

My Response/Prayer and Date

Space For You To Record Responses To Questions, Make Notes, Etc.

Study 13 - Undertake Acts of Service/Generosity

Study 13 - Undertake Acts of Service/Generosity

Study 13 - Memorising the Structure

Can you fill in the blank boxes without looking at the figure displayed at the beginning of this study?

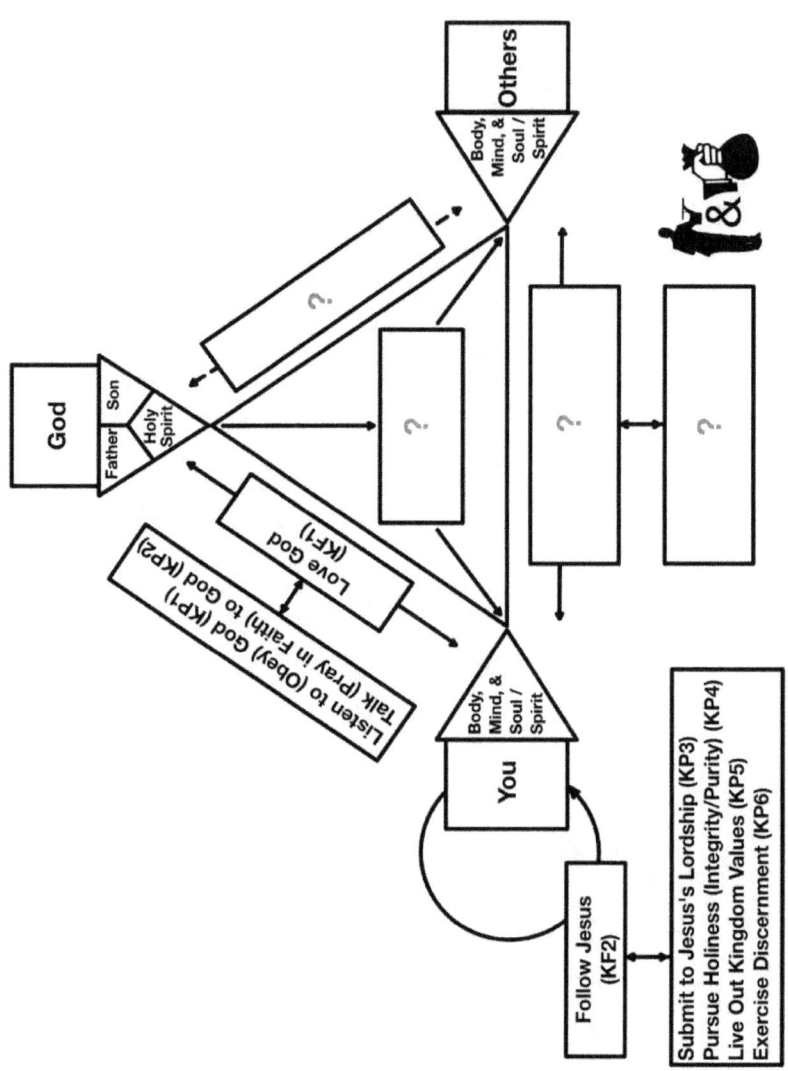

Study 14 - Outcomes from Putting These Things into Practice

Subtitle: Drawing Together the Various Components of the Last Thirteen Studies

Study 14 - Introduction

Reflecting back on Studies 1 to 13, we can see each Kingdom Fundamental and Kingdom Practice illustrated in Figure 17. It demonstrates that there are three things we need to concentrate on in terms of our relationship with God (the Trinity), five things we need to be mindful of in our own personal development, and four things that will define our relationships with other people. All of these are directly driven by our understanding and responses to our reading and application of the Scriptures and how we react to the promptings of the Holy Spirit.

Figure 17 - The Kingdom Fundamentals and Kingdom Practices Jesus Wants Us to Practise and to Teach to Other Followers

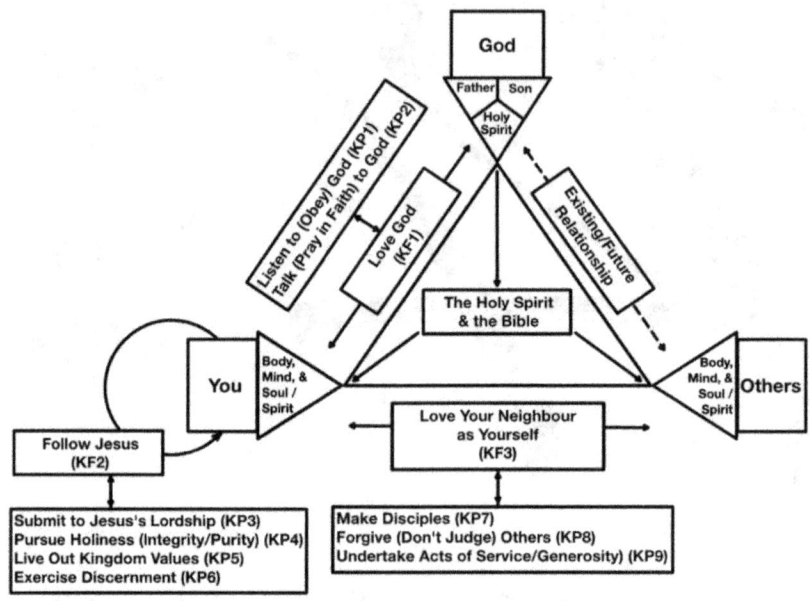

Study 14 - Outcomes

We have looked at the challenges that Jesus presented to those who would be his disciples and have considered these in the context of three Kingdom Fundamentals and nine Kingdom Practices to help us remember what he would have us do. As we seek to emulate his example, we can draw upon the Holy Spirit to help us live victorious but humble lifestyles as salt and light in our communities.

If we obey and practise Jesus's commands, the implications are that we should:

- Have life in all its fullness.
- Demonstrate more Fruit of the Spirit.
- See other people come into the kingdom as disciples of Jesus.
- Develop a deepening relationship of faith, trust, and understanding with God the Father, Son, and Holy Spirit.
- Do greater things than Jesus did.

Taking each of these points in turn, the following scriptures provide biblical support for these potential outcomes.

14.1 - Have Life in All Its Fullness

Jesus indicates that we should experience life to the full through coming to him, particularly in terms of having a living relationship with God rather than a promise of worldly pleasures:

> A thief comes only to steal and to kill and to destroy. I have come so that they may have life and have it in abundance. (John 10:10)

14.2 - Demonstrate More Fruit of the Spirit as an Outcome, Not an Objective

As we become more like Jesus in our walk of faith, others should notice that our character and behaviours exhibit greater amounts of each of the spiritual fruit listed below:

> But the fruit of the Spirit is love, joy, peace, patience, kindness, goodness, faithfulness, gentleness, self-control. Against such things there is no law. (Galatians 5:22-23)

14.3 - See Other People Come into the Kingdom and Flourish as Fellow Disciples of Jesus

If we live out our role of being salt and light to those around us, we should see a harvest of others coming into the kingdom:

> Therefore, pray to the Lord of the harvest to send out workers into His harvest. (Matthew 9:38)

> He told them: "The harvest is abundant, but the workers are few. Therefore, pray to the Lord of the harvest to send out workers into His harvest." (Luke 10:2)

> Don't you say, "There are still four more months, then comes the harvest"? Listen to what I'm telling you: Open your eyes and look at the fields, for they are ready for harvest. (John 4:35)

14.4 - Develop a Deepening Relationship of Faith, Trust, and Understanding in God the Father, Son, and Holy Spirit

As we seek to strengthen our relationship with and dependence on God in Christ, our knowledge and experience of him will become deeper:

> And I pray this: that your love will keep on growing in knowledge and every kind of discernment, so that you can approve the things that are superior and can be pure and blameless in the day of Christ, filled with the fruit of righteousness that comes through Jesus Christ to the glory and praise of God. (Philippians 1:9-11)

> I pray that the God of our Lord Jesus Christ, the glorious Father, would give you a spirit of wisdom and revelation in the knowledge of Him. I pray that the perception of your mind may be enlightened so you may know what is the hope of His calling, what are the glorious riches of His inheritance among the saints, and what is the immeasurable greatness of His power to us who believe, according to the working of His vast strength. He demonstrated this power in

the Messiah by raising Him from the dead and seating Him at His right hand in the heavens — far above every ruler and authority, power and dominion, and every title given, not only in this age but also in the one to come. And He put everything under His feet and appointed Him as head over everything for the church, which is His body, the fullness of the One who fills all things in every way. (Ephesians 1:17-23)

14.5 - Do Greater Things than Jesus Did

Jesus states explicitly that his followers as they are empowered through the indwelling Holy Spirit should do more than he was able to do while on earth. This remains a challenge for all of us:

> I assure you: The one who believes in Me will also do the works that I do. And he will do even greater works than these, because I am going to the Father. (John 14:12)

Study 14 - Our Context

If you have completed all of the study material to this point, well done! You may have found yourself challenged along the way and even found certain parts of the material difficult to deal with. Jesus tells us certain things about being his disciples:

We will find rest.

> Come to Me, all of you who are weary and burdened, and I will give you rest. All of you, take up My yoke and learn from Me, because I am gentle and humble in heart, and you will find rest for yourselves. For My yoke is easy and My burden is light. (Matthew 11:28-30)

We considered this briefly in Study 5 on Follow Jesus and to some degree in Study 12 on Forgiveness.

We will experience suffering.

> I have told you these things so that in Me you may have peace. You will have suffering in this world. Be courageous! I have conquered the world. (John 16:33)

We will experience blessing, persecution, and eternal life.

> "I assure you," Jesus said, "there is no one who has left house, brothers or sisters, mother or father, children, or fields because of Me and the gospel, who will not receive 100 times more, now at this time –houses, brothers and sisters, mothers and children, and fields, with persecutions –and eternal life in the age to come. But many who are first will be last, and the last first." (Mark 10:29-31).

There will be a cost.

> Now great crowds were travelling with Him. So He turned and said to them: "If anyone comes to Me and does not hate his own father and mother, wife and children, brothers and sisters –yes, and even

his own life –he cannot be My disciple. Whoever does not bear his own cross and come after Me cannot be My disciple." (Luke 14:25–27)

We considered this briefly in Study 5 (Follow Jesus).

Study 14 - Application Section

Jesus as Our example

As we have worked through Studies 2 to 13, we have seen that Jesus does not ask us to do anything he has not already done himself. The things Jesus requires from us are things that he undertook as an integral part of his life in ministry. He is our unblemished example of each of the Kingdom Fundamentals and Kingdom Practices we have been considering and is the only role model for any follower. Jesus loves the Father perfectly. He was confident in himself and did not need the approval of others (John 5:41). His aim for us is that in him we do things that bring glory to the Father:

> My Father is glorified by this: that you produce much fruit and prove to be My disciples. (John 15:8)

So as we are challenged to put all these things into practice in our daily lives, it is appropriate to remind ourselves once again that Jesus is still calling us to be his followers:

> "Follow Me," Jesus told them, "and I will make you fish for people!" (Mark 1:17)

The conclusion we can draw here is that we must first do the former (i.e., follow Jesus). Only then will God work through us to do the latter (i.e., fish for people) as we submit to his leading.

Some Brief Personal Reflections on Living as Jesus Intends Us to Live

Living the life that God wants us to have and fitting into his plan and will for us is not an easy process. I have sought to be obedient to God on a daily basis, but inevitably I do not live up to my own expectations, let alone God's. The question I sometimes have to ask myself is what is my heart's desire. Is it to be available to God in his service or available to myself and my own agenda? Like most of us, I suspect, the answer varies according to place, time, and situation. It's about the decisions I make concerning work, service, and being with others, whether fellow disciples or non-believers. So far as the general direction of my life and my day-to-day activities are concerned, I believe that I am currently where God wants me to be. If he needs me to do something else, then he not only needs to bring this to my attention but also my wife's!

If I can get to the end of each day and have no particular regrets about what I have or have not done, whether for my family, for others, or for "kingdom" activities, then I believe this is the best outcome I can hope for.

Too much self-analysis is not good either, as I need to receive God's grace when I fail, confess any wrongdoing, and move forward to the next task. Ultimately, I, like you, am a work-in-progress, and God is not finished with either of us yet!

Study 14 - Health Check - Questions and Issues to Consider

Outcomes Section

- In what way do you identify with the outcomes presented in 14.1 to 14.5?
- Is there anything you feel is missing from that list?
- What is your reaction to the overall Kingdom Fundamentals and Kingdom Practices as defined in Studies 2 to 13? Are they what you would have expected?
- If you had to choose a different title for any of the studies, which ones and what would the titles have been?

Our Context Section

- In your cultural context, how are disciples of Jesus regarded? Is this influenced by stereotypical attitudes rather than experience of seeing real disciples loving others as they would wish to be loved?
- Are any of the four bullets in the Our Context section relevant to you at this time (or in the past)?
- How have you reacted/responded to them?

Application Section

- Look back over the previous studies. What things has God been bringing to your attention?
- Have you ignored these things, wrestled with them, or responded in a way that can move you forward to deepen your relationship with Jesus?
- What are you going to do next? Will you put this book down and forget about it? Or will you begin to develop and build in the areas where God has been challenging you?
- Have you committed to memory the three Kingdom Fundamentals and nine Kingdom Practices we have looked at over Studies 2 to 13 as well as how they all fit together? If you need to check, look at Figure 18.

Another Challenge

If you have been working through this material as part of a group, why not consider if there is something you could do together as a practical application of your study? You could choose to serve a group in need within your community that would not be able to repay you. Or you might raise funds for a people group experiencing ongoing difficulties, whether at home or abroad. Or there are many other such possibilities of service and giving you might consider.

If you have worked through this material alone, consider whether you could encourage other believers to work with you to serve your community in some new way.

Health Warning

Remember that you should not approach the Kingdom Fundamentals and Kingdom Practices presented in this book in a legalistic way. It is much more about serving God as part of our love for him because of our salvation in Jesus. We will become more like Jesus the more we allow the Holy Spirit to lead and guide us day by day, and God will get the glory.

Final Thoughts

The complete set of Kingdom Fundamentals, Kingdom Practices, and Kingdom Behaviours is illustrated in Figure 19 at the end of this section with a different representation of the Kingdom Fundamentals and Kingdom Practices in Figure 20.

God is not in a hurry, so don't set yourself impossible timetables or workloads that will lead you into increased stress and potential failure. As Paul says in Ephesians 2:8-10:

> For you are saved by grace through faith, and this is not from yourselves; it is God's gift –not from works, so that no one can boast. For we are His creation, created in Christ Jesus for good works, which God prepared ahead of time so that we should walk in them.

It is important to recognise that we will only reach perfection when we are promoted to glory in heaven, as the apostle Paul expresses in 2 Corinthians 3:18:

> We all, with unveiled faces, are looking as in a mirror at the glory of the Lord and are being transformed into the same image from glory to glory; this is from the Lord who is the Spirit.

Figure 18 - The Overall Structure of Kingdom Fundamentals and Kingdom Practices under the Book's Main Theme

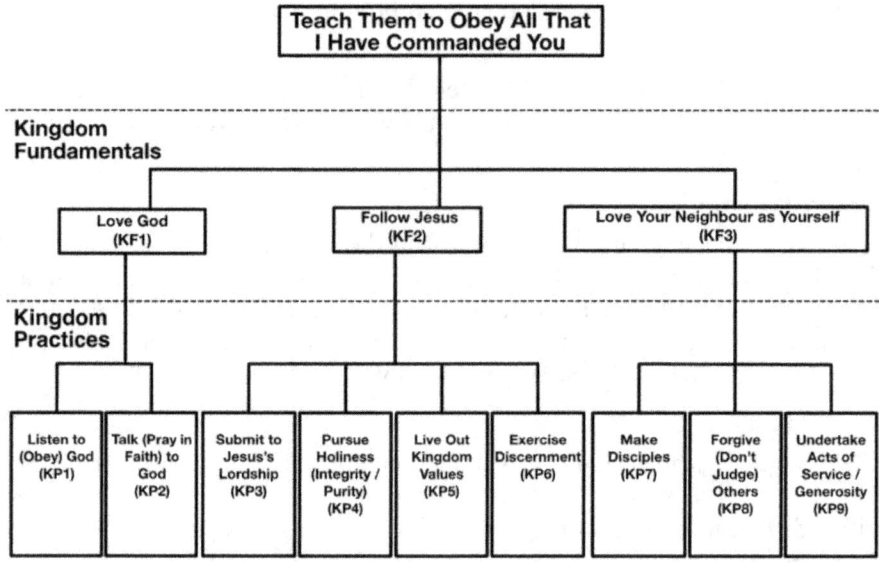

If you have used the provided text boxes in each study or in a separate journal to write out your responses to the questions and material, why not set some dates in your diary to review and reflect upon how your relationship with God has developed. You can also use these to consider to what extent you have altered your attitudes and behaviours, hopefully in a positive way. Allow a reasonable period of time between these assessments (three months is a good time frame), and don't allow yourself to fall into condemnation if you have not achieved all you aimed to do. God is gracious and understands our human nature because he experienced it in Jesus's life on earth.

Ultimately, remind yourself about what it says in Romans 8:37-39:

> No, in all these things we are more than victorious through Him who loved us. For I am persuaded that not even death or life, angels or rulers, things present or things to come, hostile powers, height or depth, or any other created thing will have the power to separate us from the love of God that is in Christ Jesus our Lord.

As we grow in our faith and the practice of the Kingdom Fundamentals and Practices we have considered, others should be able to see changes in us. In reaching out to others in love, we should be more prepared to:

- Turn the other cheek (Matthew 5:39).

- Give our shirt as well as our coat (Matthew 5:40).
- Go the extra mile (Matthew 5:41).
- Give to those who ask of us (Matthew 5:42).
- Return good for evil (1 Peter 3:9, Romans 12:17).

We should also display more of the Fruit of the Spirit (Galatians 5:22-23 above). Additionally, our relationships with others should be characterised by increasing hospitality, grace, forgiveness, faith, generosity, and practical service. As you move forward as a disciple, try to always keep in mind the two "greatest commandments"—love God and love your neighbour as yourself—along with the call to follow Jesus. We have seen here that they are supported by a total of nine Kingdom Practices which it would be good to remember.

Memorising Tip for the "Kingdom" Outline Structure

One method that helps me remember the sub-points under the three Kingdom Fundamentals is to pick letters from the Kingdom Practices and form something memorable from them. For example:

- Under "Love God", I think of London Transport (Listen and Talk) or Obey and Pray, which rhyme in English.
- Under "Follow Jesus", I think of the word SOLD, or Submit, hOliness, Live, Discern.
- Under "Love Your Neighbour as Yourself", I think of DFS (the name of a UK furniture company) or Disciple, Forgive, and Serve.

Collectively, these Kingdom Practices can be a guide to help you remember the core of what Jesus wants you to practise as his disciple. Recall also that the Holy Spirit and the Bible are central to this, which is why you see them in the middle of each diagram that accompanies each of the studies.

As we have already highlighted, this is not about us earning salvation. That is why Jesus came. Nor is it about getting "heaven points" through undertaking good works. It is about entering into a relationship with the Father, Son, and Holy Spirit as a way of living our lives day by day in dependence upon God's grace and leading so that he gets the glory.

Figure 19 - The Complete Set of Kingdom Fundamentals, Kingdom Practices, and Kingdom Behaviours Developed from Jesus's Commands

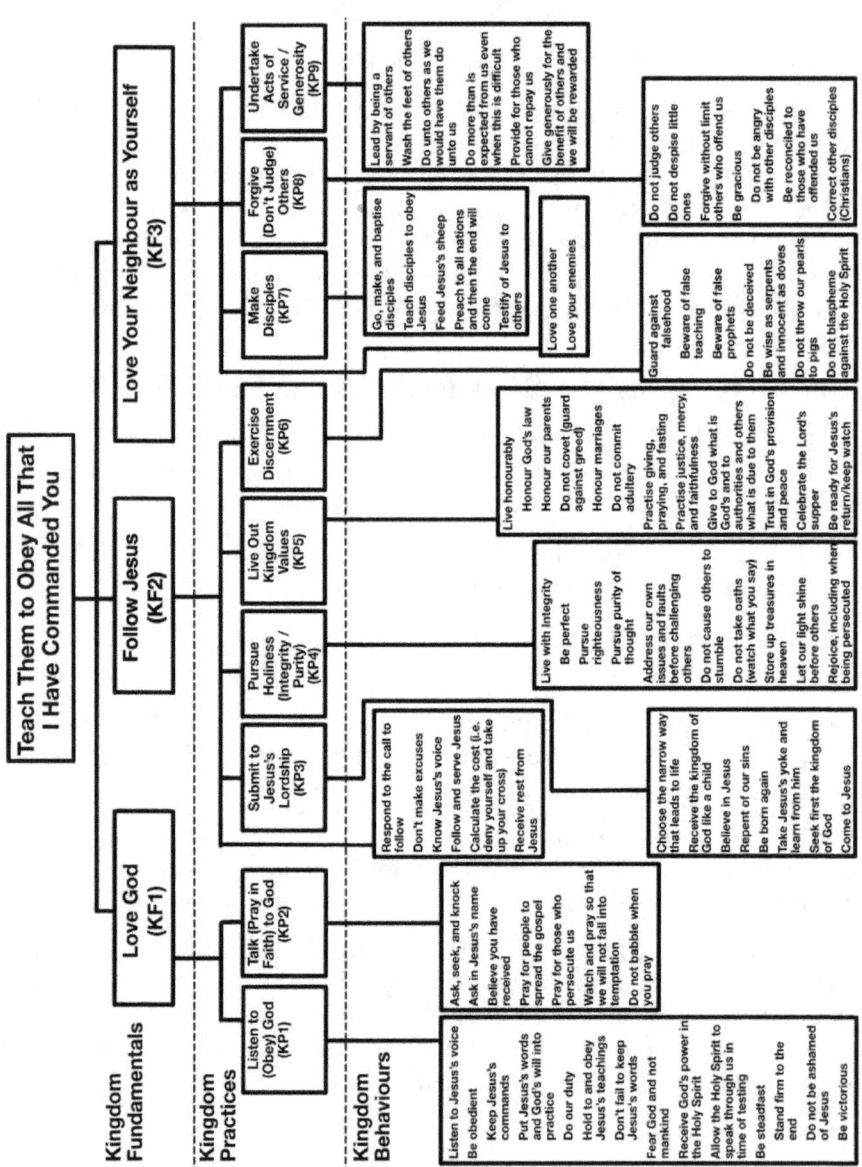

Study 14 - Outcomes from Putting These Things into Practice

Figure 20 - The Complete Set of Kingdom Fundamentals and Kingdom Practices

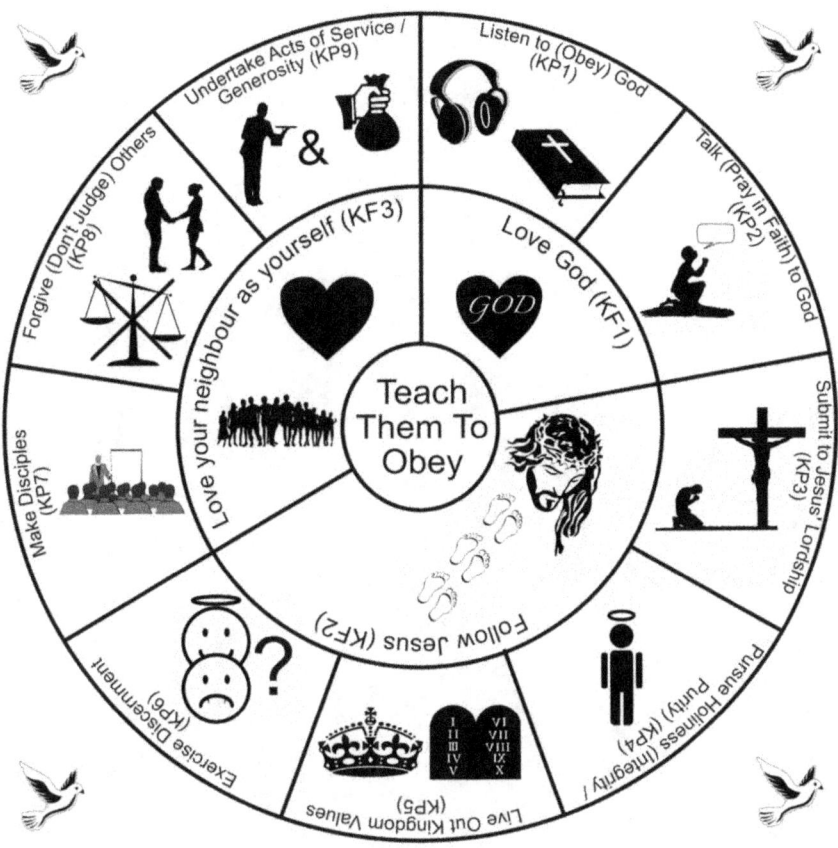

Space For You To Record Responses To Questions, Make Notes, Etc.

Study 14 - Outcomes from Putting These Things into Practice

Study 14 - Outcomes from Putting These Things into Practice

Study 14 - Memorising the Structure
Can you fill in the blank boxes without looking at the figure displayed at the beginning of this study?

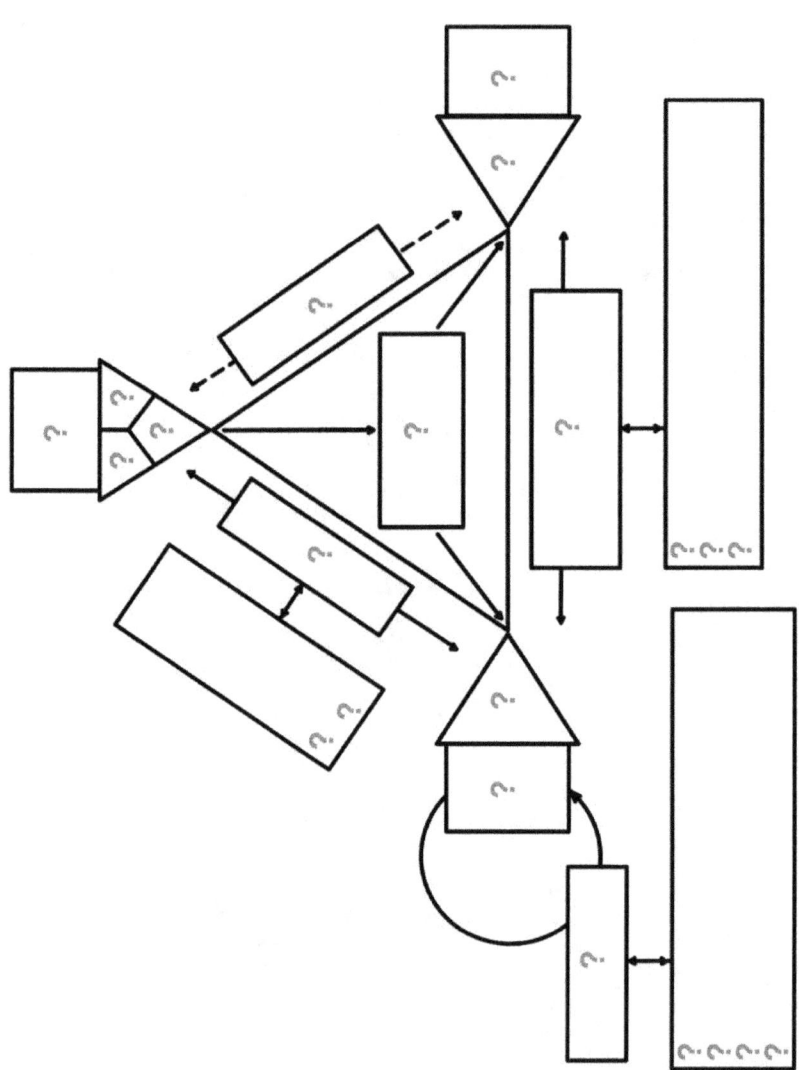

242

Appendix 1 – Further Reading on Discipleship

Space within these studies has been limited in order to make the material manageable. For those wanting to look deeper into the implications of being a follower of Jesus, it would be worthwhile to consider other bodies of work that focus on the principles of discipleship and the commands of Jesus in particular. Some examples are provided below:

- *What Jesus Demands from the World* by John Piper
- *Celebration of Discipline: The Path to Spiritual Growth* by Richard J. Foster
- *Discipleship* by David Watson
- *Discipleship: Living the Fifty Commands of Christ* by Leah Ramirez
- *Hear Him! the One Hundred Twenty-Five Commands of Jesus* by Peter Wittstock
- *The Commands of Christ: What It Really Means to Follow Jesus* by Tom Blackaby
- *The Great and Beautiful God, The Great and Beautiful Life*, and *The Great and Beautiful Community*, three excellent books by James Bryan Smith
- *The Great Omission: Jesus' Essential Teaching On Discipleship* – Dallas Willard

- *Disciples are Made Not Born* by Walter Hendrichson
- *The Lost Art of Disciple Making* by LeRoy Eims

Other sources that list different numbers of commands of Jesus include the following references (in addition to further searches that can be made on the internet):

- "The Fifty Commands of Jesus" by Matthew Robert Payne - http://ezinearticles.com/?The-Fifty-Commands-of-Jesus&id=468177
- "The Commandments of Jesus" by JS McConnell - http://www.earthsite.org/commandments.htm
- http://aplaceforyou.org/upload/Commands-of-Christ_2017.pdf
- http://www.historymakers.info/sermons/50-commands-of-christ.html

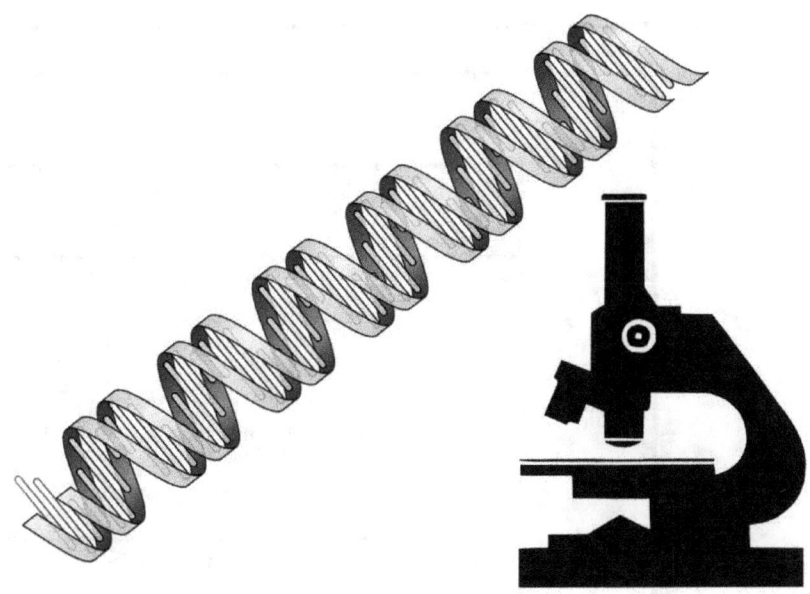

Appendix 2 - Summary of the Biblical Analysis

Kingdom Fundamental	Kingdom Practice	Kingdom Behaviour	Commands & Bible References
Love God			Mark 12:30, Matthew 22:37-38
	Listen to (obey) God		
		Listen to Jesus's voice	Matthew 11:15, Matthew 13:9, Matthew 13:43, Mark 4:9, Mark 4:23, Luke 8:8, Luke 10:16, Luke 14:34-35
		Be obedient	Keep Jesus's commands - John 14:15 Put Jesus's words and God's will into practice - Matthew 7:21, Matthew 7:24-25, Luke 6:46-49 Do Our Duty - Luke 17:7-10 Hold to and obey Jesus's teachings - John 8:31-32, John 8:51, John 14:23-24 Don't fail to keep Jesus's words - John 12:47-48
		Fear God and not mankind	Matthew 10:28, Luke 12:4-5
		Receive God's power in the Holy Spirit	Luke 24:49, John 14:26, John 20:22-23, Acts 1:8
		Allow the Holy Spirit to speak through us in time or testing	Matthew 10:19-20, Mark 13:11, Luke 12:11-12
		Be steadfast	Stand firm to the end - Matthew 10:22-23, Matthew 24:13, Mark 13:13 Do not be ashamed of Jesus - Mark 8:38, Luke 9:26, Luke 12:8-9 Be victorious - Revelation 2:7, Revelation 2:11, Revelation 2:17, Revelation 2:26-28, Revelation 3:5, Revelation 3:12, Revelation 3:21

Kingdom Fundamental	Kingdom Practice	Kingdom Behaviour	Commands & Bible References
Love God	Talk (pray in faith) to God		
		Ask, seek, and knock	Matthew 7:7-8, Luke 11:9
		Ask in Jesus's name	John 14:12-14
		Believe you have received	Matthew 6:6, Matthew 21:21-22, Mark 11:24 , John 15:7
		Pray for people to spread the gospel	Matthew 9:37-38, Luke 10:2
		Pray for those who persecute us	Matthew 5:44, Luke 6:27-28
		Watch and pray so that we will not fall into temptation	Matthew 26:41
		Do not babble when you pray	Matthew 6:7-8

Kingdom Fundamental	Kingdom Practice	Kingdom Behaviour	Commands & Bible References
Follow Jesus			
		Respond to the call to follow	Matthew 4:19, Matthew 9:9, Mark 1:17, Mark 2:14, Luke 5:27, John 1:43, John 21:19, John 21:22
		Don't make excuses	Matthew 8:18-22, Luke 9:57-62
		Know Jesus's voice	John 10:27-29
		Follow and serve Jesus	John 12:26
		Calculate the cost (deny yourself and take up your cross)	Matthew 10:38-39, Matthew 16:24-25, Mark 8:34-35, Luke 9:23-24, Luke 14:25-33
		Receive rest from Jesus	Matthew 11:28-30

Kingdom Fundamental	Kingdom Practice	Kingdom Behaviour	Commands & Bible References
Follow Jesus	Submit to Jesus's lordship		
		Choose the narrow way that leads to life	Matthew 7:13-14, Luke 13:24-30, John 14:6
		Receive the kingdom of God like a child	Mark 10:15, Luke 18:17
		Believe in Jesus	John 14:1, John 5:24, John 6:29
		Repent of our sins	Matthew 4:17, Mark 1:14-15, Luke 13:3, Luke 13:5
		Be born again	John 3:7
		Take Jesus's yoke and learn from him	Matthew 11:29-30
		Seek first the kingdom of God	Matthew 6:33, Luke 12:27-31
		Come to Jesus	John 7:37-39

Kingdom Fundamental	Kingdom Practice	Kingdom Behaviour	Commands & Bible References
Follow Jesus	Pursue holiness (integrity / purity)		
		Live with integrity	Be perfect - Matthew 5:48 Pursue righteousness - Matthew 5:20 Pursue purity of thought - Mark 7:20-23
		Address our own issues and faults before challenging others	Luke 6:41-42, Matthew 7:3-5
		Do not cause others to stumble	Matthew 18:6-7, Mark 9:42, Luke 17:1-2
		Do not take oaths (watch what you say)	Matthew 5:33-37
		Store up treasures in heaven	Matthew 6:19-21, Luke 12:33-34
		Let our light shine before others	Matthew 5:16
		Rejoice, including when being persecuted	Matthew 5:11-12, Luke 6:22-23, Luke 10:20

Kingdom Fundamental	Kingdom Practice	Kingdom Behaviour	Commands & Bible References
Follow Jesus	Live out Kingdom values		
		Live honourably	Honour God's law - Matthew 5:17-19, Matthew 19:18-19, Mark 10:19, Luke 18:20
			Honour our parents - Matthew 15:4
			Do not covet (guard against greed) - Luke 12:15
			Honour marriage - Matthew 19:6, Matthew 19:9
			Do not commit adultery - Matthew 5:27-28
		Practise giving, praying and fasting	Matthew 1:1-18
		Practise justice, mercy and faithfulness	Matthew 23:23
		Give to God what is God's and to authorities and others what is due to them	Matthew 22:19-21, Mark 12:17, Luke 20:25
		Trust in God's provision and peace	Matthew 6:25-26, John 14:27, John 16:33
		Celebrate the Lord's Supper	Matthew 26:26-27, Luke 22:17-20
		Be ready for Jesus's return/ keep watch	Matthew 24:42-44, Matthew 25:13, Mark 13:32-37, Luke 12:35-40, Luke 17:22-25, Luke 21:8-9, Revelation 22:12-14

Kingdom Fundamental	Kingdom Practice	Kingdom Behaviour	Commands & Bible References
Follow Jesus	Exercise discernment		
		Guard against falsehood	Beware of false teaching - Matthew 16:6, Matthew 16:11-12 Beware of false prophets - Matthew 7:15-20
		Do not be deceived	Matthew 24:23-28, Matthew 24:4-5, Mark 13:5-9 and Mark 13:20-23
		Be wise as serpents and innocent as doves	Matthew 10:16
		Do not throw our pearls to pigs	Matthew 7:6
		Do not blaspheme against the Holy Spirit	Mark 3:29-30, Luke 12:10

Kingdom Fundamental	Kingdom Practice	Kingdom Behaviour	Commands & Bible References
Love your neighbour as yourself			Mark 12:31, Matthew 22:39
		Love one another	John 13:34-35
		Love your enemies	Luke 6:35, Luke 6:27-29, Matthew 5:44
	Make disciples		
		Go, make, and baptise disciples	Matthew 28:19, Mark 16:15-20
		Teach disciples to obey Jesus	Matthew 28:20
		Feed Jesus's sheep	John 21:15-17
		Preach to all nations and then the end will come	Matthew 24:14, Mark 13:10
		Testify of Jesus to others	John 15:26-27

Kingdom Fundamental	Kingdom Practice	Kingdom Behaviour	Commands & Bible References
Love your neighbour as yourself	Forgive (don't judge) others		
		Do not judge others	Matthew 7:1-2, Luke 6:37
		Do not despise little ones	Matthew 18:10
		Forgive without limit others who offend us	Matthew 6:14-15, Matthew 18:21-22, Mark 11:25, Luke 17:3-4
		Be gracious	Do not be angry with other disciples - Matthew 5:22 Be reconciled to those who have offended us - Matthew 5:23-25, Luke 12:58-59
		Correct other disciples (Christians)	Matthew 18:15-17

Kingdom Fundamental	Kingdom Practice	Kingdom Behaviour	Commands & Bible References
Love your neighbour as yourself	Undertake acts of service / generosity		
		Lead by being a servant of others	Matthew 20:26-28, Mark 9:35, Mark 10:44-45, Luke 14:10-11, Luke 22:24-26
		Wash the feet of others	John 13:14
		Do unto others as we would have them do unto us	Matthew 7:12, Luke 6:31
		Do more than is expected from us even when this is difficult	Matthew 5:38-41
		Provide for those who cannot repay us	Luke 14:12-14
		Give generously for the benefit of others and we will be rewarded	Matthew 5:42, Luke 6:30, Luke 6:38

Appendix 3 – Leaders' Notes and Advice
Introduction to the Material

The whole of this book builds upon a unique analysis of the commands of Jesus (set out in the related *All That I Have Commanded You* book), which have been grouped and presented in a simple structure. This is primarily for the benefit of all followers of Jesus, seeking to group and prioritise Jesus's teachings into a form that can be remembered readily as Kingdom Fundamentals supported by Kingdom Practices and underpinned by Kingdom Behaviours (individual commands from Jesus).

If you are a leader of a group or a mentor for an individual student working through the studies in this book, it would be helpful to be familiar with the scriptural analysis set out in Appendix 2 before leading each study. In addition, you should ideally read through the study material in advance, structured in most cases in terms of:

- Introduction to the subject matter.

- Biblical support of material. This section gives the reasoning for the Kingdom Fundamental or Kingdom Practice being discussed based upon the comprehensive scriptural analysis from the related *All That I Have Commanded You* book.

- Our Context. This is an outline of how the Kingdom Fundamental or Kingdom Practice and their supporting scriptures might be interpreted in our current cultural context (which may differ greatly depending on where and by what people group this material is being studied).

- Kingdom Fundamental or Kingdom Practice Application. This section looks at Jesus as the prime example of how to live out his teaching, using Jesus's own parables and other relevant references to illustrate how he practised the Kingdom Fundamental or Kingdom Practice in question. There are also some author perspectives on each Kingdom Fundamental or Kingdom Practice. As leader, you might want to think about and be prepared to share some of your own experiences or thoughts.

- Kingdom Fundamental or Kingdom Practice Health Check. This includes a series of questions related to each study, together with a Possible Action challenge, space to record responses to questions, and a memory diagram to help students remember the structure being developed throughout the book.

If possible and as time permits, use different translations of the individual Scripture passages to enhance and enrich your considerations and discussions. You may want to lead discussions around the scriptures themselves, as some of them are challenging on their own.

How you approach each study within a group depends to some extent on how much time you have available and how chatty (or otherwise) the group may be. One option is for everyone in the group to agree to read the material beforehand so that they are familiar with the subject matter. They may choose to make notes and develop questions of their own on the content they have looked at. They can also think about their responses and ideas to the questions at the end of each study.

Reading the body text in each study out loud (leading up to the study questions) typically takes around 20-25 minutes, and you may choose to encourage different people to contribute to sharing that task.

It is not essential that the material in each study be covered in just one meeting. Depending upon group makeup and dynamics, it may be beneficial to dwell on a particular study for more than one discussion period. This could help ensure that all participants get an opportunity to contribute as well as allow time to address any particular issues or concerns that may arise.

There are no specific right or wrong answers to the Kingdom Fundamental or Kingdom Practice Health Check subsections within each study. If you are the leader, it would be good to think about the questions in advance and have some possible answers ready for the group discussion. There may be surprises, but trust in the Holy Spirit to guide you as you lead.

Focus Some Time on Reinforcing the Structure

The figures presented in each study offer a particular perspective on how the Kingdom Fundamentals and Kingdom Practices can be considered to work together in a relationship context between us, God, and other people. This is summarised in Figure 3 and 17.

In addition, Figures 18 and 19 illustrate an alternative pyramid-style structure for considering the Kingdom Fundamentals, Kingdom Practices, and Kingdom Behaviours.

No claim is being made here that the material in these studies is in any way definitive. It is simply one way of organising Jesus's commands. But in terms of living out practically the studies in this book, it would be helpful for group leaders to spend some time ensuring that participants try to memorise the structure in some way. This has been one of the prime purposes of organising the material as a series of studies.

Participants have the opportunity at the end of each study to fill in the blanks on the various figures, which will reinforce what they are learning. Committing the content of these figures to memory will help their ongoing walk as disciples.

Lead Study 7—Bribery and Corruption Exercise

As the leader, consider whether it is appropriate to undertake this exercise before beginning the study. If you are working alone, you may wish to consider the questions raised and work out your reaction and response to them. There are no specific guidelines for the exercise itself, and the way that you approach this may be dependent upon your cultural, political, and social context.

Bribery and Corruption Exercise

In looking at the subject of integrity across your wider society, either in a group or as an individual or a couple, consider the following questions:

- How do you define corruption? What kind of acts do you think are corrupt?
- What is your understanding of corruption/bribery in your country/context?
- What do you think are the main causes of corruption/bribery in your country/context?
- What do you think are the consequences of corruption/bribery your country/context?
- In what way does your faith influence your attitude and response to each of the above questions?

Lead Study 12—Confidential Forgiveness Exercise

For the confidential exercise on forgiveness in Study 12, you will need to undertake some preparation. Ideally, please source in advance some water-soluble paper (you can find it on Amazon, eBay, etc.), ensuring that there is enough for each participant to be able to write something relevant to them. You might also want to consider some small token to give each participant at the end of the exercise as a reminder of what they have done. For example, in two such courses I ran in India, I gave each attendee a small stainless-steel tumbler, in common use there, so that each time the attendees drank from them they would remember the exercise. This turned out to be a popular element of the study programme, not only because there was a gift, but also in terms of the symbolism and release participants received from the exercise.

Prior to the study, you should arrange a bucket or bowl of water into which the participants will subsequently drop the "Forgiveness Commitment" they have written out (see below for details). Once all participants have placed their "Forgiveness Commitment" in the water, the whole set of papers can be stirred to make sure they are fully dissolved, illustrating that this is a confidential action between each individual and God (see below for some alternative methods).

Forgiveness Exercise

This exercise is to help every reader/participant to address any ongoing un-forgiveness in their life in a confidential manner so that this issue is between them and God alone.

- Each participant should be given a piece of soluble paper by the leader.
- The leader should pray on the group's behalf, inviting the Holy Spirit to speak to each person about anything for which they need to forgive one or more people or forgive themselves. This could be something obvious or something hidden — whether from the distant past or perhaps a more recent issue or concern.
- Group members should then sit quietly, thinking, listening to the Holy Spirit, and praying if appropriate.
- When all are ready, each participant should write on their paper something along the following lines: "From this day (date) forward, I will forgive XXXX for YYYY and allow God to restore me."
- Group members should then fold their paper.
- The group can then be led in prayer again, after which each person is invited forward to place their paper in a bowl of water for dissolution (or a paper shredder or flame, safely, of course, for the latter!).

- The leader may then give each person a predetermined "token" (glass, beaker, polished stone, semi-precious gemstone etc.) to remind them of their commitment to forgive.

- Once all group members have come forward, the leader can again lead in prayer, the group might sing a hymn of praise, or some other appropriate choice(s) to close the session.

If you are studying alone:

Follow a similar process to that outlined above.

- Pray for the Holy Spirit to reveal anything to you for which you need to forgive yourself or others. The issue may be obvious and already known to you or something that the Holy Spirit reveals.

- As with group session above, write this down: "From this day (date) forward, I will forgive XXXX for YYYY and allow God to restore me."

- Pray this through, then when you are ready, destroy the paper by shredding, cutting, or burning it safely.

- Consider choosing something modest as a token to remind you of your commitment.

- Set your mind to carry through this process of forgiveness through the power of the Holy Spirit.

Tips for Leading Groups

Participants within any group will have varying ways in which they prefer to learn. For example in https://www.learning-styles-online.com/overview/, we see listed a set of seven different learning styles:

- Visual (spatial): prefers using pictures, images, and spatial understanding.
- Aural (auditory-musical): Prefers using sound and music.
- Verbal (linguistic): Prefers using words, both in speech and writing.
- Physical (kinaesthetic): Prefers using body, hands, and sense of touch.
- Logical (mathematical): Prefers using logic, reasoning, and systems.
- Social (interpersonal): Prefers to learn in groups or with other people.
- Solitary (intra-personal): Prefers to work alone and use self-study.

In contrast, the approach in the Manual of Learning Styles[58] offers four classifications of learning styles:

- Activist
- Reflector
- Theorist
- Pragmatist

Other theories exist and can be sourced online and elsewhere.

What this means is that some participants of these studies may prefer reading the text and hearing the words of each study being read. Others may find the diagrams helpful, while others may look for ways to try out things in practice. Some will gain a better understanding from group discussion, whereas other will benefit from private time to read and reflect about the

---

[58] Honey, P. & Mumford, A. (1982) Manual of Learning Styles London: P Honey.
https://www2.le.ac.uk/departments/doctoralcollege/training/eresources/teaching/theories/honey-mumford

material. These are not mutually exclusive as we can all benefit from using different approaches to reinforce our understanding.

The following might be useful guidelines when planning and leading a group study of this material:

Be clear who is leading each study.

You may wish to lead throughout each session or share the responsibility with others. Whatever you decide to do, make sure that the expectations of the group are managed effectively.

Aim to have groups of a manageable size.

This keeps the group from becoming too unwieldy and permits all to have the opportunity to contribute. If the group is too large, this becomes a training study rather than a discussion forum where all can really participate. If too small, there can be pressure on people to speak when they are not comfortable doing so. Four to eight participants is a good balance. But this depends on personalities and whether people already know each other as new acquaintances are less prepared to share.

Agree to keep group discussions confidential.

Those things of a personal nature shared during the group study should be kept within the group only and not discussed outside without the specific consent of those concerned. Committing to maintain confidentiality, in writing if necessary, is important. The only exception should be in a safeguarding context (where a minor or adult at risk has been impacted in some way) where there may be legal duty to report to an appointed Designated Person that some form of disclosure has been made.

Agree on a format for addressing the material.

This may involve reading the study text and considering the questions beforehand, or alternatively reading the material as a group, then addressing the questions together. Choice of format will depend upon how much time participants are prepared to put aside and that has been allotted to each meeting.

Pray in advance about the materials and subjects likely to be raised

If the participants are known to you, then you may have some understanding of their personal circumstances and whether sensitivities are likely to be heightened. Ask the Holy Spirit to lead and guide you. His prompting of you and others may raise issues that you don't expect. If the matter is urgent, please consider putting the study materials on hold for the next meeting and addressing the issues raised first. Alternatively, arrange to follow up in a separate meeting with the person/people involved.

For the actual group meeting, plan on a few minutes of silence once participants have arrived and are settled. This allows the issues of the day participants are dealing with to be put to one side. After the period of silence, commit the time to the Lord in prayer and ask that the Holy Spirit will lead and guide your discussions.

Seek to ensure that all participants have the opportunity to contribute.

Some people can be relied upon to share their thoughts whereas others will be less confident about participating in group discussion and questions. Encourage less verbal group members to share their perspectives. If necessary, be prepared to politely ask more vocal members to give others an opportunity to contribute.

Use open questions during discussion.

This means questions that require something other than yes or no as a response. Options could include:

➢ What do you think about …?

➢ How did that make you feel?

➢ Why did you do that?

➢ Can you explain/tell us about …?

Try to stay on topic.

That said, be flexible if it is clear that the Holy Spirit wants a particular issue different from the subject to be explored.

Be prepared to call out bad behaviour.

Hopefully, people will be cooperative, but if discussions get heated, don't hesitate to intervene. As appropriate, consider setting out in advance some rules for the meeting that all will agree to, such as:

- Endeavour to arrive on time.
- No walk-outs/unplanned exits.
- No one person dominating the discussion.
- Treat viewpoints of all participants with respect.
- No personal attacks or criticism of individuals.
- No "Bible bashing", i.e., forceful reference to particular scriptures that support your argument.
- No interrupting when others are speaking, especially when it is on topic and relevant.

- Keep to time frame unless the group consents to continue discussions.

Be prepared to re-visit material.

It may take more than one session to sufficiently cover a particular study topic. This should be subject to group consent and will depend upon whether the group has been organised for a fixed period or meets regularly outside the context of these particular studies.

Conclude each study with prayer.

This should include the materials and issues discussed as well as a request that all might seek the Holy Spirit's guidance on applying and practising the commands of Jesus moving forward.

Teach Them To Obey – All That I Have Commanded You

ISBN: 978-1-9164405-0-0 (paperback version).

ISBN: 978-1-9164405-3-1 (eBook version).

All the commands of Jesus presented in a simple structure of three high-level (Kingdom Fundamentals) and nine lower-level (Kingdom Practices) themes for leaders to create their own Intentional Discipleship or sermon programme.

This reference source for pastors, teachers and disciplers presents a comprehensive biblical foundation for the material in this *Studies for Disciples* book to address our (the church's) "failure" to teach disciples to obey all the commands of Jesus.

A detailed analysis of all of the commands of Jesus in the New Testament forms the basis for this work, grouping and summarising them into twelve themes that collectively present over eighty distinct commands (Kingdom Behaviours).

The main material is grouped under three Kingdom Fundamental headings. Two are outward focused - commands that relate to our need to Love God and the requirement to Love Your Neighbour As Yourself. The third addresses commands directed at our inner motivations and behaviours as individuals, under the title Follow Jesus.

Each chapter includes Kingdom Practice sub-headings: two under Love God, four under Follow Jesus and three under Love Your Neighbour As Yourself.

At the lowest level (Kingdom Behaviours), related commands of Jesus are quoted with any parallel texts highlighted.

Figures are included throughout to build and demonstrate the structuring of Jesus's commands that is the focus of this material.

This is for anyone with an interest in Jesus's teaching. Above all, it is for those who are discipling fellow followers of Jesus and/or who want to understand how Jesus's commands can be grouped into a simple to remember form.

www.ingramcontent.com/pod-product-compliance
Lightning Source LLC
Chambersburg PA
CBHW071335080526
44587CB00017B/2841